COVENANT OF LIBERTY

COVENANT OF

Liberty

The Ideological Origins
of the Tea Party Movement

Michael Patrick Leahy

BROADSIDE BOOKS
An Imprint of HarperCollins *Publishers*
www.broadsidebooks.net

HarperCollins books may be purchased for educational, business, or
sales promotional use. For information, please write: Special Markets Department,
HarperCollins Publishers, 10 East 53rd Street, New York, NY 10022.

Broadside Books™ and the Broadside logo are trademarks of HarperCollins Publishers.

FIRST EDITION

Designed by Jennifer Daddio / Bookmark Design & Media Inc.

Library of Congress Cataloging-in-Publication Data
Leahy, Michael Patrick.
Covenant of liberty : the ideological origins of the Tea Party movement / by Michael Patrick
Leahy.—1st ed.
p.   cm
Includes bibliographical references.
ISBN 978-0-06-206633-6
1. Tea Party movement. 2. United States—Politics and government. I. Title.
JK2391.T43L43   2012
320.520973—dc23   2011044449

12 13 14 15 16   OV/RRD   10 9 8 7 6 5 4 3 2 1

To Courtenay and Honor

Contents

FOUR BROKEN PROMISES: WHY THE TEA PARTY AROSE

The story of civilization can be told in the conflict between the individual's desire for liberty and the state's need to establish social order. Every government, once established, seeks to centralize and consolidate its own power at the expense of individual liberty. This is as true for a democratic republic as it is for a constitutional monarchy, an absolute monarchy, an oligarchy, or a dictatorship.

From the moment the citizens of a country bind themselves in a constitutional covenant that guarantees the rights of the individual and defines and limits the powers of the government, the battle lines are drawn between the faithful defenders of that covenant and those who seek to corrupt it.

The Tea Party movement arose in 2009 because the political class of the United States—in the form of members of the legislative, executive, and judicial branches of our government—broke four promises found within the Constitution, thereby accelerating the natural tendency to centralize and consolidate power at the expense of individual liberty.

The first promise—to abide by the written words of the Constitution—was broken before the ink was dry on the last documents that sealed the uniquely American secular covenant contained in our

Constitution and Bill of Rights. The second promise—to refrain from interfering in private economic matters—was broken when the modern party that routinely pays homage to "free markets" first came to power.

The third promise—to honor the customs, traditions, and principles that make up the "fiscal constitution"—was broken by Herbert Hoover and Franklin Delano Roosevelt 143 years after the Constitution was ratified.

Had not the fourth and final promise—that members of the legislative branch would exercise thoughtful deliberation while giving respectful consideration to the views of their constituents—been broken in such a disdainful and audacious manner in January and February 2009, the grassroots activists who came to be known as the Tea Party movement would never have been compelled to action.

But like the proverbial frog that jumps out of a suddenly boiling pot of water when a slow, steady increase of temperature would have left him unaware, the activists were finally alerted to the danger they were in by the rushed passage of the $787 billion stimulus bill during the Obama administration's first thirty days in office.

In this book, I explain why the ideas found in the covenantal promises of the Constitution were held in the minds of Americans at the formation of the republic, how they passed down largely intact from generation to generation, how those promises were broken by a corrupted political class, and how average citizens remained faithful to the covenant and the promises contained within it.

On my desk is a small old framed black-and-white photograph that provides a vivid reminder of my personal connection to the origins of our secular constitutional covenant. The photo, taken around 1927 outside a modest building that once served as a general store in a small upstate New York community, shows four generations of my family. My grandmother, then around ten years old, displays a bright smile, and holds hands with her mother, who stands next to her grandmother and great-grandmother, the latter a wizened gray-haired woman well past eighty for whom the effort of a smile seems too much to ask. As the four look at the camera, they form a visual link between me, my children, and the founding of the republic.

The old woman is Miranda Scott Dickinson, the great-granddaughter of Captain Andries Bevier, a veteran of the Revolutionary War, and the original recipient of the land grant that brought his sons and their children to this small town in upstate New York. The census of 1790, taken before this familial migration occurred, shows Captain Bevier, aged fifty, as the owner of a midsize farm in Wawarsing, thirty miles to the west of Poughkeepsie on the other side of the Hudson River.

Captain Bevier had voted in the 1788 election that picked a delegate to represent Ulster County in the ratification convention for the U.S. Constitution, held in nearby Poughkeepsie that summer. It was there that Alexander Hamilton cynically professed his undying commitment to republican values, turned the tide in favor of ratification in a tight 30–27 vote, and along with the other delegates signed a letter confirming that Congress had no implied powers beyond those specifically enumerated in Article I, Section 8 of the Constitution. Perhaps, given his prominence in the local community, Captain Bevier had ventured the thirty miles east to sit in the galleries and watch as Mr. Hamilton waxed eloquent. If he did, I wonder if he believed Hamilton's speeches were sincere.

Later, Captain Bevier voted in the election in New York's 4th Congressional District that put John Hathorn in the First Congress, which passed the Bill of Rights in September 1789. In 1790 he voted for the members of the state assembly and state senate who voted to ratify the Bill of Rights that year.

Eight generations ago, this ancestor of mine was one of a million or so regular American citizens whose active participation in the ratification debates gave them a share in the title Founding Father.

In what way am I and my fellow citizens bound today by the same secular covenant as my ancestor? The answer lies in the rights guaranteed me in that document. Just as Captain Bevier had the ability to help form that secular covenant, so have I and millions like me exercised that right through direct participation in the political process, and by the knowledge that we can follow the same process to update and amend that covenant.

Whether I choose direct electoral and social engagement, or participation in amendment campaigns—either through lobbying Congress or by persuading the state legislatures to hold another Constitutional Convention—the opportunity to have "skin in the game" is the social contract by which I remain bound to that original covenant, just as the executive, judicial, and legislative branches are bound, along with the respective state governments.

In the aftermath of what we constitutional conservatives saw as the electoral debacle of 2008, I chose direct engagement. The means of engagement was the formation of an online conservative community called Top Conservatives on Twitter.

The question that intrigued me was this—were there any conservatives on Twitter? If there were, then perhaps we could form an online community and develop a common strategy. On November 28, 2008, I put together a list of twenty-six conservative people I knew who were on Twitter, placed it on a blog, and sent out a tweet inviting other conservatives to join. Almost immediately, I was hit with an avalanche of requests. In the first twenty-four hours, I received more than five hundred requests from conservative Twitter users around the country to be added.

The mere presence of a list, and in particular the fact that it was growing, served to instantly create and grow an online community. And because conservatives now could see a list of like-minded folks they could "follow," the collective visibility of all conservatives individually increased as well.

As the list grew, an interesting phenomenon developed. Conservatives would go to the list and follow all of the top one hundred on the list. Then they would engage them in dialogue, either public or private. Without intending to do so, we had created a real-time, online digital version of the New England town meeting.

About this time, many of those on the now-growing Top Conservatives on Twitter list suggested that we needed to adopt a "hashtag," that it would be easier for anyone on Twitter to follow the ongoing conservative conversation. One of our members, a seventy-eight-year-old grandmother from Weslaco, Texas, Beulah Garrett, suggested that we use the abbreviation of the list's name, thus the hashtag #tcot. By the end of the second full week, there were more than one thousand names on the list and #tcot was consistently on the Twitter top-trending topics.

Our small but vibrant and growing online conservative community arrived on the scene just as the Republican Bush administration abandoned constitutional principles. We began to experiment with ways in which we could stop what we saw as this headlong rush toward socialism. Barack Obama was still more than a month away from being inaugurated as president, but the trend for liberty was wrong. And in fact we suspected it was about to get significantly worse.

The secular covenant earned through battle and fine-tuned by years of deliberative debate more than two centuries ago requires constant attention. Its participants must honor its terms through vigilant attention to their duties and obligations as citizens, legislators, and officials. They must also be alert to the periodic need to update it, and to safeguard its integrity by calling to account those who would seek to corrupt it. If we remain faithful to our inheritance, and carry forward the core values of the Tea Party movement with authentic grassroots intensity over the next generation, the future of our country is bright indeed. Based on my personal experiences over the last three years, I have no reason to doubt that we will succeed in this effort, and that our posterity will be able to say of us, They restored the covenant of liberty.

Chapter 1

THE ENGLISH ROOTS
OF AMERICAN LIBERTY

The first Tea Party movement was launched from a Tower of London prison cell in January 1647.* It was there that John Lilburne, a former officer in the Parliamentary Army who had been imprisoned for publicly insulting the integrity of a member of the House of Lords, set to paper concepts of the natural rights of the individual, constitutionalism, and the sovereignty of the people that would resonate through the centuries. His handwritten notes were smuggled out to a network of like-minded political and theological pamphleteers, friends, and colleagues based in London's nearby Coleman Street Ward, the clandestine center of England's burgeoning illegal press. Working in secret, Richard Overton, the proprietor of one of England's most prolific illegal print shops, quickly edited Lilburne's notes, set the type, and began producing thousands of copies of *The Cause of Regal Tyranny Discovered.*

---

* While you can't draw a straight line from the Leveller Movement of 1647–1649 to the Tea Party Movement of 2009–2011, there are several similarities. Both were grassroots movements, powered by the energy of the common man. Both movements grew because of clever use of new media, printed pamphlets, and social media, respectively. Finally, both movements were focused on similar general principles. Levellers sought guarantees of individual liberty, property rights, expanded franchise, and an accountable, democratic republic. Tea Partiers seek constitutionally limited government, free markets, and fiscal responsibility.

ndred pages, *The Cause of Regal Tyranny Discov-*
ʼy long. Despite its bulk, the pamphlet circulated
rns and meetinghouses of London where gath-
emerging grassroots movement championing the
ˌˌˌˌs of the individual known as "The Levellers."* After several
ˌˌars of writing similar pamphlets, Lilburne had developed a large and
sympathetic audience among the small merchants, journeymen, and
apprentices of London, in addition to the rank-and-file members of the
Parliamentarian Army. Few among this group, whom today we might
call the middle class, were able to vote in Parliamentary or local elections. That privilege was limited to the 200,000 or so landholders of
property valued at forty shillings† or more, not more than 5 percent of
England's population of five million.

His newest pamphlet was an incendiary attack upon both the
monarchy of Charles I and the aristocratic lords who served him. The
youngest son of minor gentry, Lilburne had come from the rustic north
of England to London as a teenager to serve as an apprentice to a cloth-
maker. Already steeped in Puritan Christian theology, Lilburne was a
voracious reader and writer who began to independently develop the
notion that adherence to Christian principles meant everyone was born
with natural rights.

Lilburne argued that all English kings and their subordinate lords
since the Norman Conquest in 1066 had illegally held and exercised
power. He not only attacked royalty for its origins in Norman tyranny;
he also boldly asserted that the members of the House of Lords who
had imprisoned him should be stripped of their powers. It was time,

---

* This term would be introduced several months later by the group's antagonist, Oliver Cromwell, who wanted to falsely label them as favoring wealth redistribution, and a "level" society
socially and economically. In reality, these "so-called Levellers" supported private property rights
and the abolition of trade monopolies. The three most prominent leaders were Lilburne, the
printer Richard Overton, and William Walwyn, a prosperous weaver.

† There were 20 shillings to a pound, so this equaled two pounds. Owners of property (usually
land) valued at forty shillings or more were called "forty shilling freeholders." The requirement
to own property valued at forty shillings or more in order to be able to vote was introduced in
England around 1430, and was still in effect until the early twentieth century.

Lilburne argued, for England to return to its republican origins of Anglo-Saxon antiquity. The concept of the "Norman yoke," imposed upon freedom-loving Englishmen for centuries by tyrannical monarchs, had been written of in earlier pamphlets, but Lilburne's reputation gave it a vastly wider audience and significant credence.

The lords, Lilburne wrote, had inherited their titles "from their predecessors whom William the Conqueror, alias 'Thief and Tyrant' made Dukes, Earls, and Barons for helping him subdue and enslave the free nation of England, and gave them by the law of his own will the estates of the inhabitants."[1]

Since the House of Lords itself was illegitimate, he concluded, his own imprisonment was illegal, and he should be released immediately. One hundred miles to the north of Lilburne's Tower of London cell, in the small English town of Southwell, another prisoner plotted his release. Charles I, the king whose reign was the complete embodiment of the Norman yoke Lilburne so deeply desired to break, had been held for six months by the Scottish Army. He had led his own army in four years of bloody civil war against an army raised on the authority of Parliament. Having lost the war, he was now reduced to the scheming intrigues of a prisoner with few cards to play.

For the past decade, Charles and Lilburne had been at opposite ends of a great and often violent national battle about the proper relationship between the rights of the individual and the powers of the state. Their fates would be influenced, if not controlled, by the decisions of two powerful men, as bitterly opposed to each other as they were divided in their views of the relationship between the rights of the individual and the powers of the state.

Less than a mile from Lilburne's cell, in the House of Commons at Westminster Palace, Denzil Holles sat as a member of the Long Parliament, now in its seventh year. A protégé of the late jurist Sir Edward Coke, inventor of the concept of "the Ancient Constitution," Holles too believed that "from time immemorial" England had been governed as a constitutionally limited monarchy where the power of the monarch was constrained by the aristocracy in the House of Lords and the gentry in the House of Commons. Individual rights were guaranteed by the rule of law. The crown had its prerogatives, but individuals at every level of society had their rights as well. Holles had paid the price for his devotion to Coke's "Ancient Constitution," having been briefly imprisoned by Charles I in 1642. Now, in Parliament, he found himself in opposition to those who wanted to eliminate the monarchy entirely.

The second powerful man, Oliver Cromwell, sat at the head of the victorious New Model Army, 40,000 strong, now encamped in the north of England. The war brought the opportunity for him to rise to national prominence as he molded a highly organized and effective army. Previously, his obscurity was distinguished only by a genuine devout conversion to Independent Puritanism. He viewed his victories over the king's Royalist forces in battle as evidence that he had been called by God to use the power of the sword to install a virtual Christian military dictatorship over all of England.

The personal battles between Lilburne, King Charles, Holles, and Cromwell reflected the four distinct philosophies, prevalent in England at this time, about the relationship between individual liberty and the power of the state. This divergence of thought would have been unknown in England a century earlier.

Throughout the four and a half centuries that followed the Norman Conquest, all of England had but one view of that relationship. The land had been governed by an unwritten constitutional compact between the monarch, the aristocracy, and the landed gentry, blessed and sanctified through the formal participation of the state-authorized church—Roman Catholic until 1534, Church of England thereafter.

When William conquered England in 1066, he claimed all the land and gave one-third of it to the church. Everyone—king, lord, gentry, commoner, yeoman, and laborer—belonged to the Catholic Church. All but the king paid their tithes and followed the theology proclaimed from the pulpit each Sunday. No individual discernment was allowed, or even possible, since the few Bibles that existed were handwritten in

Latin, a language only the clergy could read. Church and state were inseparable.

Kings and parliaments, good and bad alike, had ruled through the ages, but always there had been an "agreement of conventions" whose terms were never comprehensively articulated in a single document. They existed instead in a complex set of relationships formed by years of tradition, common law, and custom. Conflicts between the rights of the individual and the powers of the state had been resolved, more or less, by using these long-established conventions.

It was this "agreement of conventions" around which formed widespread support for the notion of an unwritten constitution, a notion that would be strongly held on both sides of the Atlantic for centuries. Calls for improvements to this unwritten tradition in a constitution with greater specificity—written in a single document visible to and understood by all—arose in England periodically, but never succeeded. It was only in America that such a written constitution—our secular covenant—was finally introduced and accepted. But even in America, the idea of an "agreement of conventions" whose terms were not specified in the written constitution was accepted by all the Founding Fathers when it came to the important matter of fiscal responsibility.

With the rise of the Reformation and Henry VIII's decision to break from the Catholic Church in Rome, this singular view began to fracture. As English-language Bibles were printed and distributed, every Englishman was now capable of determining for himself his own views on the great covenantal relationships: between man and God, between the individual and the state, and between the individual and his local church.

Kings and bishops throughout Europe were wary of the possible effects from widespread distribution of the Bible written in the vernacular. Many believed that Martin Luther's German-language Bible—one of the first vernacular Bibles available—had been one of the causes of the Peasant Wars, populist uprisings in Germany in the 1520s in which an estimated three hundred thousand people were killed. Luther himself was sufficiently concerned with such claims that he publicly separated himself from the actions of the peasants. English translations came decades later, and were possible only because of the shifting religious loyalties of the English monarchy.

When the Catholic Mary Tudor ascended to the English throne in 1553, leading Protestant theologians, including William Wittingham and the Scottish reformer John Knox, fled to exile in John Calvin's Geneva Republic, which tolerated only Presbyterian Calvinism. There they undertook a new English translation from the Hebrew and Greek originals, one that would be more dynamic and easily understood by the common man than the first English translation, created by the scholar William Tyndale nineteen years earlier.

Their translation was deeply influenced by the works of Calvin. In his magnum opus, *The Institutes of the Christian Religion*, Calvin described his system of Protestant theology, including the covenantal relationship between man and God, but also the relationship between the church and civil governance. The *Institutes* provided a biblical justification for Christian resistance to the rule of tyrannical monarchs. It also laid the framework for the establishment of a biblically based civil government, as practiced in Geneva, then a city of 20,000. Its republican form of government tolerated but a single theological perspective: Calvinism. Under the five theological points of Calvinism—the total depravity of man, unconditional election of the saints, limited atonement given only to the predestined saints, God's irresistible grace and total sovereignty, and the perseverance of the saints—only the predestined "elect" who were members of the established Presbyterian church enjoyed full civil rights.

Calvin's predestination theology was at odds with later Christian theologies that emphasized "free will" and made no distinction between the "saved" and "doomed," such as those of Arminius,[*] Grotius, and Roger Williams. All men had the potential to be saved, they argued, and it was that potential that formed their original natural rights.

---

[*] Lilburne's tormentor, Archbishop of Canterbury William Laud, subscribed to some, but not all, of Arminius's views.

When the Geneva Bible was finally published in 1560, it had the same effect in England as the French-language Olivétan Bible, published in 1535, had had in France and Switzerland. The new Protestant queen, Elizabeth I, allowed its printing and distribution, even though a careful reading of the text and the extensive margin notes encouraged challenges to her royal authority. Englishmen who had previously thought little about the relationship between the individual and the state now had reason to contemplate what God had to say on that matter. Following Calvin's thinking, the Geneva Bible made the concept of a covenant—a solemn agreement between God, who promised eternal salvation, and man, who promised obedience—now seem relevant and applicable to other relationships, such as the individual and the state, and the individual and his local church.

With their divine task in Geneva completed, the expatriate English theologians returned to their homelands. In England, some returned easily to their prior roles in the Church of England, while others began to see the need to "purify" that institution along the Calvinistic lines they had observed in Geneva.

In Scotland, John Knox returned with copies of the Geneva Bible and a determination to install a Calvinist version of the Geneva Republic. Inspired by Knox, the Scottish Parliament rejected Catholicism. They established a General Assembly of Presbyters, modeled on Calvin's consistory of church leaders, who set the policies that the elected civil magistrates were to follow to manage the governance of the Church of Scotland,* rejecting the episcopacy of the Church of England.

Mary, Queen of Scots returned briefly to Scotland from France to assume her crown after the death of her first husband, Francis II, but by 1567 her troubled reign ended with her exile. Her one-year-old son, James, was named king. Until he reached his majority, the country was

---

* The reaffirmation of this covenant by the Scottish Parliament in 1638 was the proximate cause of Charles I's initiation of the Bishops' Wars between England and Scotland.

ruled by a series of regents. James's education was supervised by the severe and demanding George Buchanan, a renowned Presbyterian scholar and a follower of Knox, who supported the concept of limited constitutional monarchy. In 1579 his *Dialogue Concerning the Rights of the Crown in Scotland* was published. Its purpose was to instruct his now thirteen-year-old charge that the source of political power was the people. Monarchs, Buchanan argued, must honor the terms by which they are given authority. Where Calvin had merely argued that tyrannical monarchs could be lawfully resisted, Buchanan went further. Tyrannical monarchs, he wrote, could be lawfully overthrown.

James feared and hated Buchanan. Even when he was an adult the mere mention of his childhood taskmaster's name would send him into a dark and combative mood. Two decades later, in 1598, he publicly rejected his former tutor's philosophy. In *The True Law of Free Monarchies*, James set out the doctrine of the divine right of kings. James argued that his authority as a monarch derived directly from God, in an apostolic succession that extended back to Jesus himself. Monarchs owed none of their authority to the aristocracy, the gentry, or the people. The monarch was accountable not to the people, but to God, and he alone was the arbiter of God's will. The people were accountable to him.

In England, challenges to the royal prerogative were also raised, but the politically astute Elizabeth dealt with them so adeptly that none rose to the level of constitutional crisis.

When Elizabeth I died in 1603, the change that took place in England as James VI of Scotland became James I of England was dramatically illustrated by a troubling event that occurred as the new king traveled with his entourage south from Scotland for his coronation. A thief had followed the caravan as it proceeded toward London. At Newark-on-Trent, the thief was caught, and confessed to the crime of stealing purses. James had him hanged on the spot. The unfortunate criminal had neither trial nor hearing, the rule of law that would have certainly been applied had the incident occurred during Elizabeth's reign. The new king's subjects took note. This was a very different ruler from Elizabeth.[2]

Now thirty-seven years old, James finally had the opportunity to use the church and throne of England to consolidate his absolute powers. For James, the hierarchical structure of the Church of England was far better suited to this doctrine of governance than the Presbyterianism of his native Scotland. In England, God directed the king, who in turn directed the archbishop of Canterbury. As a practical matter, however, James spent little time trying to discern God's will, and assumed that because something was his will, it was also God's.

Early in his reign, he joined several Puritan preachers and bishops of the Church of England at the Hampton Court Conference in 1604 to discuss ecclesiastic matters. A major purpose of the conference was to secure the cooperation of biblical scholars from all factions to undertake and complete a more "royal-friendly" English translation of the Bible. There he confirmed that Presbyterianism was not consistent with the type of absolutist monarchy he intended to practice:

"I know what would become of my supremacy [if there were no bishops]. . . . No bishop, no King. When I mean to live under a presbytery I will go into Scotland again."[3]

One worthy at the conference reported James gave this caveat:

that no marginall notes should be added, having found in them which are annexed to the Geneva translation . . . some notes very partial, untrue, seditious, and savouring too much of dangerous and trayterous conceites. As for example, Exodus 1:19, where the marginal note alloweth disobedience to Kings, and 2 Chronicles 15:16, the note taxeth Asa for deposing his mother, only, and not killing her.[4]

This conference resulted in the publication of the authorized version of the King James Bible in 1611, but the popularity of the Geneva Bible and its antimonarchical margin notes kept it in wide circulation for several decades.

Soon after the Hampton Court Conference got under way, Sir Edward

Coke came to the king's attention, after his successful prosecution of Guy Fawkes and several other Catholics who conspired to blow up Parliament. At fifty-two, Coke was already one of the most respected and wealthy common lawyers in the country. After the convicted traitors were hanged, drawn, and quartered, no man in England not of royal blood was held in higher regard than Coke.

Impressed with Coke's legal skill and tenacity, James appointed him chief justice of the Court of Common Pleas in 1606, but he underestimated the extent of Coke's devotion to English legal traditions and the rule of law. He had expected Coke to bend to his own exercise of divine royal authority, but Coke was unyielding in defense of his judicial independence. James claimed the right—the royal prerogative—to adjudicate any cases he wished in any courts he desired. Coke responded forcefully, as J. C. Tanner reports in *The Constitutional Documents of the Reign of James I*, that such a royal prerogative was nowhere to be found in English common law:

> [T]he King in his own person cannot adjudge any case, either criminal . . . or betwixt party and party . . . but this ought to be determined and adjudged in some Court of Justice, according to the Law and Custom of England.

It was the first of many conflicts between, on the one side, Coke and others in the landed gentry like him who knew that centuries of English common law tradition had imposed limitations on the conduct of kings, and, on the other, the Stuart kings, who saw the authority of God in all they did or wanted to do. Soon a divide arose throughout England between Court—the aristocracy and gentry who sought advancement and wealth by royal favor and sided with the Stuart kings—and Country—the landed gentry who sided with Coke. As the leader of the gentry, Coke found himself in constant conflict with the king, even serving some time in the Tower of London.

When James I died in 1625, England did not weep. His son and successor, twenty-four-year-old Charles I, brought with him his father's devotion to the supremacy of arbitrary royal prerogative and a disdain for Parliament. Further conflict with Coke was inevitable.

In need of money, Charles hit upon a tactic that previous monarchs had used with some success—a program of forced loans. Aristocrats and landed gentry whom the king could not tax without Parliamentary agreement were instead forced to "loan" the crown funds, knowing such loans would never be repaid.

The scale and scope of Charles's forced loan program were unprecedented. Never before had so many gentlemen been forced to pay, and never had so many refusers been thrown in jail,[5] including five knights, a decision that did not sit well with the populace. The king finally released the jailed knights when, in need of even more money, he was forced to call Parliamentary elections, and knew that they would not turn out favorably until the knights were free.

Coke now used the concept of the "Ancient Constitution" as a rhetorical spear for Parliament's attack upon the king's arbitrary rule.[6]

The traditions of the "Ancient Constitution" had been practiced from "time immemorial," Coke argued, when the ancestors of the English people—the Angles, Jutes, and Saxons—lived in the forests of Germany. These ancient Germanic tribes were ruled by an elected king whose powers were limited by an elected parliament and a second institution of powerful chiefs. Citizens were guaranteed a string of liberties, which included trial by jury. When the Angles, Saxons, and Jutes invaded England, they imposed this form of governance on the native Britons, and it thrived until 1066, when the conqueror William I imposed feudalism through force and Norman law.

In Coke's view, William tempered the Norman law with the acceptance of many of the elements of his Anglo-Saxon predecessor, Edward the Confessor.* Lilburne's "Norman yoke" concept was one that Coke

---

* As mentioned earlier, John Lilburne and other members of the Leveller movement took a very different view of William the Conqueror. To them his imposition of feudalism represented not a continuation of the Ancient Constitution, but a complete rejection. The Norman yoke of absolute rule and feudalism, which installed all subsequent monarchs in England, was therefore illegitimate. Coke would have thoroughly rejected this concept, but by the beginning of the American Revolution, these two views had been conflated.

would have completely rejected. According to Coke, this Ancient Constitution was periodically improved, starting with the Magna Carta in 1215. Over the next four centuries the natural balance found in the Ancient Constitution was continually improved in fits and starts until the rule of James I.

The king, Coke argued, was subject to the rule of law as much as any of his subjects were. Coke would find many precedents to support that argument, and in doing so, he gave his fellow members of Parliament the courage to publicly stand with him in opposition to the king.

As Coke and his allies gathered in the spring of 1628, they decided to make a stand for the rights of Englishmen against Charles I's arbitrary rule. The bill they set forward, the Petition of Right, included the prohibition of taxation without Parliament's consent, as well as prohibition of forced loans and arbitrary arrest, the right of habeas corpus, the prohibition of forced billeting of troops, prohibitions against the imposition of martial law, and rights of due process.[7] Significantly, the very name of the bill—a petition to the king—acknowledged that it was the sovereign who held the ultimate authority, and that Parliament could only ask for his favor.

When Charles finally gave his assent, he did so disingenuously. Though the Petition of Right was now law, he almost immediately breached its provisions. In the spring of 1629 he closed down Parliament and began the eleven years of arbitrary exercise of power known as the era of personal rule.

Coke soon retired, and in the quiet of his private life, he wrote the four volumes of the *Institutes of the Lawes of England*. When Coke died in 1634, Charles confiscated the books but, notably, did not burn them. They would be published posthumously in 1642, and Lilburne would put them to good use in his writings.

The eleven years of personal rule from 1629 to 1640, when Parliament did not meet, were the culmination of Stuart absolutism. Reactions among Puritans were strong. One group, led by John Winthrop, determined to leave England and establish a Christian Bible-state that could be a "city upon a hill" and an example to all Christians of the proper godly way to organize and manage a country. From 1629 to 1640, an estimated forty thousand Puritans made the trek to Massachusetts, where Winthrop and other elders established the first Christian theocracy in the new world—the Massachusetts Bay Colony.

Others, either through lack of resources, lack of boldness, or devotion to the mother country, chose to stay in England and press for their rights there. Among this group was the young John Lilburne.

The tall and charismatic Lilburne entered the public eye in 1638, at the height of Charles I's era of personal rule. Only twenty-four at the time, Lilburne was arrested and tried for smuggling "unlicensed" Christian books from Holland to England. His courageous conduct at his trial and subsequent public punishment established his reputation.

He was not tried in a common law court by a jury of twelve peers, where he would have been granted the right to his own legal counsel. Instead his case was brought before the Star Chamber. Previously, this special court had been used for expedited hearings on matters involving important figures who might have influenced the outcome of common trials. Charles transformed the Star Chamber into his personal vehicle for eliminating enemies and forcing compliance with established regulations limiting dissent. By the time Lilburne was brought in chains before it, the Star Chamber had become the symbol of the abuse of power that characterized Charles's rule.

Addressing Lilburne in the customary "Law French" of the Star Chamber,* the judges demanded to hear his plea. Lilburne refused to plead until he heard the charges in English. Angered by his defiance, the court ordered him to be stripped of his shirt and tied to an oxcart, behind which he walked for two miles. Crowds gathered to watch as he was lashed more than two hundred times with a three-tailed whip. When he arrived at his destination—the front yard of Westminster—he was untied from the cart and placed into a pillory.

Defying his captors, Lilburne removed the banned religious books

---

* At the time, the official business of all courts in England was conducted in "Law French," a holdover from the Norman Conquest in 1066.

he had hidden in his pockets, threw them into the crowd, and loudly proclaimed that his punishment was a violation of his rights as an Englishman. His captors quickly gagged him, but he had won the hearts of his countrymen and become a symbol of resistance to the arbitrary power of the king. The price for this demonstration of courage was high. He remained in prison under severe conditions for more than two years, released only when Charles I was compelled to call Parliament into session to finance his "Bishops' Wars" against Scotland. He emerged severely malnourished. He no longer could use two of his fingers, casualties of two years of wrist chains.

Had he faded from the scene in 1640, his place in history would have been secure. More than three centuries later, U.S. Supreme Court justice Hugo Black cited Lilburne's refusal to enter a plea to unknown charges in the Star Chamber proceedings as the basis for the Fifth Amendment—the protection against self-incrimination.[8] Lilburne's Star Chamber trial was also cited as a significant historical precedent in the Supreme Court's majority opinion in the landmark case *Miranda v. Arizona.*

But Lilburne spent the rest of his life embroiled in controversies, displaying a knack for getting thrown into prison. England was less than a decade into an era of explosive growth of printing that featured widespread distribution of one-page broadsheets, slightly longer pamphlets, and books. A prolific and compelling writer, Lilburne quickly became one of the brightest stars in this "new media" explosion.

When the English Civil War broke out in 1642, he fought at Edgehill, and quickly rose to the rank of lieutenant colonel. He was captured by the Royalists, imprisoned for several months, and scheduled for execution. His brave, resourceful, and very pregnant young wife, Elizabeth (known to history as "Bonnie Bess"), rode through the night to persuade Parliament to put to death a number of its royal prisoners if her husband was executed. She completed the return trip just in time to begin negotiations for a prisoner exchange, which were successful.

Over the next five years, Lilburne continued to write at a prolific pace, gathering around him other like-minded Englishmen who believed in the cause of individual liberty. For him these views were a natural extension of his Puritan Christian faith. As his personal popularity grew he rankled the Parliamentary powers just as much as he had Charles I.

As the cold winter of 1647 turned to spring, three competing philosophies—Stuart absolutism, Coke's constitutionally limited monarchy, and Lilburne's constitutional republicanism—had now been firmly established. The fourth—the authoritarian Bible-state of Cromwell—was about to be fully revealed. Cromwell would soon assert his control over the New Model Army, which in turn would use its power of the sword to assert its control over Parliament.

The army was now the most important player in the developing drama to reestablish a working English government. England had no tradition of standing armies, but the Civil War had spawned one. Parliament had raised it five years earlier, and Cromwell had turned it into the highly efficient war machine that had defeated the king. Now Lilburne watched from his prison cell window as 20,000 soldiers of the New Model Army marched into the city of London in a line that stretched for a mile and a half. Later, Cromwell visited him in his cell, promising to work through Parliament to gain his release,[9] but in October 1647, he still languished in the Tower as preparations for the critical Putney Debates began.

These debates were designed to hash out differences between the Grandees and the Agitators on the formation of a new government and the treatment of the imprisoned king. Parliament, though in session, was an increasingly weak and ineffective counter to the New Model Army, whose senior officers, the "Grandees," came from the same landed gentry who populated Parliament. Cromwell, the most prominent Grandee, had served in Parliament, as had many of his fellow Grandees. They sought to establish a government where the privileges of the aristocracy and landed gentry of "purified" Christian beliefs were preeminent.

The "Agitators," elected representatives of the rank and file, were supporters of Lilburne's much more republican view, in which the people were sovereign, the right to vote was extended to almost all adult males, and individual rights—especially with regard to religious worship—were respected.

The role played by the imprisoned king—if any—in a new government was an issue on which the two sides were uncertain. Neither the Grandees nor the Agitators trusted the king, but the Agitators, driven as they were by the desire to expand individual rights for all but "wage-earners and beggars," seemed willing to accept either a republic or a constitutionally limited monarchy, provided their individual rights were acknowledged.

Cromwell wanted to hold the debates while Lilburne was still in prison so that he would be unable to participate. The Grandees' plan—one that failed to advance the people's sovereignty—was more likely to prevail if the most effective champion of those liberties, "Free-borne" John Lilburne, was unable to make the argument in person.

Drawing upon Lilburne's writings, John Wildman, a young Leveller attorney whose origins were more modest than even Lilburne's, penned a 900-word constitution called "The Agreement of the People." The document called for the establishment of a biennially elected unicameral Parliament of four hundred representatives, elected by every adult male in the country (excepting servants and "wage-earners"),* limitations on Parliament's power to compel religious worship, and the abolition of the state-authorized episcopacy and the dreaded tithe that supported the Church of England.

As a sign of the government's accountability to the people (rather than the other way around), its adoption as the new basis of England's constitutional governance required acceptance by the people—civilians

---

* The exception of wage-earners is most notable. It belies Cromwell's subsequent demeaning characterization of Lilburne and his supporters as those who sought to "level" all men to the same wealth and social standing. Levellers were dominated by those in the middle and lower middle classes—small independent farmers in the rural areas, and artisans, small merchants, and proprietors of small "industries" in London and other urban areas.

as well as soldiers—in a national referendum. In essence, the Agreement of the People called for a congregational covenant, freely entered into by all, that would provide the authentic basis for the government of the entire nation.[10]

More than three centuries later, in his dissenting opinion in *Goldberg v. Kelly*, Supreme Court Justice Black paid tribute to this document as one of the early precursors of our own Constitution:

> The goal of a written constitution with fixed limits on governmental power had long been desired. Prior to our colonial constitutions, the closest man had come to realizing this goal was the political movement of the Levellers in England in the 1640's. . . . In 1647, the Levellers proposed the adoption of An Agreement of the People which set forth written limitations on the English Government. This proposal contained many of the ideas which later were incorporated in the constitutions of this Nation.[11]

The Putney Debates came to an end, without resolution, in part because Charles I escaped from his house arrest in Hampton Court. But the most compelling reason for the termination is that Cromwell feared Lilburne's possible arrival, which held out the potential of turning the tide in favor of the Agreement of the People among the army.

By the time Lilburne was finally released on November 7, 1647, it was clear that the debates would never reconvene. While Charles I languished in his royal imprisonment, Lilburne used his time of freedom wisely, working to organize the Leveller movement. He held regular meetings in taverns and inns around London, established an organizing committee, helped organize a weekly publication of Leveller thought and tactics called *The Moderate*, and improved the printing and distribution of pamphlets and broadsheets. The number of Levellers grew dramatically, making it truly the first significant grassroots political movement in Anglo-American history. Representatives were selected to spread the message throughout the country, which they did with great vigor, inspired by Lilburne's enthusiasm.

Fearing the popularity of Lilburne's message, Cromwell contrived in January 1648 to have Lilburne arrested and imprisoned in the Tower of London again. This time he was joined by other Leveller leaders, including young John Wildman. Though deprived of freedom, Lilburne was comforted in the knowledge that his organizational efforts had succeeded. The thousands of Leveller sympathizers who had gathered throughout London at the time of his first release had grown in two short months to tens of thousands around the country. Their ranks continued to swell during his second imprisonment.

In early 1648 King Charles undertook actions that would soon unravel his chances of returning to the throne. He cut a deal with the Scots to introduce Presbyterianism as the ecclesiastic policy in England for a period of three years. That summer the Scots invaded England, fighting against their former Parliamentary allies, and were defeated at the Battle of Preston in August 1648.

The majority Presbyterian faction in Parliament wanted to negotiate a settlement. For several months, Parliamentary representatives negotiated the Treaty of Newport with Charles, which would have restored him to the throne under conditions that limited his authority. The Grandees of the New Model Army and the Puritan Independents in Parliament didn't trust the king.

But Cromwell refused to let Charles retain any power. Instead Cromwell swung his mighty sword in the name of the Lord, and the only military coup d'état in English history was launched. On a December morning in 1648, New Model Army colonel Thomas Pride surrounded the Houses of Parliament with a regiment of one thousand soldiers. As those members of Parliament aligned with the Presbyterian faction attempted to enter the building, he checked their names off a list. Those who supported reconciliation with the king were refused entry and arrested. Soon, more than seventy members of Parliament were in prison, and another two hundred chose not to attempt entry to the building. Denzil Holles, already targeted by Cromwell and his allies in Parliament, got wind of the coup. Knowing he would be arrested, he fled to France.

The remaining members—barely 200 out of the 500 elected in November 1640—were all inclined to support the Grandees. This "Rump Parliament" continued to conduct business as if they maintained the same constitutional authority as before.

On January 6, 1649, the Rump Parliament appointed 135 members to a "High Court of Justice," which tried King Charles I for treason, convicted him in a three-day trial, and had him beheaded on January 30, 1649. The next week, the Rump abolished both the monarchy and the House of Lords, and set up a forty-one-member Council of State. Cromwell was named chairman.

To the constitutionally minded Lilburne, every action taken by the Rump Parliament was illegal. This new "Commonwealth" was a greater violator of individual liberties than Charles I had ever been, even at his most tyrannical. Its authority was maintained not by law, but by the might and force of the standing army.

When the king's sentence was confirmed, Lilburne had proclaimed, "Why stop at one execution? Why not hundreds or even thousands?" The point was echoed by the conduct of the army. One Colonel Hewson is said to have proclaimed, "[W]e can hang twenty before they can hang one."[12] To which Lilburne rejoined, "And thus, after these fair blossoms of hopeful liberty, breaks forth this bitter fruit, of the vilest and basest bondage that ever English men groan'd under."[13]

Lilburne, free once again, set forward his indictment of Cromwell's tyrannies in a new pamphlet, aptly titled *England's New Chains*. It spread through the Leveller distribution system at a rapid rate. The Rump Parliament was not pleased, calling the document "false, scandalous, and reproachful" as well as "highly seditious." Cromwell knew that he had a pending revolt on his hands, and moved quickly to crush it. At four in the morning on March 28, 1649, one hundred horsemen surrounded Lilburne's lodgings, and dragged him off to the Tower once more.

But public sentiment stood behind him. For much of the decade, he had been the most popular man in England, and his supporters did not desert him. In April his wife led more than a thousand women, all wearing sea-green ribbons,* in a march that ended at the doors of Westminster, where they delivered a petition, signed by 10,000 people, demanding Lilburne's freedom. The Rump Parliament refused to accept it.

Hugh Perry, an emissary from Cromwell, visited Lilburne in the Tower that month, attempting to secure a public statement of support for the new government in return for his freedom. The two engaged in a sharp exchange. Sovereignty, Lilburne argued, derived from the people. Pshaw, laughed Perry. The only legitimate authority derived from the might of the sword. Cromwell soon exercised that sword once more in a vicious and brutal way to finally suppress the well-intentioned but poorly organized and ill-financed Levellers.

Unhappiness with the new government continued to grow among Leveller supporters in the army. In April, a mutiny erupted among soldiers concerned about a planned invasion of Ireland, their late pay, and the failure to secure new Parliamentary elections. The uprising was quelled, its ringleader executed at St. Paul's Cathedral. His funeral was attended by thousands of Levellers wearing their sea-green colors.

The next month, Leveller William Thompson led a mutiny at Banbury, calling for the release of Lilburne and the acceptance of the Agreement of the People. Cromwell led a disciplined charge of loyal cavalry that surrounded and captured several hundred mutineers, who were imprisoned for several days at Burford Church. Thompson was killed in the skirmish. After their capture, three other ringleaders were executed and buried on the grounds of the church. The militarily hapless Levellers had been crushed.

In October 1649, the Rump Parliament convened an "extraordinary" court of forty-one specially selected judges to try Lilburne on charges of violating the Treason Act, a law passed a few months earlier for the specific purpose of creating a crime for which they could convict Lilburne. After a three-day trial, he was found not guilty and released. Bonfires

---

* The popular press referred to these Leveller women as "Bonnie Besses in their sea-green dresses."

of celebration lit the skies from London to the English countryside. The victorious Lilburne was lionized as a hero throughout the land.

But when the Levellers' military efforts ended, so too did their political ones.[14] The Rump Parliament reinstituted censorship of the press, and the repressions of the Commonwealth regime continued. Lilburne, though free, was unable to organize among the former Levellers, many of whom rightly feared for their lives. The grassroots movement for a democratic republic of constitutionally limited government in England was over.

Lilburne never regained his position of prominence. He continued his opposition to Cromwell and was in and out of English prisons for the rest of his short life. Near the end, he became a Quaker.[15] On a short parole from Dover Prison in the spring of 1657, Lilburne died of "gaol fever" in the arms of his long-suffering wife, Elizabeth. Of his passing, and her life with him, Elizabeth said it had brought her only "seventeen years' sorrows."[16]

Though a failure in its own time, the Leveller movement was a spectacular success when viewed through the prism of posterity. More than three centuries later, seventeen of the twenty key proposals in the Agreement of the People would be incorporated in English statutes and the English Constitution, and the eighteenth—the call for a written constitution—would be adopted in the new United States.

Having crushed the only significant popular opposition to the Commonwealth, Cromwell went about consolidating his power. His methods, however, became increasingly unpopular. The Calvinistic authoritarian Bible-state he headed delivered brutal justice and limited personal liberties in ways that were even more objectionable than those used by Stuart tyrants.

Lilburne's protégé, young John Wildman, was able to read the tea leaves of political and military power more clearly than his mentor. Recognizing the futility of the Levellers' cause in the face of the overwhelming financial and military resources of Cromwell, he quietly removed himself from the scene. He would wait for another day when the political winds might be aligned more in his favor.

When the monarchy and the Ancient Constitution were restored in 1660 and Charles II took the throne, so great was the unhappiness with Cromwell's rule that his body, which had been entombed at Westminster Abbey after he died in September 1658, was exhumed, hung in public chains, and decapitated. The headless body was disposed of in a pit, and his severed head "was displayed on a pole outside Westminster Hall"[17] for the next twenty-four years.

The Stuart genetic predisposition toward absolutism, however, remained. Chastened by the fate of his father, Charles II proceeded with more political caution toward the complete realization of his grandfather's divine right of kings. Fortunately for Charles and the kingdom, he was so preoccupied by the pursuit of his own dissolute pleasures (he is said to have fathered more than a dozen illegitimate children, by nearly as many mistresses), he never focused his full energy and attentions in that direction.

Opponents of Stuart absolutism rallied around the aging Denzil Holles, returned from his Cromwellian exile, and former Leveller John Wildman, who with other like-minded leaders formed what would become the first opposition political party. They were called "Whigs," a term derived from the stubborn Scottish covenanters— "Whiggamores"—who only reluctantly accepted the Restoration.

Like most political coalitions united around a common opponent, these Whigs spanned a wide spectrum of political thought. The radical minority tended toward more republican views on government, while the majority merely sought to restore the kind of balance Coke described in the Ancient Constitution.

Whig writers dusted off the Leveller tool of political pamphleteering but found themselves in need of a compelling new argument. The failure of the unpopular Cromwellian regime left philosophies of civil governance based upon Protestant covenant theology in poor repute. And while the Ancient Constitution had its place, Lilburne's Norman yoke had become so intertwined with it that absolutist apologists for the king ("Tories") could dismiss it as a factor contributing to the anti-monarchical excesses of Cromwell.

Casting about for new rhetorical weapons, the more radical Whig pamphleteers such as Algernon Sidney and James Tyrrell, a close friend and supporter of John Locke, eagerly embraced a new school of secular natural rights, articulated most successfully in the writings of the Dutch theologian Grotius and German philosopher/statesman Baron von Pufendorf.

With help from Locke and Wildman, Sidney and Tyrrell soon carried the natural law argument to the forefront. Though their arguments were secular, they acknowledged that natural law was given to man by God, and that it could be maintained only if agreements were honored. The most aggressive aspect of this natural rights argument was that it gave citizens the moral authority to resist the exercise of force that compels compliance with acts contrary to natural law.[18]

Algernon Sidney's *Discourses Concerning Government* was a response to the divine right of kings apologist Sir Robert Filmer's *Patriarcha*. Sidney "believed that the Sovereign's subjects had the right and duty to share in the government of the Realm by giving advice and counsel." Patriarchal government was not the exertion of God's will, as Filmer and others contended, because the "[c]ivil powers are purely human ordinances."[19]

Though Sidney's arguments were presented in the immediate aftermath of the Glorious Revolution and played an indirect role in the Whig pamphleteering that led up to it, John Locke's ideas of natural law were the most powerful of the day.

Among the most significant natural rights that all men possessed, Locke would argue, was the right to obtain and keep property. With property came a stake in society. For Locke, unlike his more radical Whig allies, the right to vote should be limited to those who possessed at least a modicum of property.

The Catholic James II was crowned king in April 1685 on the death of his brother Charles II by natural causes (though some of the radical Whigs unsuccessfully conspired to kill him in 1683). James II wasted little time in giving the enemies of Stuart absolutism reason to complain. Calling a new Parliament into session, he

deployed heavy-handed techniques to ensure the election would result
in a majority of members that would support his program. He continued
his brother's practices of removing opponents from eligibility to stand
for election, and, as the contemporary historian Gilbert Burnet documented, did not shy from the use of force to make sure his men won.
Reports "came from all parts of England complaining about the violence used in the elections of 1685. . . . The methods were so successful
that James II said that there were only 40 members of parliament that
he was unhappy with."[20]

Even this most supportive Parliament, however, soon gained the dis-
favor of the newest Stuart king. In November James II decided to eliminate the Test Acts, a law that prevented Roman Catholics from holding
public office or serving as officers in the army. Parliament recoiled at
this, and when the members voiced their opposition, he dismissed them
all. As historian George Henry Wakeling noted, "and thus the most
loyal Parliament a Stuart ever had was prorogued."[21]

James II quickly piled on his offenses. He assembled a standing
army of more than 34,000 soldiers without securing Parliamentary approval, and he insisted on his right to dispense with any law that he did
not like made by past or present Parliaments.

The last straw came when he published his Declaration of Indul-
gence, which in effect gave preference to Catholics over members of
the Church of England. He then compelled all the bishops in the
Church of England to read the document as part of regular church
services. Seven refused, and when he imprisoned them in 1688, their
subsequent trial and acquittal sparked Whig pamphleteers to continue their literary assaults on the latest Stuart tyrant. Many limited
their arguments to the restoration of Coke's Ancient Constitution, but
the Radicals went further. Not only did they seek freedom of conscience and religious tolerance, but they resurrected the Levellers' argument for the broad expansion of suffrage. Popular sentiment across
the country rallied to the arguments of both Moderate and Radical
Whigs.

Soon Whig leaders sent a letter of invitation to Prince William of

Orange, the Protestant leader from Holland, to rescue England from the tyrannies of James. William's wife, Mary, was James II's Protestant daughter, and she, in her own right, had a legitimate claim to the English throne.

In November of that year, William responded positively to the invitation, sending back his own Declaration of The Hague,[22] a brief statement of his intent to assist these politicians in restoring English liberties. When he landed in England with an army of 20,000, it took only two minor skirmishes with James's largely unmotivated forces to convince James that militarily he was at a disadvantage. In addition, William had cleverly arranged for the printing of 60,000 copies of his 1,300-word Declaration of The Hague in broadsheet format, and when he landed, his Whig allies on the ground saw to it that this reassuring document was widely distributed among the English population.[23] William allowed James to escape to France, and his Whig allies took that as proof that James had abdicated his throne.

A special "extralegal" Convention Parliament was called into session by the members of King James II's Privy Council.[24] The elections, held in January 1689, returned many of James's former opponents who had been deprived of their seats in the "rigged" Parliamentary election of 1685. The unhappy and unconstitutional origins of the Cromwellian "Rump Parliament" weighed heavily on the minds of members of the Convention Parliament, and the members took great pains to avoid being similarly classified.

First they needed to make the case that James II had "broken his original contract"[25] with the English people, as philosopher John Locke would later describe it. This, they argued, he had done not only by fleeing the country, but also by throwing the royal seal into the Thames on his way out. They also needed a bill of particulars that outlined the manner in which he had broken the constitutional contract—Coke's "Ancient Constitution." This they were able to prepare readily in the form of a Declaration of Rights, which passed in February.

The charges were devastating. They outlined twelve specific policies by which James had "endeavour[ed] to subvert and extirpate the protestant religion, and the laws and liberties of this kingdom";[26] these included abuse of the dispensing power, unlawful prosecution of the seven bishops, levying of taxes without the proper Parliamentary authority, raising a standing army in peacetime without Parliamentary authority, and conducting improper Parliamentary elections, among several others.

In addition, the Declaration of Rights reaffirmed in an even more expansive way the same "ancient rights and liberties" that Sir Edward Coke and Parliament had forced Charles I to confirm, if only temporarily, in the Petition of Right six decades earlier.

Added to the rights affirmed in the Petition of Right—these were the prohibition of taxation without Parliament's consent, the prohibition of forced loans, the prohibition of arbitrary arrest, guarantee of the right of habeas corpus, the prohibition of forced billeting of troops, prohibitions against the imposition of martial law, and guarantees of due process—were these "ancient rights": the right of the subject to petition the king, the right to bear arms for defense, the protection of free elections of the members of Parliament, the right of members of Parliament to engage in free and open debate, the prohibition of excessive bail and "cruel and unusual punishment," and the right to frequently hold sessions of Parliament. Some Radical Whigs expected that dramatically increased suffrage would naturally follow.

A month later, the Convention Parliament offered the crown jointly to William of Orange and his wife, Mary, conditional upon their acceptance of the limitations on the constitutional authority of the monarch implicit in the Declaration of Rights. They agreed, accepted the crown, and formally called into session the Parliament, which subsequently passed the earlier Declaration of Rights passed by the Convention Parliament, now as the constitutionally authorized English Bill of Rights of 1689.

Did the subsequent conduct of William III and the Whigs who had brought him to power perfect the rights of Englishmen under the Ancient Constitution of Coke's creation? Or did it merely represent the transfer of power from one absolutist monarch to a slightly less absolutist monarch, who shared more power with Parliament?

Historian Catharine Macaulay, writing at the time of the American Revolution, found William III and his Parliaments little different from those that preceded him. Most of his cabinet members had served similar roles during the reign of James II. Many of them were personally corrupt: "The Flaws in the revolution system left full opportunity for private interests to exclude the public good . . . [creating] a system of corruption. . . . Parliament, the great barrier of our much boasted constitution, while it preserved its forms, annihilated its spirit."[27]

Macaulay pointed to numerous violations of that spirit, including:

> the destructive grievance of a debt of one hundred and forty millions, a grievance which operates powerfully and variously against public freedom and independence; a strong military standing force, contrary to the very existence of real liberty; an army of placemen and pensioners, whose private interest is repugnant to the welfare of the public weal; septennial parliaments in violation of the firmest principle of the constitution, and heavy taxes imposed for the advantage and emolument of individuals, a grievance never submitted to by any people not essentially enslaved.[28]

Contemporary Whigs were equally dissatisfied with the outcome of the Glorious Revolution. Locke's *Two Treatises of Government*, published in late 1689—months after William and Mary were on the throne—was in all likelihood an attempt to reassert the public virtues that Whigs thought they were ushering into governance when they backed William and Mary's claim to the throne over James II's.[29]

Locke's minority voice was heard but not influential in England in the wake of the Glorious Revolution. But within the next several decades, and for the next half a century preceding the American Revolution, his arguments—as he made them and others represented them in their own names—would form part of the intellectual framework used by the colonials to justify that rebellion across the sea.

Chapter 2

AMERICAN CONSTITUTIONALISM AND THE FORMATION OF THE SECULAR COVENANT

As their English cousins battled to restore the checks and balances of the Ancient Constitution, the colonists in British America clung to a narrow fringe of land along the Atlantic Coast stretching from the port of Charleston in the Carolinas to the fishing villages of Maine. The New England colonies had been granted charters by the king and were thus largely self-governed, while the Middle Atlantic and southern colonies all had a royally appointed governor (either directly by the king or through the colonial proprietor authorized by the king) whose powers were limited, in theory, by locally elected colonial legislatures. But by 1687, rebellion brewed in the small town of Ipswich, thirty miles north of Boston. At its center was John Wise, a thirty-five-year-old, Harvard-educated Puritan minister. The revolt he led signaled the birth of a uniquely American form of constitutionalism, one created from an amalgam of Puritan covenant theology, John Lilburne's Norman yoke, and the growing secular school of natural rights.

The colonial charters of Massachusetts, Connecticut, Rhode Island, New Hampshire, and Plymouth Colony having all been revoked,* James II had installed the tyrant Edmund Andros as his governor in the Dominion of New England, a near dictatorship formed to replace colonial governments with a centralized voice of the crown.

The citizens, however, remained loyal to their local governments. In Connecticut, Andros never actually obtained possession of the charter, thanks to a resourceful citizen who smuggled the document out of the room just before Andros's arrival. It was hidden in the hollow of an oak tree until after Andros departed. According to local legend, the wood from the oak tree, felled by lightning centuries later, was used to make the desk that now sits in the office of that state's current governor. Massachusetts, the grand Christian Bible-state, the "city upon a hill" that was to be an example to Christians throughout the world, was not so fortunate. The charter, so carefully guarded by the Puritan John Winthrop, was quickly snapped up by Andros's agents.

Andros moved quickly to assert imperial control over the colonies. He installed Joseph Dudley, son of one of the Massachusetts Bay Colony's first elected governors, in a puppet council. His abuses of colonial rights were legion. He insisted that the Navigation Acts, which prohibited the colonists from trading with any country other than England and which for two decades had been honored in the breach, must now be strictly enforced. He appropriated the building and properties of the Old South Church in Boston and gave them locally to the Church of England, which had but one hundred adherents in the entire colony. He revoked property rights, forcing many families to repurchase their own properties or remove themselves from the premises. Adding to the insult, he decreed that town meetings, a well-established democratic tradition in the region, could be held only once a year.

This dictate was in direct opposition to a half century of self-

---

* The following year, New York and New Jersey would be included in the Dominion of New England. James II's plan was to consolidate all the colonies into two administrative areas—the Dominion of New England in the north, and Virginia, Maryland, and the Carolinas in the south. Only Massachusetts experienced a permanent revocation of its charter.

governance known as "the New England Way," practiced in each of the one hundred towns throughout Massachusetts, Connecticut, Rhode Island, New Hampshire, and Plymouth Colony since their founding. Each town had its own Puritan church,* based on a Calvinist theology but self-governing on the independent "Congregational" model. In the early years, only members of the church could own property in the town, and only male members of the church over the age of twenty-one—the local "saints"—had the right to vote in the town meetings. At these meetings, the civil affairs of the town and important matters of policy were discussed in an open forum where all eligible male residents had a right to express their views. For those predestined saints eligible to participate, it was the ultimate in local democratic control. Those not eligible—women, Dissenters, Deists, Quakers, Baptists—found it to be anything but democratic. In the early years, there were few who offered resistance to the Calvinist theology of the oligarchs who led the colony. Those that did, such as Roger Williams and Anne Hutchinson, were banished. Punishments for heresy became more severe over time, as half a dozen Quakers executed in the 1660s discovered.

Despite these faults, the New England colonies of British America were at the time the most democratic societies in the world. As much as a quarter of the entire population enjoyed the franchise, a vastly higher percentage than in any other country. In the mother country, as the Leveller movement had highlighted, only 3 percent to 7 percent of the population were entitled to vote. As in England, every colony limited the franchise to owners of property, but in America, where land was cheap and plentiful, that standard was far easier to meet. Any man born into complete poverty could, by dint of his own labor—which being in scarce supply was adequately compensated—rise to "freehold" status by his thirties.

In August 1687, two hundred men of Ipswich convened a town

---

* In Rhode Island, the majority of the churches had rejected the Calvinist predestinationist theology of Massachusetts and were early "free will" Baptists.

meeting of the sort that had been conducted regularly since the town's founding in 1636, to consider their response to Andros's demands, specifically to his most recent imposition of arbitrary taxes and appointment of tax collectors. Two years earlier, the town had expressed its opposition to the arbitrary rule of Andros when they unanimously rejected the call to surrender the colony's charter voluntarily. Now John Wise led the charge to oppose Andros's taxes and, with his fellow townsmen, helped give birth to the concept that would be heard round the world decades later: no taxation without representation.[1]

Andros and Dudley convened a Star Chamber–type proceeding in Boston whose sole purpose was to punish the insolent Wise. The defiant minister defended himself admirably. "The evidence in the case, as to the substance of it, [is] that we too boldly endeavored to persuade ourselves we [are] Englishmen, and under privileges,"[2] Wise told the court in words that echoed those of Lilburne five decades earlier.* But according to Andros and his fellow judges, the rights of an Englishman that Coke defended in the Petition of Right were not his to enjoy on the far side of the Atlantic.

Speaking from the bench, Dudley sneered that "[y]ou shall have no more privileges left you than not to be sold for slaves,"[3] while Andros taunted him with the rhetorical question, "Do you believe . . . Joe and Tom may tell the King what money he may have?"[4] A third judge disabused Wise of the notion that the privileges of Englishmen applied to the colonials: "Do not think the laws of England follow you to the ends of the earth."[5]

The court found Wise and five members of his congregation guilty of sedition. They were thrown into a Boston jail for three weeks; there they languished without right of release. Only after considerable efforts by their friends was bail offered. They were freed after fifty pounds were paid and a bond of a thousand pounds given. Though freed, Wise

---

* There is no indication that Wise was familiar with Lilburne. He arrived at this determination independently.

was briefly suspended from his ministry.[6] Ultimately, the town of Ipswich paid the new tax, but popular sentiment throughout the colony sided with their resistance.

Across British America, the next two years saw a rise in public support for a broader, more permanent rebellion, particularly in Massachusetts. When, on April 4, 1689, a ship from Nevis, West Indies, arrived in Boston with copies of the English-language version of William of Orange's Declaration of The Hague, the locals seized the opportunity. Once ashore, Boston merchant John Winslow circulated dozens of the broadsheets and shared what he knew of William's landing in England. Soon Boston was abuzz with rumors of a much-hoped-for change in government.

Andros, who ruled from a heavily fortified wooden fort known as "the castle," located on an island in the Boston Harbor,[7] had Winslow arrested for possessing "seditious and treasonous" papers and imprisoned in the castle's jail. When news reached a regiment of colonial militiamen stationed in nearby Pemaquid, they mutinied and marched on Boston. They were joined in the streets by more than a thousand of the city's residents.

Simon Bradstreet, eighty-six years old and the last popularly elected governor, was greeted with resounding cheers when he joined them. Bradstreet was not merely a symbol of colonial self-governance and defiance of the arbitrary rule of Andros; he was a compelling reminder of the colony's proud history. Bradstreet was a man of substance and courage, whose personal story was a living history of the Massachusetts Bay Colony. Born in England in 1603, he graduated from Emmanuel College, Cambridge, and secured employment as secretary to Thomas Dudley, one of the early organizers of the colony. He married Dudley's daughter Anne and arrived with Winthrop on board the *Arbella* in 1630, a year when the entire population of British America was no more than 5,000—barely 1,000 in nearby Plymouth Colony, perhaps 4,000 in Virginia. During the next six decades, Bradstreet saw the population grow to 250,000, still barely 5 percent of the population of the mother country, but worthy of notice and clearly poised for dramatic growth. When the crown revoked Massachusetts's charter, the old man refused to accept an appointment to Andros's new puppet government.

The insurgents arrested the unpopular Andros, took over the fort and castle, and imprisoned him along with Joseph Dudley in his own former headquarters. Within a month, both men were sent back to England in chains.

With no royally appointed governor or revised charter, the citizens of Massachusetts turned to the ancient Bradstreet to serve as their governor once again as they awaited the king's decision.

A decade and a half before Cromwell had his chance to form a Christian Bible-state on earth, Winthrop and the handful of saints who had formed the Massachusetts Bay Company received a royal charter that gave them their own chance. The charter allowed all the "freemen" of the company (independent Puritans who subscribed to the Calvinist teachings preferred by Winthrop and the other leaders) to select the governor and members of the General Court, who met four times a year to manage the affairs of the colony. Already acting in opposition to the democratic ideals on which their society was based, Winthrop kept the charter itself hidden from the rest of the freemen for years. The charter, if followed properly, would offer a model of truly democratic government. The court also possessed the power to admit individuals to the freedom of the company.[8] In practice, this gave the court the power to exclude any settlers who had different religious views, a power that it would soon exercise with vigor.

As secretary to the General Court, Simon Bradstreet experienced and documented the defining events of what historian Perry Miller would later call this "errand into the wilderness." In 1634 he witnessed the first "revolution" in Massachusetts, when the freemen called on Winthrop to produce the charter none of them had seen.[9] When they learned the full nature of the rights granted to them, the freemen insisted on their exercise. In the next election, Winthrop was removed temporarily as governor, replaced by Bradstreet's employer, Thomas Dudley.

Bradstreet also witnessed the disagreements between Winthrop and his magistrates on the one side against strong-willed thinkers who instinctually resisted the standards of conduct imposed by the select group of "saints." The General Court of Massachusetts, and each local community, had the right and the authority to develop long lists of constraints on personal behavior. Many of these constraints related to statements of faith and orthodoxy; others, especially at the local level, were extremely trivial. In one early Puritan community, for instance, young men were forbidden to marry until they had killed at least six blackbirds or three crows.[10] When it came to "liberty of community"—that is, the right of each community to establish its own laundry list of prohibited behaviors—the Massachusetts Puritans were utterly implacable. This system would not be tolerated for long. Two banishments (Roger Williams and Anne Hutchinson) and one impatient departure (Thomas Hooker) provided alternatives to the authoritarian Bible-state the Massachusetts divines intended.

As a young boy in England, Roger Williams first caught the attention of Sir Edward Coke with his skills as a translator and scribe. Coke arranged for his education at Cambridge, and, upon graduation, Williams had embarked on a career as a minister. His strongly held Separatist Christian views hastened his speedy evacuation to Boston, barely a few steps ahead of Charles's zealous Archbishop Laud. By 1635, his controversial preaching in Salem, Massachusetts, included challenges to both the king's authority in the granting of charters and the colony's new requirement of an oath of allegiance.

In October of that year, Williams was banished from the Massachusetts Bay Colony on charges of sedition and heresy. For Williams, the attempt by a central ecclesiastic or governmental authority to compel any individual to think in a certain way "stinks in the nostrils of God."[11] He and a dozen friends established a settlement on the site of what is now Providence, Rhode Island. It soon became a haven for separatists and dissenters of all types, including fellow heretic Anne Hutchinson, who was banished from the Massachusetts Bay Colony the following year.*

Rhode Island was an unwelcome anomaly in Puritan New England. For decades, the small colony fended off challenges to its autonomy from its overbearing neighbor to the north, Massachusetts, and its new, slightly less aggressive neighbor to the west, Connecticut. Thomas Hooker, a well-known Puritan preacher in England before he came to Massachusetts in the fall of 1633, established and led the new colony. Less than a year into his stay there, both he and his parishioners became restless. An expedition of six members from the church went out to the Connecticut River valley. Upon their return, virtually the entire congregation, Hooker included, left Newtown, Massachusetts, for Connecticut in 1636, the same year as Roger Williams's banishment.

While Hooker was in agreement with the General Court's decision to banish Williams, elements of the authoritarian rule of the General Court in Massachusetts did not sit well with him. He was decidedly more democratic in his notions than Winthrop of Massachusetts. This is highlighted by key areas in which the governments of Connecticut and Massachusetts differed. In Connecticut, for instance, the right to vote was not exclusively limited to church members. All male inhabitants, church members or not, were allowed to vote.[12] Also, in 1639, Hooker and Connecticut adopted the Fundamental Orders, a constitution for their community† that covered many of the points that would appear a decade later across the Atlantic in the Levellers' Agreement of the People. In that document they affirmed that the covenantal nature of a secular constitution applied to all in the community, regardless of church affiliation. It would be these more democratic principles that

---

* Hutchinson's spiritual journey continued. In 1642, after the death of her husband, she adopted a type of Christian individual anarchism and moved to what is now Westchester County, New York, where she and several of her children were massacred by Indians. Royalist governor Thomas Hutchinson of Massachusetts was her great-great-grandson.

† Justifying Connecticut's nickname, "the Constitution State."

would spread beyond New England, not the more restrictive principles of Massachusetts.

W hen England became embroiled in the Civil War during the 1640s, it largely left the colonies in British America alone, much to their liking. It wasn't until the Restoration that the mother country began its campaign to centralize the administration of British America. The autocratic nature of the Stuart kings' approach to colonial governance increased up until the time of the Glorious Revolution, and it was with great joy that all colonists in British America celebrated the rise of Parliament, the English Bill of Rights, and the ascension of the Protestant William and Mary to the throne.

It came, then, as a disappointment when the colonists discovered that the new king and Parliament, though less autocratic, desired more centralized administrative control over the colonies. As the colonists in Massachusetts sent Andros back to England in chains, they expected that the English Bill of Rights would be applied to them as fully as it was to their cousins back in the mother country. Surely the new king would restore local self-governance and allow them once again to elect their own governor and legislature.

Colonists in nearby New York had similar ideas. By the end of April 1689, news of the successful Boston revolt reached New York. There a group of local merchants headed by Jacob Leisler overthrew the Andros regime and established their own provisional government until a representative of King William and Queen Mary arrived.[13] The Leisler Rebellion in New York ended poorly. Confusion over royal authority when the royal representatives arrived led to a series of battles, culminating in Leisler's execution in 1691. The judge who ordered the execution was the same Joseph Dudley who had arrived in chains on the boat that carried Edmund Andros to England in 1689 (Dudley had quickly talked his way back into the good graces of the crown).

When news of the Glorious Revolution arrived in Virginia, it was received with equal enthusiasm, though without the plotting of rebellion against the royal governor because Virginia, more than any other colony, identified with the English monarchy. William and Mary's choice of a new royal governor for Virginia gave an indication that though the crown intended to honor the English Bill of Rights in the mother country, colonial policies were in the hands of Tories or Court Whigs, rather than radical Whigs like John Locke. The new governor who arrived in Jamestown in 1692 was the same Edmund Andros whose tyrannical rule had sparked the Boston Rebellion three years earlier.

In Virginia there was no tradition of town meetings. The social and economic structure reflected Elizabethan hierarchy—crown, aristocracy, landed gentry, yeomanry, common people. The established religion was the Church of England, not the independent Congregational Puritan churches. Royal governors exercised Stuart policy, while the first families embraced the kind of Parliamentary powers with which that champion of the Ancient Constitution, Sir Edward Coke, would have been entirely comfortable. The colony had been established for economic gain, not religious freedom.

When the Parliamentary forces prevailed over Charles I, many of his loyal cavaliers and their children fled to Virginia, where they found a safe haven. For example, George Mason fought in the Royalist Army of the future Charles II at the Battle of Worcester. He was among only a handful of Royalists who were able to escape after their loss. He was able to slip through the lines of the Parliamentary Army dressed as a peasant, boarded a ship bound for the Americas, and in the spring of 1652 landed in Virginia. There he founded one of the first families of that colony. His descendants included his great-great-grandson George Mason V, a leading figure in Revolutionary Virginia, a forceful Anti-Federalist, and the namesake of George Mason University in Virginia.

Andrew Munro, a Scotsman who had fought on the side of Charles I at the Battle of Preston and was an ancestor of James Monroe, made his way to Virginia at about the same time as Mason. They were joined in 1656 by John Washington, son of a displaced Church of England minister who made his fortune at Popes Creek Plantation, just miles from the Mount Vernon site that became home to his great-great-grandson George Washington.

First records of the ancestors of Thomas Jefferson, James Madison, and the Lees date to this period as well. They established plantations in Virginia and over the next century formed the politically and economically powerful landed gentry that came to dominate the state.

By the mid-1690s, the aftereffects of the Glorious Revolution had rippled through the colonies and a "new normal" in British-American colonial relations was established. With two notable exceptions (Connecticut and Rhode Island), most colonies now had royally appointed governors and locally elected independent legislatures.[14] So long as the crown in British America did not overreach its royal prerogatives—that is, so long as it respected the limitations upon its exercise of power as delineated in the English Bill of Rights—the system worked well enough. All the colonies of British America were experiencing a period of extraordinary population growth and economic advancement, and no one on either side of the Atlantic seemed much inclined to interfere with that success.

That is, until the crowning of Queen Anne in 1702. The period between 1702 and 1765 saw popular sentiment and political practice in British America move toward a view that natural rights extended to all nonslave colonists. The English Bill of Rights merely acknowledged those rights. The availability of vast expanses of untouched virgin land, where a man's liberty was constrained only by his ambition and creativity, seemed but an obvious manifestation of those rights. Even in Massachusetts, where the original Puritan theocracy had attempted to thwart that natural liberty, the ecclesiastic independence granted to local churches under the Congregational model worked against authoritarian constraints. Participation in civil governance that had been limited to the predestined saints now extended to the entire free white population, regardless of religious affiliation. Where the Puritan Congregational ecclesiastic tradition had once stood for a theocratic republic modeled on the narrow confines of the Geneva Republic, or even the

Cromwellian Commonwealth, it now gave birth to an expansive, widely inclusive raw form of democracy.

It was John Wise, hero of the revolt against Andros's tyrannies, who gave formal voice to these ideas. Now in his sixties, but still pastor of the Chebacco Parish in Ipswich, Wise wrote his *Vindication of the Government of the New England Churches* in 1717. That Wise was a practitioner of Puritan covenant theology and champion of "the New England Way" in civil governance was no surprise. That he understood and used the arguments of natural rights advanced by Pufendorf in *The Law of Nature and of Nations* in articulating his case for democracy, however, was revolutionary. It was another indication that in the wide-open spaces of British America, the synthesis of Protestant theology and secular political philosophies would find fertile ground for rapid growth.

From this synthesis, Wise argued that democracy was the form of government most favored by both reason and God. Of monarchy, he concluded "that God and wise nature were never propitious to the birth of this monster," and aristocracy was "a dangerous constitution in the church of Christ." He added that only "a democracy . . . is the form of government which the light of nature does highly value."[15] He believed that natural rights require democracy in both ecclesiastic and civil organization, arguing that "man's original liberty . . . ought to be cherished in all wise governments. . . . [T]hese churches of New England, in their ancient constitution of church order, it being a democracy, are manifestly justified and defended by the law and light of nature."[16]

Wise put forward the first written articulation of American constitutionalism, a concept that had been developing in the minds of the colonists of British America for decades:

"Let us conceive in our mind a multitude of men, all naturally free and equal, going about voluntarily, to erect themselves into a new Common-Wealth. Now their condition being such, to bring themselves into a politick body, they must needs enter into divers[e] Covenants."[17] He outlined the three steps necessary to establish these secular covenants. Half a century later, his grandchildren's generation would follow these steps precisely as they erected a new "Common-Wealth" in British America:

> [First], each man covenant to joyn in one lasting society . . . by a publick vote.

> [Second, a] vote or decree must then nextly pass to set up some particular species of Government over them. . . . Then all are bound by the majority to acquiesce in that particular form thereby settled, though their own private opinion, incline them to some other model.

> [Third], there will be need of a New Covenant, whereby those on whom sovereignty is conferred, engage to take care of the common peace, and welfare. And the subjects on the other hand, to yield them faithful obedience. . . . [T]he aforesaid Covenants may be supposed under God's Providence, to be the Divine Fiat, Pronounced by God.[18]

Whether Wise originated the American concept of a secular constitutional covenant or was merely the first to express it in writing, there was little doubt that the idea had already taken hold in the colonies. Benjamin Franklin, the man most historians have come to consider "the first American," would have undoubtedly been aware of Wise's works, having apprenticed in his brother's printing business. Franklin shared with Wise an antipathy for Puritan cleric Cotton Mather. It was Mather's weak attempts to establish Presbyterianism and an aristocratic theocracy in New England that had inspired Wise's first literary work (*Churches Quarrels Espoused*, 1705). Mather's general stuffiness later inspired the fifteen-year-old Franklin to write the humorous Silence Dogood series of letters, first published by his brother in 1722.

Franklin's early preference for secular philosophies of natural rights was probably fanned by his exposure to the radical republican critiques of the powers of the new Parliament and crown written by Londoners and "commonwealthmen" John Trenchard and Thomas Gordon known as *Cato's Letters*. Trenchard and Gordon wrote 140 pamphlets printed in London during the three years between 1720 and 1723. These were reprinted and widely distributed throughout America, including by Franklin's brother James's *New England Courant*. They advanced the argument that individual liberty and republicanism were the best safeguard against the ever-encroaching centralized powers of the government—any government—because governments by their nature always sought to increase their own power. It was through these letters that the works of John Locke became widely known in British America.

The arguments for individual liberty advanced in *Cato's Letters* gained credence just as a new wave of immigrants began coming to British America, around 1717. They came from Scotland, Northern Ireland, and the northern counties of England, at a rate of 5,000 emigrants a year, bringing at least 250,000 new colonists to British America over the next fifty years.[19] Unlike the New England Puritans before them, this group was largely motivated by economics. Though they were of the Scottish Presbyterian tradition, and concepts of the "covenantal" foundations of both civil and ecclesiastic society rang true with them, it was escape from the desperate economic conditions of their native lands that drove them. For this reason they found the arguments of individual liberty espoused in *Cato's Letters* and other writings very appealing.

The natural sentiments of the population in British America to believe in individual liberty, enhanced among the more literate class by the writings of John Wise and *Cato's Letters*, gained broad support across all social classes when an emotional religious fervor swept the country a little more than a decade later. The genesis of this First Great Awakening was the arrival of English preacher George Whitefield in 1739. Whitefield had been greatly influenced by John Wesley and his Methodism, which offered a vision of a loving God who promised salvation to all those willing to accept it. The two evangelical friends differed on predestination—Wesley rejected it, while Whitefield accepted a modified form of it—and slavery, which Wesley considered an abomination and Whitefield accepted. Whitefield, however, would become the first Christian preacher to systematically preach the gospel to the enslaved.

A century after the Puritan fathers had arrived in New England, religious fervor had been replaced in their churches with dour liturgy and unemotional sermons. Whitefield changed all that. He preached in open fields to crowds that often exceeded 10,000. He emphasized the personal nature of individual faith and encouraged his audiences— uninspired by the dry sermons they heard from their own preachers—to read the Bible and establish a personal love for God. While he didn't completely reject the harsh Puritan doctrines that separated people into the "saved" and the "damned," his emotional preaching led all those who heard his voice to believe that they were saved if only they would accept that salvation. In many respects, it was a reversion to the same kind of personal interpretation of the Bible that sparked the Protestant Reformation two centuries earlier.

Benjamin Franklin, more Deist than traditional Christian, became one of Whitefield's greatest supporters. Though not converted to his friend's theology, he marveled at the improvement in civic behavior that accompanied every one of Whitefield's appearances. These optimistic notions led to a further expectation of political as well as theological equality among the thousands who thronged to his outdoors sermons. If any man could be saved by his personal acceptance of Christ, standing before God equal to the most learned minister, why should any man be denied the right to vote merely because he didn't own 40 pounds' or 40 shillings* worth of property?

Within British America, white adult male suffrage, already dramatically higher than in England—where, despite the Glorious Revolution, property-owning requirements still limited suffrage to barely 5 percent

---

* The English 40-shilling freeholder requirement to obtain the privilege of voting in elections transferred to British America during the migrations of the seventeenth century. By the decade immediately preceding the American Revolution, the freeholder requirement in most colonies had increased to ownership of property that either had a value of forty pounds or generated an annual rent of forty shillings (two pounds). Despite this higher threshold, the ready availability of land combined with the high wages paid to scarce labor gave many more residents of British America the franchise than was the case in England.

of the population—continued to rise. In New England it rose to as high as 70 percent in the country, 40 percent in the city. In the South it remained lower, but the trend toward broader participation and more self-government was undeniable.

In England, however, both the Parliament and the crown were moving in the opposite direction. The adoption of policies of "salutary neglect" masked the widening transatlantic divide. The originator of that policy, Robert Walpole, the first de facto prime minister, in office from 1721 to 1742, famously remarked, "If no restrictions were placed on the colonies, they would flourish,"[20] and the colonies could not disagree. Britain was not eager to expose this gulf amid the vibrant growth of British America, which filled the coffers of both the colonies and the mother country.[21]

But foreign military and financial concerns caused the abrupt end of this policy. Britain and France were engaged in the expensive and bloody Seven Years' War (known as the French and Indian War in the colonies) between 1757 and 1763. When William Pitt the Elder took over the administration of the war, he began to conduct policies that required British control of colonial actions.

When the war ended in 1763, instead of returning to the prewar policy of salutary neglect toward the colonies, Parliament issued the Proclamation of 1763, which prohibited colonial purchase of land beyond the Appalachians and deployed 10,000 British troops on the frontier to ensure that no colonials would venture to the west of their confines.

A standing army did not sit well with the colonials. A year later, Massachusetts attorney James Otis echoed Lilburne's Norman yoke argument in his lengthy pamphlet, *The Rights of the British Colonies Asserted and Proved*:

> Liberty was better understood and more fully enjoyed by our an-
> cestors before the coming in of the first Norman tyrants than ever
> after, till it was found necessary for the salvation of the kingdom to
> combat the arbitrary and wicked proceedings of the Stuarts.[22]

Otis's argument received little attention outside New England, but in the following year, 1765, when Parliament passed the Quartering Act, which required the forced billeting of British troops in colonial residences, and the Stamp Act, requiring a tax on all legal documents, newspapers, and other printed documents, Americans began to realize that the British Parliament no longer considered them fellow Englishmen. The colonists believed that, as Englishmen, they deserved their own voice in determining whether and how they should be taxed. The reaction in the colonies was predictable to anyone who understood the colonies and had followed these trends toward common national interests and more popular support for the guarantee of individual rights. Otis's invocation of the Norman yoke was the first of what soon became a veritable onslaught of prerevolutionary pamphleteers citing this concept, though the idea's reception was initially rather chilly in the more crown-friendly colony of Virginia.

In Boston, John Adams's radical cousin Samuel joined a newly formed group of agitators called the "Sons of Liberty"; the name was bestowed upon them by Sir Isaac Barré, an Irish-born member of Parliament who had fought alongside the colonials during the French and Indian War. The Sons of Liberty instigated the burning in effigy of Lord Bute, the British chancellor of the exchequer responsible for enforcing collection of the taxes. On August 14, 1765, a boisterous crowd, perhaps including an octogenarian with a memory of the 1689 rebellion, descended upon the houses of Royal Lieutenant Governor Thomas Hutchinson and Royal Governor Francis Bernard and destroyed them.

As informal chapters of the Sons of Liberty spread throughout the colonies, Benjamin Franklin had not yet given up on the idea of a British America in which colonists enjoyed the same rights as all Englishmen. In 1768, while serving in London as the agent of the Assembly of Pennsylvania, Franklin set forth a proposal to Lord Hillsborough, the secretary of state for colonial affairs in Prime Minister George Grenville's cabinet. Let the colonies be allowed to elect representatives to the British House of Commons, Franklin suggested. This straightforward proposal was rejected by a condescending Hillsborough, who went so far as to reject Franklin's authority to represent the colony of Pennsylvania in London, since his appointment came only from the colonial legislature and did not have the stamp of approval from the governor appointed by the colonial proprietor.[23]

In June 1770, Franklin tried again, arranging for the publication of a letter he wrote to Samuel Cooper setting forth an even bolder proposition. Colonial assemblies, he argued, should not be subservient to Parliament; instead they should report directly to the king.[24] There was so little hope that this proposal would be entertained, Franklin never had the opportunity to formally present it directly to either Hillsborough or any other representative of the king. Now even Franklin gave up his dreams of becoming an American-English gentleman. He would be an American, plain and simple. The ultimate dissolution of British America as part of the English colonial system was unavoidable.

In 1772, Boston publisher John Boyle reprinted John Wise's *Vindication* at the request of the town of Boston, the Sons of Liberty, and Colonel Artemas Ward, the first leader of the Massachusetts militia during the revolution and Washington's second in command from 1776 to 1777. The first edition sold out, and a second edition was rushed to print. All told, more than 1,100 copies were sold.[25]

Samuel Adams, journalist and revolutionary, stood at the bright center of the revolutionary movement. He served as one of Boston's two representatives to the General Court, the colonial legislature, and was an influential leader of the Boston town meeting, having served as the moderator and now as chairman of the newly named Committee of Correspondence, a group of twenty-one charged unanimously by the town meeting with articulating Boston's view of the rights of the colonists, and communicating that view to other towns in Massachusetts, the other colonies, and the world.

The resulting document—*The Rights of the Colonists*—was published by the town of Boston in November 1772 and widely circulated throughout the colonies. Written largely by Adams himself, the document drew heavily from both John Locke and—indirectly—John Wise's *Vindication*. Significantly, the manner in which the colonists declared their independence from Great Britain and established their new "species of government" mirrored the three steps Wise outlined in *Vindication*.

The first step was taken with the establishment of the Continental Congresses of 1774 and 1776, and the public vote by the delegates that resulted in the Declaration of Independence from Great Britain in 1776.

The second step, that of selecting the species of government, was taken twice: first in the midst of war by the Second Continental Congress, with the Articles of Confederation; and then by the Constitutional Convention in 1787, with the U.S. Constitution.

The third step, the establishment of the new secular covenant, was undertaken during the war when the state legislatures ratified the Articles of Confederation. When that secular covenant failed and a new species of government was introduced in 1787, the establishment of that new covenant took place in an even more elaborate process—authorized not by state legislatures, but instead by state ratification conventions.

Though the oppressive Townshend duties enacted by Parliament had largely been repealed, the onerous tax on tea remained, and when Royal Governor Hutchinson refused to allow three ships laden with tea to return to Boston, Samuel Adams having informed the ship captains on behalf of the town of Boston that they wouldn't be allowed to unload their cargo so long as the tax was required, the stage was set for the first American tea party.

Samuel Adams used his role as the town's de facto chairman of the Committee of Correspondence to take Wise's first step, that "each man covenant to joyn in one lasting society . . . by a publick vote."

Adams chaired a town meeting on December 16, 1773, that was attended by several thousand. That evening, about one hundred men disguised as Mohawk Indians boarded the ships and dumped overboard more than three hundred chests, containing all together about 90,000 pounds of tea. At modern prices, the total value of the tea was in excess of $1 million. Later, American merchants offered to reimburse the British merchants for their losses, but the offer was refused.

Adams, whose own *Rights of the Colonists* had dwelled heavily on John Locke's devotion to property rights, wrote an impassioned defense

for the acts of the tea partiers. The responsibility for the destruction of
the property, he argued, lay with the governor and the consignees, who
refused to allow the ships to return safely to England, knowing they
would not be allowed to unload if the taxes were required.[26]

In Virginia, news of the tea party met with mixed reviews. The
fiery backcountry Scotsman Patrick Henry celebrated it, but the more
established families, with their Cavalier heritage and plantation privileges, were hesitant to express support. Henry, along with Richard
Henry Lee, and twenty-nine-year-old Thomas Jefferson had been only
recently appointed by the House of Burgesses to serve in that colony's
Committee of Correspondence. These three, then, were the properly
authorized representatives assigned to develop a response to the actions in Boston.

Jefferson, who since his years as a law student at the College of
William and Mary had been fascinated by the Norman yoke concept,
having tried to advance it to anyone who would listen, with little success,
now found an opportunity to connect the fiery natural liberty of Patrick
Henry to the staid Ancient Constitution of the first families. Jefferson
now argued that the Stuart tyrant who embodied Lilburne's Norman
yoke had been replaced by a new form of tyrant—those 160,000 electors in Great Britain who selected that nation's Parliament.

Whether Jefferson was influenced by his familial connection to
Lilburne in introducing the Norman yoke argument we don't know.
(His great-great-grandfather on his mother's side, William Lilburne
[1636–1681], was John Lilburne's first cousin.)* We do know that
Jefferson, like Samuel Adams before him, blended the authority of
John Locke into the mix in 1774 to argue for full independence in his
Instructions to the Virginia Delegates to the Continental Convention,
printed for the public under the title of *A Summary View of the Rights
of British America*:

---

* Historians are uncertain if Jefferson was aware of this familial connection. Fred Donnelly, a
professor of history at Canada's University of New Brunswick, recently argued that Jefferson
may have been aware of his connection to Lilburne and chose to play it down.

Can any one reason be assigned why 160,000 electors in the island of Great Britain should give law to four millions in the states of America, every individual of whom is equal to every individual of them, in virtue, in understanding, and in bodily strength? Were this to be admitted, instead of being a free people, as we have hitherto supposed, and mean to continue ourselves, we should suddenly be found the slaves, not of one, but of 160,000 tyrants, distinguished too from all others by this singular circumstance, that they are removed from the reach of fear, the only restraining motive which may hold the hand of a tyrant.[27]

It was this intellectual bridge that enabled the first families of Virginia, long loyal to the crown and the Church of England, to join forces with the natural liberty arguments of rough-hewn Scotch-Irish backcountry leaders like Patrick Henry and Calvinist/Congregationalist Puritans like Samuel Adams.

Two years later, John Adams, the less radical of the Adams cousins, impressed by Jefferson's ability to synthesize the disparate themes of American thought on the subject of independence, insisted that Jefferson draft the document that became the Declaration of Independence. Jefferson's famous second paragraph was the perfect blend of Locke, Protestant covenant theology, and the Ancient Constitution, all prepared to throw off the Norman yoke:

We hold these truths to be self-evident, that all men are created equal, that they are endowed by their Creator with certain unalienable Rights, that among these are Life, Liberty and the pursuit of Happiness.

The delegates from the thirteen colonies—now states—covenanted among themselves that together they would fight for their independence from Great Britain, but they did not yet bind themselves together into a new country, as Jefferson's withering critique of George III in the Declaration made clear:

He has combined with others to subject us to a jurisdiction foreign
to our constitution, and unacknowledged by our laws; giving his
Assent to their Acts of pretended Legislation . . . we, therefore . . .
declare, that these united colonies are and of right ought to be free
and independent states; that they are absolved from all allegiance
to the British Crown . . . and that as free and independent states,
they have full power to levy war, conclude peace, contract allian-
ces, establish commerce, and to do all other acts and things which
independent states may of right do. And for the support of this declaration, with a firm reliance on Divine Providence, we mutually
pledge to each other our lives, our fortunes and our sacred honor.

On the evening of July 4, 1776, immediately after the Second Continental Congress declared independence in Philadelphia, the Congress authorized Philadelphia printer John Dunlap to print a one-page
broadside of the Declaration of Independence. Within two days he
had printed and distributed two hundred copies, which were sent far
and wide.

That the concept of throwing off the Norman yoke was a powerful
symbol of the new revolution was confirmed later that month when delegates of the new state of Pennsylvania met in Philadelphia on July 15
to draw up that state's new constitution.

Within a week of the publication of the "Dunlap Broadside"* of the
Declaration of Independence in Philadelphia, a prominent Pennsyl-
vanian wishing to influence the proceedings of that state convention,
using the pseudonym "Demophilus,"† and most likely the radical Whig
George Bryan, quickly had a small book published titled *The Genuine
Principles of the Ancient Saxons, or English Constitution: Carefully Collected from the Best Authorities*.

The book totaled 12,000 words and consisted of three parts: an in-

---

* Twenty-nine copies of the Dunlap Broadside exist today.

† Demophilus was the general of 1,000 Thespians who stood with the 300 Spartans at the Battle
of Thermopylae.

troduction and commentary by Demophilus; excerpts from a 1771 book titled *Historical Essay on the English Constitution* (written by an obscure radical English Whig, Obadiah Hulme), which laid out in detail the Norman yoke interpretation of the Ancient Constitution; and a complete reprinting of the Dunlap Broadside version of the Declaration of Independence.

Judging by the results of the 1776 Pennsylvania Constitutional Convention, many delegates were influenced by Hulme's argument that

> there are many customs, forms, principles and doctrines, that have been handed down to us by tradition; which will serve as so many landmarks, to guide our steps to the foundation of this ancient structure, which, is only buried under the rubbish collected by time, and new establishments. Whatever is of Saxon establishment is truly constitutional; but whatever is Norman, is heterogeneous to it, and partakes of a tyrannical Spirit.[28]

The state adopted a radically democratic constitution that reflected the delegates' understanding of that idyllic pre-Norman Anglo-Saxon governance. It included a unicameral legislature, a weak governor, and innumerable protections of individual rights. It was so democratic, in fact, that it made any action virtually impossible, and in 1791 the state replaced it with a new constitution more in line with the newly passed federal constitution. Pennsylvania's trouble hitting the right note the first time around on a constitution would soon be mirrored by the new nation as a whole, when the Articles of Confederation, adopted in 1781, proved to be, as John Wise might have said, "the wrong species of government."

Chapter 3

ALEXANDER HAMILTON AND THE BROKEN PROMISE OF PLAIN MEANING

The tragedy of Alexander Hamilton's life of greatest significance to the newly formed United States of America was not his premature death in 1804 from his duel with Aaron Burr. Instead it was his inability to abandon his "quasi-monarchist" English aristocratic worldview and accept the Constitution and the Bill of Rights as the secular covenant it was. This philosophy led him as secretary of the Treasury to break the first of the four promises contained within that secular covenant before the ink was even dry on the ratified Bill of Rights—the covenant that the federal government would abide by the written words of the Constitution.

If you were to ask average Tea Party activists what "constitutionally limited government" means, they would point you to two things: Article I, Section 8 of the Constitution, which enumerates the powers of Congress; and the Bill of Rights, those first ten amendments to the Constitution, which guarantee the rights of all individuals.

These limitations on federal power and guarantees of individual rights are the core of the secular covenant by which we have all agreed to be bound.

The Constitution, as it has been subsequently amended, is a secular covenant of the type John Wise first described in 1717, whose terms have been agreed to by the federal government, the states, and the people. This covenant was formed over a four-and-a-half-year period that began on May 25, 1787, when the Constitutional Convention convened in Philadelphia, and ended on December 15, 1791, when Virginia became the eleventh state to ratify the Bill of Rights and the first ten amendments were added to the Constitution.

By this time a government and cabinet had already been established, a first Congress had been elected and convened, and a second Congress had been elected under the terms of the ratified Constitution. The secular covenant, however, was not fully established until the fulfillment of a promise made during the ratification process by the new constitution's advocates: that a Bill of Rights would be added to it.

Following the plan John Wise set forward more than half a century earlier, the American colonies had created a new nation, formed by a citizenry that had independently agreed to be bound by a secular covenant, the first time in history this had been done. This agreement has held us together ever since, updated through the amendment process on seventeen occasions during the more than 220 years that have followed.

T hough he participated in its formation, and campaigned for its adoption, Alexander Hamilton did not consider himself bound by this secular covenant.

Smart, ambitious, creative, and articulate, Hamilton was a man of remarkable accomplishments. The youngest of the Founding Fathers, Hamilton was the only member of that group besides Benjamin Franklin who could call himself "self-made." His ascent from poverty toward national leadership was even greater than that of Franklin, who came from a well-respected, if modestly successful, family.

Born in 1755* in the small port city of Charlestown on the island of Nevis in the British West Indies, he was the product of the common law marriage between Rebecca Faucette Lavien, a young woman of French Huguenot and English descent, and James Hamilton, fourth son of a minor Scottish lord. He and his older brother James had a Dickensian upbringing in the Caribbean. Abandoned by his father when he was eleven, orphaned at thirteen when his mother died, the scrappy Hamilton showed intellect, talent, energy, and a bent for literary adventures and self-improvement.

In 1773 he arrived in New York City, on a scholarship provided by businessmen in his native British West Indies, and enrolled in King's College (soon to become Columbia University). In February 1775, less than two years after his arrival as an immigrant to the American colonies, he penned an eloquent defense of the democratic-republican ideals of the revolution in a pamphlet titled *Refuting the Farmer*.

That summer he joined the militia, quickly rising to the rank of captain in the Continental Army. By the end of the war he had risen to the rank of lieutenant colonel, and served much of the time as General Washington's chief of staff. On the battlefield, Hamilton distinguished himself on only one occasion, performing admirably in the final victory at Yorktown in 1781.

By 1783, the twenty-eight-year-old who had returned to study and practice law in New York City was now firmly committed to an aristocratic worldview. Driven by his desire for martial glory, as an aide to Washington, the commander of the army, he had witnessed firsthand the foibles of the elected Continental Congress. When he left the army, Hamilton in his heart was more Cromwell than Lilburne, more William III than Locke, more Walpole than Jefferson.

Perhaps the very steepness of his own personal ascent developed in him a philosophy of governance more dependent on the power of per-

---

* There appears to be uncertainty as to whether Hamilton was born in 1755 or 1757. Biographer Ron Chernow accepts 1755, while biographer Richard Brookhiser accepts 1757. Either seems plausible, with 1755 slightly more so.

sonal will than on those underpinnings of American constitutionalism that were of such bedrock importance to the other Founding Fathers. Puritan covenant theology interested him little. Secular theories on the natural rights of man—those which were found in the writings of Locke, and which so inspired Jefferson—he found uninspiring. In the common law of Sir Edward Coke he found a model for civil governance, but Lilburne's Norman yoke left him cold.

The lawyer trained in precedent, Hamilton cherished the sanctity of contract, but of John Wise's concept that civil government must be based on a secular covenant freely entered into, he was entirely unsupportive. That he lacked confidence in the wisdom of the common man there was little doubt. He said as much in the one speech he gave at the Constitutional Convention:

> All communities divide themselves into the few and the many. The first are the rich and well born, the other the mass of the people. The voice of the people has been said to be the voice of God; and however generally this maxim has been quoted and believed, it is not true in fact. The people are turbulent and changing; they seldom judge or determine right. Give therefore to the first class a distinct, permanent share in the government.[1]

In one area, Hamilton would have agreed with John Wise's *Vindication*. When a species of government, such as the federation under which the United States operated during the revolution, has failed, the old covenant should be buried and a new covenant formed.

At the poorly attended Annapolis Convention called in 1786 to suggest improvements to the weak Articles of Confederation, Hamilton and Madison were among the few delegates who showed up. Prodded by Hamilton, the delegates sent a bold proposal to the Continental Congress. A convention ought to be held, they said, to determine how to improve our means of governance.

In the spring of 1787, the Continental Congress agreed, and another convention—ostensibly for the purpose of improving the Articles of Confederation—was called to meet in Philadelphia that May. All thirteen states were invited to send delegates. Hamilton managed to have himself named as one of New York's three.

So began the first of four phases in the four-year process of creating the secular covenant by which our nation is governed. At the Constitutional Convention held in Philadelphia in the four months between May and September 1787, the fifty-five delegates prepared a new species of government—in the form of our Constitution.

The second phase was the ratification conventions. This first required the participation of the entire eligible voting population in each state, to elect delegates to that state's convention. Across the thirteen states, two thousand delegates were elected by about one million voters. The first such convention was held in Delaware, which ratified the Constitution in December 1787. The ninth convention, and the one that put the document into effect, came in June 1788, when New Hampshire ratified the document.

The third phase—the fulfillment of the promises made at the ratification conventions of Massachusetts, New Hampshire, Virginia, and North Carolina by the Federalists to the Anti-Federalists that Congress would pass the Bill of Rights—involved about 800,000 voters in the eleven states* and the sixty members of the House of Representatives they elected, as well as the thousand or so members of the eleven state legislatures and the thirty senators they elected. This phase was successfully completed in September 1789.

The fourth phase—the ratification of that Bill of Rights by those eleven states, which began in September 1789 and ended more than two years later, in December 1791, when Virginia became the eleventh state to ratify the amendments—involved the thousand or so members of the eleven state legislatures of those states, and by extension the voters who elected them.

During these four phases every eligible voter had the opportunity to

---

* Rhode Island and North Carolina didn't send representatives to Congress until after September 1789.

freely choose to join the covenant on three distinct occasions. As many as 1 million out of a population of 3 million participated.

When we speak today of the Founding Fathers we tend to think only of the seven great men pointed to by historians—Washington, Adams, Jefferson, Madison, Jay, Franklin, and Hamilton[2]—but sometimes include "the Framers," those fifty-five delegates who attended the Philadelphia Constitutional Convention or the thirty-nine who signed the Constitution.

But the select club known as the Founding Fathers must be thought of as larger than these few dozen. Every eligible voter in the thirteen original states who participated in the elections, conventions, and legislative sessions of 1787–1791 could authentically be called a Founding Father, for the assent of these voters was required to form the covenant.

The disturbing truth is that one of these seven storied Founding Fathers—Alexander Hamilton—intended from the very beginning to subvert the secular covenant of the Constitution and the Bill of Rights by knowingly misrepresenting what was meant by the plain meaning of three simple words found within it—"necessary and proper."

Between the first and last words of Article 1, Section 8 of the Constitution can be found a list of nineteen powers specifically enumerated and granted to Congress. They include the power to tax, pay debts, provide for the common defense, provide for the general welfare, borrow money, regulate commerce, establish uniform rules of naturalization, set bankruptcy law, coin money, punish counterfeiters, establish post offices, establish copyrights and patent protection, establish federal courts, punish piracies on the high seas, declare war, raise and support armies, maintain a navy, provide rules for state militias, and govern the capital city.[3]

The very last clause of Article I, Section 8, the famous "necessary and proper" clause, reads:

> [The Congress shall have power] To make all Laws which shall be necessary and proper for carrying into Execution the foregoing Powers, and all other Powers vested by this Constitution in the Government of the United States, or in any Department or Officer thereof.[4]

The most significant rule of the Constitutional Convention was the one that swore all delegates to silence outside the rooms of the convention. No printed documents could be issued, no conversations retold to any nondelegate. The intent, Madison said, was "to secure unbiased discussion within doors, and prevent misconceptions and misconstructions without."[5] Due to this rule, it was impossible for the ratifying conventions to rely upon "the intent" of the Framers. They were left to determine the plain meaning of the words enclosed in the document. A century later, "Living Constitution" proponents such as Woodrow Wilson and Oliver Wendell Holmes Jr. attempted to cloak their own extraconstitutional notions of federal government activism in the "intent" of the Framers, but such efforts were as transparently dishonest then as they are today. As Georgetown University constitutional law professor Randy Barnett notes:

> The necessary and proper clause was added to the Constitution by the Committee on Detail without any previous discussion by the Constitutional Convention. Nor was it the subject of any debate from its initial proposal to the Convention's final adoption of the Constitution.[6]

The Committee on Detail was formed on June 23, 1787, for the purpose of creating a draft of the Constitution based on the discussions of the convention to that point. A month later, on July 26, the convention adjourned to give this committee time to prepare the draft. It took them ten days, and when the convention reconvened on August 7, the "necessary and proper" clause had been inserted at the end of Article I, Section 8.

John Rutledge of South Carolina chaired the committee. The other four members were Edmund Randolph, Oliver Ellsworth, James Wilson, and Nathaniel Gorham. Presumably, discussion among all five of these men led to the inclusion of the "necessary and proper" clause. Later, as attorney general, Randolph would interpret Hamilton's legislation for the First National Bank of the United States as unconstitutional, an interpretation rejected by Washington in February 1791.

The same committee had previously rejected a clause proposed by Delaware delegate Gunning Bedford that Congress shall have power to "legislate in all cases for the general interests of the Union, and also in those to which the States are separately incompetent, or in which the harmony of the United States may be interrupted by the exercise of individual legislation."[7] As Randy Barnett explains, "in other words, the Convention had before it an almost completely open-ended grant of power to Congress and rejected it, without discussion, in favor of enumeration of particular powers and the ancillary Necessary and Proper clause."[8]

Congress has no powers—implied or invisible—beyond these stated in plain words. Any attempt to increase the power of Congress, or any other branch of the federal government, beyond these enumerated powers represents a usurpation of the secular contract that is the Constitution.

By introducing the unconstitutional First National Bank of the United States legislation to Congress, then persuading President George Washington to sign it into law in February 1791, Hamilton not only revealed his own deceptive nature; he also ignited a controversy about the proper role of the federal government that continues to this day.

The most damning evidence of thirty-two-year-old Hamilton's deception was the six-hour speech he gave to the convention on June 18, 1787. A delegate from New York, he had been quiet during the first three weeks of deliberations, suspecting that his own idealized vision of government was likely to draw criticism.

Hamilton wanted a highly centralized, powerful national government based on the British model. Instead of a hereditary king, he proposed what amounted to an elected monarch for life. Instead of a House of Lords, he proposed a senate whose members had lifetime appointments and were not directly elected by the people, but instead selected by "electors" selected by the voters. Instead of a House of Commons, he proposed an assembly of directly elected representatives who would serve three-year terms. Hamilton's executive would have veto power over any laws passed by the legislature. National power would be further curtailed by prohibiting the states from controlling their own militias.

> Let one body of the legislature be constituted during good be-
> havior or life. Let one executive be appointed who dares execute his
> powers. It may be asked, is this a republican system? It is strictly so,
> as long as they remain elective.
>
> It may be said this constitutes an elective monarchy! Pray what
> is a monarchy? May not the governors of the respective States be
> considered in that light? But by making the executive subject to
> impeachment, the term monarchy cannot apply.[9]

Hamilton's proposal was met with only forced politeness upon its conclusion. The next morning, when the convention reconvened, no one mentioned the speech or even discussed its merits.

Hamilton, being politically attuned, knew it was time to drop the proposal and support whatever plan emerged from the convention. But we know, based on his subsequent actions, that the "Hamilton Plan" he proposed that day was the true plan of governance he wished to implement. He would accept the constitution that emerged from Philadelphia as the best interim step that could be hoped for. Though he argued vigorously in public on behalf of ratification, he did so with great insincerity, always on the alert for opportunities to subvert the Constitution and replace it with the Hamilton Plan.

Perhaps chastened by the poor response to his June 18 speech, Hamilton left the Philadelphia convention on June 29 and remained away for more than two months, not returning until September 2, a mere two weeks before the final document was signed.

When he finally returned to the convention, it was clear that a final document was close to completion. He thought it "better than nothing," but would later concede that "no man's ideas were more remote from the plan than my own." Patiently waiting for his chance to advance his own agenda, he signed the final document with thirty-eight other delegates on September 17, 1787, kept his misgivings to himself, and vigorously promoted its merits in public.[10]

Thirty-nine delegates signed the document that emerged from that convention on September 17, 1787. Fourteen had returned home and three—George Mason and Edmund Randolph of Virginia and Elbridge Gerry of Massachusetts—had remained to the end but refused to sign because of its failure to include a Bill of Rights. Now it was time for that document to receive the willing consent of the states and the people of those states through an extraordinarily interactive process of ratification that engaged the people—recognizing their sovereignty and their right to freely give or withhold their consent. It was this freely given consent that formed the bond by which the secular covenant of the Constitution was made.

The Framers were wise in the manner they sought that consent. Rather than give the ratification process to the state legislatures, the Constitution called for a ratification by conventions held by the state-wide delegates elected specifically for the purposes of either granting or withholding their assent. Article VII laid this process out:

> The Ratification of the Conventions of nine States, shall be sufficient for the Establishment of this Constitution between the States so ratifying the Same.[11]

Within days of the end of the Philadelphia Convention, ink was flowing forth on both sides of the question with arguments for and against the Constitution. The public supporters of the Constitution—known as Federalists for their support of a federal system that gave certain powers to the centralized national government while leaving other powers to the state governments—were better organized and more systematic in their approach. This was largely due to the energetic efforts of Hamilton, who persuaded James Madison and John Jay to join him in writing a series of eighty-four articles in support of the Constitution. The Federalist Papers are the best-known political documents from this era. Jefferson and John Adams favored the new constitution but neither was seriously involved in the dialogue, Jefferson serving as our minister to France, and Adams as minister to England.

Most historical accounts of the process by which the secular covenant of the Constitution and the Bill of Rights were agreed to by the states and people of America describe the Constitutional Convention of 1787, and the subsequent discussions concerning state ratification, as a competition between two schools of thought. One school, again, the *Federalists*, argued for ratification of the Constitution because it offered the right level of centralized control to hold the new nation together. The second school, the *Anti-Federalists*, argued against the Constitution because it granted too much power to the federal government, at the expense of the rights of the states and of the individual.

Historian Robert Scigliano elaborated on the fights between the two groups over both the Constitution and the name attached to each group. The Anti-Federalists claimed that they were the real Federalists. "We're the ones standing by the Articles of Confederation, our federal Constitution, and you have stolen the name 'Federalist' from us," as Scigliano puts it. There's some truth in that, and yet the Federalists' argument was that they had been in favor of strengthening the Articles of Confederation, getting a stronger federal government, and therefore they were the real Federalists. Hamilton also had a special definition of a Federalist, a person who could support a consolidated, unitary national government so long as the states existed in some subordinate role within it. His was a special definition of federalism.[12]

Hamilton, who considered the Constitution a poor document indeed, became one of the most stalwart public advocates for its ratification. Even before he began work on the Federalist essays, he set down his own thoughts about the likely ratification success in a document he wrote titled "Conjectures About the New Constitution," which revealed his monarchist worldview. Fortunately for Hamilton, this document was not seen by the public until long after his death. It's unlikely, for instance, that Madison saw it, because had he done so, it's hard to imagine he would have consented to join Hamilton.

A reading of the highlights explains the wisdom of that course of action.

In this unpublished document Hamilton's contemporary assessment of the odds of the Constitution's adoption was guarded:

> It is almost arrogance in so complicated a subject, depending so entirely on the incalculable fluctuations of the human passions, to attempt to even conjecture about the event. It will be eight or nine months before any certain judgment can be formed respecting the adoption of the Plan.[13]

Hamilton continued, now almost pining for reunification with Great Britain under a monarchical system:

> A reunion with Great Britain, from universal disgust at a state of commotion, is not impossible, though not much to be feared. The most plausible shape of such a business would be the establishment of a son of the present monarch in the supreme government of this country with a family compact.[14]

While Hamilton was penning these hidden conjectures, the Continental Congress, convening in New York, and operating under the authority of the Articles of Confederation ratified in 1781, after some deliberation, forwarded the Constitution to the governors and legislatures for the purpose of calling state conventions to consider ratification.

The first such convention was held three months later in Delaware, and it ratified the Constitution. Other states' conventions would drag on over the next several months. By the summer of 1788, when New Hampshire, New York, and Virginia finally held their ratification conventions, eight states had ratified the Constitution. Should one of these three ratify, nine states would then form a new government, and the other four would be left to fend for themselves.

Opponents of the Constitution—the Anti-Federalists—were less organized but equally prolific. Patrick Henry of Virginia opposed it—he had refused to attend the Philadelphia convention because he "smelled a rat," but he didn't put pen to paper. Hamilton's New York colleague at the convention, Robert Yates, wrote as Brutus, and New York governor George Clinton wrote *Cato's Letters*—borrowing the name from the well-known series in the 1720s from the British Commonwealthmen Trenchard and Gordon. James Winthrop, great-great-grandson of the Puritan founder of Massachusetts, wrote *The Letters of Agrippa*, and Pennsylvania's William Findley wrote under the name "An Officer of the Late Continental Army."

From the beginning the main theme coming from the Anti-Federalists was a real concern about what the Constitution would do to institutionalize power over individual liberty and private conduct of economic activity.

Historians, however, have tended to overemphasize the significance of the competing pamphlets and underemphasize the debates at the ratifying conventions. In examining the process by which the secular covenant of the Constitution and the Bill of Rights were first formed, the public authority derives from the ratification debates, not the pamphleteering dialogues. There we learn that it is impossible to consider the Constitution without the Bill of Rights as the core of this secular covenant.

Hamilton's private prediction was on target. Nine months later the Constitution was ratified by the requisite ninth state, New Hampshire, and the wheels were set in motion to establish the new government, with each of the nine states beginning elections of representatives.

Hamilton, however, failed to understand or acknowledge the key role that acceptance of the Bill of Rights would play in this process. This is not surprising, given his steadfast arguments that no such document was needed. Given his future lawyerly manipulation of the "necessary and proper" clause to accomplish the centralized ends he desired, and his unqualified support for the Sedition Acts of 1798, we can only be everlastingly grateful to the Anti-Federalists who made addition of the Bill of Rights a condition of their support of the new constitution.

The breakthrough came five months after Hamilton's conjectures, on a wintry Massachusetts day in February 1788. Five states—Delaware, Pennsylvania, New Jersey, Georgia, and Connecticut—had already ratified the Constitution, but the odds against adding an additional four states to the ratification rolls were long indeed. Sentiment among the 350-plus delegates to the Massachusetts convention was decidedly Anti-Federalist.

The most optimistic Federalists expected that the entire secular covenant could be finalized within a year but that prospect quickly vanished when Massachusetts, in its January and February 1788 ratifying convention, became the sixth state to ratify the Constitution on the explicit promise by Federalists in attendance that a Bill of Rights would be added to it.

The level of direct citizen connection with the delegates elected to decide the fate of the Constitution in each state was extraordinary. In North Carolina, for instance, 271 convention delegates were elected to represent a population of 393,000—one delegate for every 1,300 residents. At the other extreme, in New York, 57 convention delegates were elected to represent a population of 340,000, one delegate for every 6,500 residents.

The proceedings in each state were at times raucous affairs, with delegates on each side cheered on or booed by crowds in the galleries. Locations varied—statehouses, churches, other large buildings—and the comfort of delegates and galleries alike was often an afterthought.

After ratification sped through five state conventions, the Federalists ran into a buzz saw of Anti-Federalism opposition in Massachusetts. It was here that the amendment process contained in the document itself provided a solution. Article V provided:

The Congress, whenever two thirds of both Houses shall deem it necessary, shall propose Amendments to this Constitution, or, on the Application of the Legislatures of two thirds of the several States, shall call a Convention for proposing Amendments, which, in either Case, shall be valid to all Intents and Purposes, as part of this Constitution, when ratified by the Legislatures of three fourths of the several States, or by Conventions in three fourths thereof, as the one or the other Mode of Ratification may be proposed by the Congress.[15]

Only after Anti-Federalists Samuel Adams and John Hancock secured promises from the Federalists that (1) the First Congress would immediately propose a package of amendments (ultimately the ten amendments known as the Bill of Rights) guaranteeing individual rights and (2) they would support the ratification of those amendments throughout the state legislatures did the Massachusetts convention narrowly ratify the Constitution, by a 187–168 margin.

I n New York, where Hamilton was a delegate to the ratification convention, he presented himself as the most ardent friend of the republicans. During June and July, Hamilton argued vigorously on behalf of the new constitution, not as the "monarchist" he was at heart, but almost as a Jeffersonian Democrat-Republican. In order to secure the support of Anti-Federalists, Hamilton and other Federalists agreed to include a "circular letter" recommending specific amendments to the Constitution. Hamilton attached his signature to the "Circular Letter" that emerged from the New York state ratification convention in July 1788, as part of the official report of that convention. This act was insincere in the extreme on Hamilton's part, but he considered it a necessary concession designed to ensure the convention ratified the Constitution.

That letter said, in part, "WE . . . [d]o declare and make known . . . that those clauses in the said Constitution, which declare that Congress shall not have or exercise certain powers, do not imply that Congress is entitled to any Powers not given by the said Constitution."[16]

After the ratification squeaked through the convention by a 30–27 vote, Hamilton conveniently developed an entirely different view of the implied powers given Congress in the Constitution. This letter is yet another example of Hamilton's long-term deceptions and his view that the Constitution was but an interim step to accomplish his ultimate purpose of installing a highly centralized government of his own design in the United States.

There was a third school of thought, however, and from the moment the new government was formed, this school set about to usurp the Constitution. I speak of the *Faux-Federalists*, a party of one, which was headed by Alexander Hamilton during the convention and which would over time gain many adherents. Its ideological descendants continue to plague the republic to this day.

Hamilton never viewed the Constitution and the Bill of Rights as a secular covenant that bound the federal government, state governments, and the people into a solemn and mutual contract. He had little reverence or respect for the Constitution other than as the best interim arrangement that could help him advance his permanent purpose—the establishment of a nationally centralized government ruled by an elite class of meritocrats, in turn headed by a chief executive who enjoyed a lifetime appointment.

Hamilton's own words during and after the convention give us more than enough evidence to know that his support for the Constitution— the arguments he advanced in the Federalist Papers—was insincere. Words, of course, are not the strongest evidence of intent. Actions, on the other hand, are. By his actions, Hamilton indicated that he did not consider the Constitution binding. Once the Constitution was in effect, Hamilton was placed in a position of executive power second only to President George Washington. During the five years he served as the secretary of the Treasury—from September 1789 to January 1795, but especially during the period from December 1790 to January 1795—Hamilton's unconstrained and unconstitutional exercise of power, his establishment of the precedent of federal powers far beyond those articulated in the Constitution itself, set a pattern of infringement on individual liberties that was unmatched until the administrations of Franklin Delano Roosevelt in the 1930s and 1940s and Barack Obama in the twenty-first century.

While Hamilton is to be admired for his intelligence, energy, ambition, and vision, he was deficient in constitutional fidelity. His much-heralded authorship of the Federalist Papers, and vigorous advocacy of the Constitution at the New York state ratification convention, derived not from a genuine commitment to the Federalist system of checks and balances but instead from political pragmatism. This coauthor of the Federalist Papers was, again, a Faux-Federalist, not an authentic Federalist. He accepted the Constitution as a temporary, interim step that brought him closer than did the weak, decentralized Articles of Confederation to his goal of establishing a powerful centralized government headed by a powerful magistrate appointed for life.

That Hamilton was a monarchist at heart was conceded by his close friend and fellow Founding Father, Gouverneur Morris, who confessed in his diary in 1804 that "[Hamilton] was on Principle opposed to republican and attached to monarchical government."[17] Had Hamilton's six-hour speech favoring "an elected monarch" at the Constitutional Convention and his pro-monarchy "Conjectures About the New Constitution" been known, it is difficult to see how Washington could have appointed him secretary of the Treasury.

But in September 1789, with a busy agenda ahead for a government that was but six months old, mere rumors of possible monarchist tendencies were not sufficient to keep Washington from giving his brilliant and ambitious thirty-four-year-old protégé the job. The nomination sailed through the Senate in an afternoon, and the next morning, Hamilton was at his desk in the new office of the secretary of the Treasury.

Within days, a busy Congress, fresh off the vote that sent the Bill of Rights to the states for ratification, asked Hamilton for a Report on Public Credit. Four months later, he delivered that report, which included an ingenious plan for establishing the new country's public credit. The nation—through both the prior Continental Congress of the Articles of Confederation and the thirteen states individually— had taken on very high levels of debt in order to finance the Revolutionary War.

Hamilton's proposal was to combine the state debts of about $25 million with the federal debt of $54 million into one large debt assumed by the new federal government and totaling $79 million.[18] The new federal government would then issue securities to the holders of this combined debt, and pay them interest, while leaving the door open as to when—and if—the principal would ever be retired. This action would create a market for these public securities. Then Hamilton proposed the creation of a "sinking fund"—with capital from excess federal revenues (revenues at that time consisted largely of custom duties paid on imported goods) and a new loan from Europe. This fund was designed to support the market value of the new public securities—buying them when the price was considered too low, selling them when the price was considered too high—thereby increasing public confidence in the reliability of the public debt as an investment vehicle.[19]

Hamilton's proposal stalled in Congress during the spring and early summer, until a "chance" encounter with Thomas Jefferson on the street in June 1790. Moved by Hamilton's despair at his proposal's progress, Jefferson invited both Hamilton and James Madison, the effective leader of the House of Representatives and a leading opponent of the assumption plan, to a private dinner at his new lodgings at 57 Maiden Lane, just a few blocks from Wall Street. The result of the dinner was a compromise: Hamilton agreed to support a move of the national capital from New York City to an unspecified site on the Potomac River (which would become Washington, D.C.), with an interim ten-year stop in Philadelphia. Madison, in turn, agreed not to argue aggressively in opposition to Hamilton's assumption plan. The dinner meeting would later be described by historians as "The Compromise of 1790"—perhaps the only significant compromise in American history whose terms were honored based on the word of the participants, and not codified in legislation, as was the case with the more well known Compromises of 1820 and 1850.

In July 1790 Congress passed Hamilton's plan, as outlined in the Assumption Bill.* Washington signed it, and the full faith and credit of the United States became a reality. The plan was spectacularly successful, and Hamilton's star was on the rise.

Though New Yorkers grumbled the next month when the second session of the First Congress ended and the capital moved permanently to Philadelphia, Hamilton was the dominant player in Washington's new administration. Flush with victory, Hamilton astonished the third session of the First Congress when it reconvened in the new temporary capital of Philadelphia in December 1790 with a proposal to establish a national bank.

There was little doubt the country—and the new federal government—needed a banking system. Without banking, industry could not grow, and the government would be unable to fund future wars, should they occur. As secretary of the Treasury, Hamilton clearly saw this as his next important task.

Each of the thirteen states had chartered banks, and the Continental Congress had established a national bank in 1781 under the direction of Hamilton's friend and mentor, Robert Morris of Pennsylvania, who now served in the United States Senate. Though that first bank had not succeeded as a national bank and was subsequently converted to a private state-chartered bank, Hamilton thought a new national bank was the right direction to go in.

It was here that Hamilton began to stumble. The plan he had in mind was modeled on the Bank of England, which, ironically, was the first major institution to emerge from the Glorious Revolution. Considered in the first Parliament held under William and Mary, the bank would be a private entity. Its first order of business would be to loan £1.2 million to the new monarch's government. Coming off a near century of Stuart penury, and facing expensive wars against the

---

* In the House, it was a narrow 32–29 victory.

much wealthier nation of France, William found the idea appealing. Parliament approved of the plan in the Tonnage Act of 1694, and the foundation for financial stability of the British Empire for the next two centuries was set in place.

Hamilton envisioned a Bank of the United States that would repeat the success of the Bank of England. It would be a "public-private partnership," the ancestor of the ubiquitous "public-private partnerships" of the twentieth and twenty-first centuries in which a favored elite benefits from the full faith and credit of the United States government at the expense of the vast majority of citizens.

As an instrument of public finance to aid in the development of the new nation's economy, Hamilton's idea had great merit. There was a problem, however. Parliament had been able to establish the Bank of England because, under the unwritten English Constitution, any act of Parliament signed by the king was by definition constitutional. In the newly formed United States of America, Congress could pass only acts that were constitutional. The Framers and the state ratification conventions had been quite clear in stating that Congress could exercise only powers that had been clearly enumerated in the Constitution. Hamilton himself had signed a letter at the New York state ratifying convention agreeing to that point not three years earlier.

The same Hamilton who, as a delegate to the New York state ratification convention, had signed the letter proclaiming "those clauses in the . . . Constitution, which declare that Congress shall not have or exercise certain powers, do not imply that Congress is entitled to any Powers not given by the said Constitution" would now become the champion of the doctrine of implied powers. Hamilton knew full well that neither the Constitution nor the Tenth Amendment of the proposed Bill of Rights granted the federal government the authority to charter corporations.

But since Hamilton did not believe in or respect the secular covenant of the Constitution, this was now an unimportant obstacle. What mattered was that he had the wind at his back and he knew that he could secure congressional approval of the proposal with ease.

A more sincere believer in the Constitution would have approached the matter quite differently. Instead of discussing the merits of the bank bill with his fellow cabinet members—Jefferson at State and Randolph at Justice—and the effective House leader Madison prior to his introduction in December 1790, he sprang it on them unannounced. Their opposition to the bill on constitutional grounds should not have come as a surprise to him. And if he did anticipate that opposition, a private conversation, similar to the dinner in June with Madison and Jefferson that had led to the Compromise of 1790 and the success of the Assumption Bill, would have yielded productive results.

One can imagine Madison and Jefferson pointing out the lack of constitutional authority and suggesting that instead of introducing the unconstitutional legislation, Hamilton craft a constitutional amendment that would allow him to accomplish the purposes he envisioned for the bill. There would soon be precedent for the approach. In 1793, when the Supreme Court decided in *Chisholm v. Georgia* that individuals could sue state governments in federal courts, an irritated Congress quickly passed what would become the Eleventh Amendment, prohibiting the suing of states in federal courts. The amendment sped through the ratification process in less than a year.

But Hamilton, sensing his worldview on the ascent, chose not to have that discussion. Instead he went full steam ahead, lobbying both houses of Congress on behalf of his bill. In January it sailed through the Senate. In February it easily passed the House, by a 39–20 margin.[20] He had gained nine votes from his Assumption Bill victory in July. Many members of the First Congress, it seemed, were more than willing to ignore the Constitution and follow the winner.

It was a destructive victory for the long term, however. Only five of those thirty-nine votes came from south of Maryland. A sectional rivalry was starting to heat up and it would intensify when the bank became operational.

Hamilton proposed that the federal government should put up 20 percent of the proposed capital of the bank, with private investors putting up the remaining 80 percent. At a total initial capitalization of

$10 million, this meant that the federal government's $2 million was matched by $8 million from private investors. However, since the federal government actually had no money, that $2 million was "loaned" by the bank itself . . . which meant the federal government was given ten years to put up the $2 million in equal installments.

The bank's charter would be for twenty years and could be renewed by Congress at the end of that period. Though it would serve as a provider of short-term loans to the government and would be the institution in which the government would deposit its receipts, the primary purpose of the bank would be to engage in commercial and private lending.

With the success of the Assumption Plan, Hamilton found that his views of a powerful, central government seemed to be gathering a following, especially among some of the members of Congress from the northern states. The secret centralized "elected monarchy" plans of which he had spoken at the Constitutional Convention, and which he had written down for himself in the fall of 1787, seemed to be in the ascendant.

Former opponents who had previously considered Hamilton far too monarchical now began joining his camp. In the Senate, his friends Robert Morris, Rufus King, Oliver Ellsworth, and George Read, all of whom had attended the Constitutional Convention as delegates and applauded only politely during his ill-advised speech proposing an elective monarch, were more inclined than ever to publicly back any plan he proposed. In the House, the nine opponents to the Assumption Bill who had embraced the Bank Bill began moving toward the Hamiltonian worldview.

That the tide was turning in Hamilton's favor has been confirmed by modern scholars. The late Thornton Anderson, a political scientist at the University of Maryland, undertook an analysis comparing the debate at the Constitutional Convention[21] with the debates of the First Congress and concluded that what he called "state Federalists," who argued for more national control than did "state sovereignists" and less national control than did the "nationalists," had been very significant in the creation of the "balanced federal system" articulated in the Constitution. Anderson found that this group of "state Federalists" had been surprisingly weak in the First Congress, and that this led to "legislation and an evolved ideology that irrevocably changed the operation of the U.S. Constitution to a system significantly at variance with that agreed upon at the Convention."[22] The "state Federalists," under Hamilton's sway, had become "nationalists." Together they routed the "state sovereignists."

After the bank bill passed both houses, Washington was uncertain about signing it. Though he leaned in favor of it, he wanted to cover all his bases. Giving Hamilton a tactical advantage, he asked for written opinions from the two members of his cabinet he knew were not favorably inclined toward the bill—Jefferson and Randolph.

In his February 12, 1791, advisory opinion to the president, Attorney General Randolph concluded the bank bill was unconstitutional; he focused especially on the Constitution's "necessary and proper" clause. Since he had been on the Committee on Details that inserted the clause into the Constitution, it is likely he had a very keen understanding of the intent of the convention. Randolph told the president:

> The phrase, "and proper," if it has any meaning, does not enlarge the powers of Congress, but rather restricts them. For no power is to be assumed under the general clause, but such as is not only necessary but proper, or perhaps expedient also. But as the friends to the bill ought not to claim any advantage from this clause, so ought not the enemies to it, to quote the clause as having a restrictive effect: both ought to consider it as among the surplusage which as often proceeds from inattention as caution.

> However, let it be propounded as an eternal question to those who build new powers on this clause, whether the latitude of construction which they arrogate will not terminate in an unlimited power in Congress?

> In every aspect, therefore under which the attorney general can view the act, so far as it incorporates the Bank, he is bound to declare his opinion to be against its constitutionality.[23]

Washington had cleverly asked both Jefferson and Randolph to submit their opinions to him before asking Hamilton to weigh in. This gave Hamilton the advantage of knowing his adversaries' complete argument prior to developing his own counterattack.

On February 22, 1791, Hamilton submitted a lengthy response to Washington. The core of his argument was that

> [i]n entering upon the argument it ought to be premised, that the objections of the Secretary of State and Attorney General are founded on a general denial of the authority of the United States to erect corporations. The latter indeed expressly admits, that if there be anything in the bill which is not warranted by the constitution, it is the clause of incorporation.[24]

Hamilton concludes by arguing in direct opposition to the letter he had signed only three years earlier in which he concurred in the view that no congressional powers existed beyond those strictly enumerated in the Constitution:

> [E]very power vested in a Government is in its nature sovereign, and includes . . . a right to employ all the means requisite, and fairly applicable to the attainment of the ends of such power; and which are not precluded by restrictions and exceptions specified in the constitution, or not immoral, or not contrary to the essential ends of political society.[25]

On February 25, 1791, Washington signed the Bank Bill into law. When the initial subscription of the bank stock, offered to the public in July 1791, sold out in less than an hour, Hamilton was triumphant. But his triumph came at a cost. Stock was offered only in Philadelphia, Boston, and New York, where it was mostly snapped up by northern merchants and their European partners. This struck many southerners as yet another example of one group benefiting over another.

Hamilton had earned a temporary political victory but had plunged the country into a debate that would last for more than two centuries. Jefferson, Madison, and modern Tea Partiers support the plain meaning of the words of the Constitution. Hamilton and the modern expansionists of government power support a meaning of the Constitution that can be expanded to justify virtually any action the federal government seeks to undertake.

Thomas Jefferson was swept into office a decade later, in 1800, by popular revulsion at the overextension of federal power exercised by the Federalist administration of John Adams. Though Hamilton and Adams despised each other, Adams was thoroughly Hamiltonian in his commitment to the superiority of centralized power over the rights of the individual.

When Benjamin Franklin died at the age of eighty-three in the fall of 1790, his grandson, Benjamin Franklin Bache, inherited his printing equipment.[26] Barely twenty-one years old, he had been extremely close to the old man, having lived with Franklin while the latter was ambassador to France and traveled throughout Europe. Bache shared his grandfather's passion for journalism and immediately set about to found a newspaper, which he published in Philadelphia under the name *Aurora*. Young Bache's newspaper became one of the fiercest Jeffersonian critics of the administrations of first George Washington, and then John Adams.

The inclination of the majority members of the Federalist Congress to ignore the Constitution, first evidenced in the Bank of the United States Bill vote of 1791, became even more strongly evident in 1798, when Congress passed yet another set of unconstitutional laws—the Alien and Sedition Acts.

The ostensible purpose was to ensure the security of the government in light of a possible war with France. But the real purpose—at least the purpose for which it was used—was to shut up political opponents from the Jeffersonian Democratic-Republican Party. Officially "An Act for the Punishment of Certain Crimes Against the United States," it was one of four laws passed at the same time known as the Alien and Sedition Acts.

On July 14, 1798, President Adams signed into law the bill that had passed the Senate on a 22–9 party line vote, and the House of Representatives on a 60–46 party line vote. The modern reader, looking at the plain language of the bill, recoils in horror at its utter unconstitutionality. It read, in part:

> [I]f any person shall write, print, utter or publish, or shall cause or procure to be written, printed, uttered or published, or shall knowingly and willingly assist or aid in writing, printing, uttering or publishing any false, scandalous and malicious writing or writings against the government of the United States, or either house of the Congress of the United States, or the President of the United States, with intent to defame the said government, or either house of the said Congress . . . then such person, being thereof convicted before any court of the United States having jurisdiction thereof, shall be punished by a fine not exceeding two thousand dollars, and by imprisonment not exceeding two years.[27]

It was unfortunate for the country that the doctrine of Supreme Court judicial review had not yet been established. Future Supreme Court chief justice John Marshall, a Federalist, was known to have opposed the law, and one can only speculate on the possibility that had he been in office, this test case, rather than *Marbury v. Madison*, would have established that principle.

Among the public critics was Benjamin Franklin Bache. President Adams, he wrote in the *Aurora*, "has appointed Alexander Hamilton inspector general of the Army, the same Hamilton who published a book to prove he is an adulterer. . . . Mr. Adams ought hereafter to be silent about *French* principles."[28]

Soon Bache was arrested for violating the law. He died of yellow fever in the summer of 1799, before his case was brought to trial, but during the more than two years the law was in effect, twenty-five Americans were prosecuted and imprisoned based upon its provisions.

In Newark, New Jersey, a man who watched President Adams's entourage pass by heard a cannon blast in salute to the president. When one in the crowd commented that "there goes the President and they are firing at his ass," Luther Baldwin replied that he didn't care "if they fired through his ass." Incredibly, Baldwin was arrested, convicted, and imprisoned for this remark. He remained in prison until he paid the hefty fine specified in the law, as well as the associated court fees.[29]

In the fall of that year, another equally unjust trial took place in Dedham, Massachusetts, where a man named David Brown and a group of his friends put up a liberty pole that read "No Stamp Act, No Sedition Act, No Alien Bills, No Land Tax, downfall to the Tyrants of America; peace and retirement to the President; Long Live the Vice President."[30]

For this affront, Brown was arrested, convicted, and sentenced to eighteen months in prison. He appealed twice to President Adams for a pardon but was denied both times. Finally, when Jefferson assumed the presidency in March 1801, Brown and the twenty-four other Americans imprisoned for violating the Sedition Law were pardoned. The law expired on that day, and no one had the desire to renew it.

It had been so unpopular it fueled Jefferson's 1800 presidential victory over Adams and, equally important, it swept the Federalists out of their majority in both houses. The Senate, with a 22–9 Federalist majority before the election, was now 17–15 in favor of the Democratic Republicans. The switch in the House was even more dramatic. A 56–50 Federalist majority in the Sixth Congress became a 72–33 Democratic-Republican majority in the Seventh. Before the election, the Federalists had 53 percent of the seats in the House. After it they had a mere 31 percent. It was the biggest percentage loss of control ever in the House of Representatives.

It was also the first time in American political history that the people had risen up in an election and "thrown the bums out." The degree of public repudiation of Adams's Federalist agenda is not nearly captured by the Electoral College vote results. Jefferson won the presidency by a 73–65 Electoral College vote margin over Adams (notwithstanding the intrigues of vice presidential candidate Aaron Burr to supplant Jefferson at the head of the ticket),* but in this election only five of the sixteen states cast their Electoral College ballots based on the direct popular vote. In eleven of the sixteen states, Electoral College electors were selected by the state legislatures. In those five states, Jefferson stomped Adams at the ballot box 59–37 percent.[31]

The Senate was also elected by state legislatures, so the results there did not show the people's wrath as quickly. It was in the House of Representatives that it was most clearly seen. By more than a two-to-one margin—69–31 percent—the people rejected the unconstitutional policies of the dysfunctional Adams-Hamilton Federalist Party.

The Federalist Party would never again hold a majority in either house of Congress. Though the body would not be buried officially for another decade, the Federalist Party of Washington, Adams, and Hamilton was dead.

For the next two decades, Jeffersonian principles formed the basis for what became one national party, to which all the great leaders belonged. Jefferson's two consecutive terms as president were followed by two for Madison, and then two for Monroe.

The First National Bank served the purpose that Hamilton had intended for twenty years. Its charter was not renewed in 1811, during the first term of James Madison's administration. Five years later, facing the extensive debts incurred during the War of 1812,

---

* In 1803, the Twelfth Amendment was ratified, a direct response to preventing any future such vice presidential intrigues.

Madison reluctantly agreed to the establishment of a Second National Bank, also with a twenty-year term.

Over the next decade, under the leadership of the acquisitive and arrogant Nicholas Biddle, the second iteration of the Bank of the United States dominated the economic life of the country, rewarding its political friends and punishing its opponents. But America in the 1820s was undergoing dramatic changes, and Biddle's empire would soon experience the consequence of those changes.

The first was driven by the westward expansion of the new nation. The thirteen original states that hugged the Atlantic coast were joined by nine that filled the valleys between the Appalachian Mountains and the Mississippi River. To Tennessee and Kentucky were now added the states of Ohio, Indiana, Illinois, Missouri, Alabama, Mississippi, and Louisiana.

The experience of the settlers was the same in each new state. Virgin land was claimed, plowed, and transformed into productive farmland. Without established churches and clergy, a new wave of itinerant preachers brought the gospel west, in a vibrant camp meeting environment. Thousands would gather to hear a message even more hopeful and democratic than that of the First Great Awakening, which had swept the country in the decades preceding the revolution.

Gone was even the muted Calvinism of Whitefield and Edwards. In its place was the optimistic and hopeful message of love and free will, delivered by Methodist and Baptist preachers schooled more in the art of oratory than scholarship.

Salvation, they preached, was open to all. There were no elect and unwashed. Everyone could be saved. One only had to accept Jesus Christ as savior.

The class differences of the stuffy original colonies evaporated further now in the West. The commonality of the hard life, and the increasingly shared religious conversion experiences, served to reinforce the natural egalitarian tendencies of these western pioneers.

Democratic concepts of theology naturally applied to the political arena.

The first evidence of this egalitarianism came, state by state, in the removal of property-owning requirements for the exercise of the vote. By the mid-1820s the country as a whole could claim near-universal white male suffrage. No other nation on earth had achieved such widespread democracy.

The Tennessean Andrew Jackson was the natural champion of this budding populist movement, devoted as it was to the primacy of every individual in his own actions and strict adherence to the secular covenant of the Constitution. Later historians would call this political movement of Jacksonian Democrats the first "conservative" populist movement, and though such a label is not misleading, it could just as easily have been called the "stay out of my business" populist movement. These were ordinary people who stubbornly resisted any efforts to invade or constrain their natural liberty to do as they darn well pleased, anytime they wished to, within the constraints of the rule of law, as it was loosely enforced in those days.

Democratic concepts began to permeate every phase of life, and the method by which presidential candidates were selected was no exception. Popular conventions arose in this era, replacing the selection by an elite group of political leaders. It was by such popular methods that Andrew Jackson came to challenge John Quincy Adams for the presidency in 1824.

Though Jackson won the popular vote, he lost in the Electoral College. He was convinced that Biddle had bankrolled John Quincy Adams's presidential campaign in 1824, costing him the presidency. He was also convinced by the first arguments of Jefferson, Edmund Randolph, and James Madison that Congress did not have the right to incorporate a business.

When, four years later, Jackson won the presidency, the Tennessean was determined to crush the National Bank and its dictator, Biddle. His election had been fueled by the spirit of the common man, as voter participation increased from 30 percent in 1824 to 60 percent in 1828.

By withdrawing federal deposits and successfully vetoing the renewal of its charter, Jackson succeeded in putting a dagger in the heart of the Second National Bank, which died an unmourned death in 1841.

As Jackson said in his veto statement:

> [S]ome of the powers and privileges possessed by the existing Bank are unauthorized by the Constitution, subversive of the rights of the States, and dangerous to the liberties of the people. . . . One Congress, in 1791, decided in favor of a bank; another, in 1811, decided against it. One Congress, in 1815, decided against a bank; another, in 1816, decided in its favor. Prior to the present Congress, therefore, the precedents drawn from that source were equal. If we resort to the States, the expressions of legislative, judicial, and executive opinions against the Bank have been probably to those in its favor as four to one.[32]

The Jeffersonian view was in the ascendant, but weak leadership after Jackson and sectional rivalries spawned a new party that drank deeply from the Hamiltonian tradition. When it gained power, it would be decades before the Jeffersonians could reclaim it.

Chapter 4

THE REPUBLICAN PARTY
AND THE BROKEN
PROMISE OF FREE
MARKETS

As much as Abraham Lincoln is admired for his leadership during the Civil War, constitutional conservatives must admit that he was a true Hamiltonian. As such, he undertook the first projects by the federal government to break the second promise of the Constitution—that of a commitment to free markets. Lincoln successfully advocated policies that gave federal benefits to selected "winners" in business. These "internal improvements" were sold as a benefit to all. It would be left for Woodrow Wilson, Franklin Roosevelt, and Barack Obama to infringe upon the conduct of individuals exercising their free will.

In March 1791, fresh off two stunning political victories, Alexander Hamilton turned his attention to the last piece of his master plan for the new republic. The Bill of Rights was still six months from final ratification, but the country needed a manufacturing sector and he intended to create one by using the power of the newly muscular federal government. Since he had just broken the first promise of the Constitution with relative ease and no regrets, the prospect of breaking a second promise did little to slow his pace or ambitions.

But this time Hamilton failed. When a speculative financial bubble he helped create burst in spectacular fashion in early 1792, the debris scattered all over the monied partners he had recruited to promote his scheme for a government-subsidized national manufacturing company. Despite this setback, Hamilton had successfully created a school of followers devoted to his early brand of "crony capitalism."

Hamilton had used his broad interpretation of the "necessary and proper" clause at the end of Article I, Section 8 of the Constitution to win the battle for the First Bank of the United States. When he attempted to secure congressional approval of direct federal investment in his pet manufacturing project, he hung his argument on the "general welfare" clause of Article I, Section 8. Madison and Jefferson were able to defeat this second expansion of federal powers, if only temporarily.

Hamilton was largely ignorant about manufacturing. But he was convinced of its national importance, having witnessed firsthand the calamities that befell our revolutionary army, which was forced to depend on scarce and unreliable imports for such staples of warfare as gunpowder, muskets, and cannons.

In March 1791, just weeks after President Washington signed the law establishing the Bank of the United States, Hamilton and his assistant, Tench Coxe, set about creating a plan for a vast privately owned manufacturing enterprise that would benefit from public subsidies and favorable charters. They called it "The Society for Establishing Useful Manufactures" (SEUM). It was modeled after a similarly named venture Coxe had helped organize in Philadelphia four years earlier, which had gone nowhere for lack of capital.

Hamilton was the driving force behind this private company's organization and funding, using his position as secretary of the Treasury and the possibility of government funding as an enticement to speculative investors. It was well known that he wrote the investor prospectus and was committed to using his powers to ensure the company's success. The prospect of such support from the highest level of the newly formed government proved irresistible to many speculators. What else would a potential investor conclude, knowing the prospectus had issued from Hamilton's pen?

The full faith and credit of the United States government was not yet behind the SEUM, but the full faith of Secretary of the Treasury Alexander Hamilton was.* That summer, Hamilton turned to his friend and former assistant secretary of the Treasury William Duer to help attract investors.

The project was of such importance to Hamilton that in July 1791 he left his offices in the new capital in Philadelphia and traveled to New York City† to meet Duer and other potential investors. Days earlier, the first offerings from his new Bank of the United States had sold out within forty-eight hours and speculators had already realized significant profits as the price of these offerings rose dramatically in a frenzy of interest.‡ Hamilton was assured a warm reception by investors in Duer's circle who were in the process of making strong profits from that offering.

On the heels of the successful Bank of the United States offering, the SEUM offering was equally well received. Within a few months, $100,000 of stock subscriptions to be paid in over four years were secured. Among the investors in addition to Duer were Secretary of War Henry Knox,§ future Supreme Court justice Henry Brockholst Living-

---

* When he resigned his position as secretary of the Treasury, Hamilton served as a director for two years and was presumably part of the group that decided to cease the SEUM's manufacturing operations in 1796. For several decades the company was virtually inactive, until its resurrection, which was largely possible due to the favorable charter granted by the state of New Jersey in 1791. There is no evidence Hamilton was ever a shareholder, though he advanced funds to the group periodically during its rockiest periods and regularly accepted and performed assignments for it while secretary of the Treasury.

† New York City had served as the new nation's capital from March 1789 to November 1790, when the capital was moved to Philadelphia. This was the result of the debt assumption compromise crafted between Madison and Hamilton, with Jefferson's assistance. The capital would remain in Philadelphia for ten years, then move to the "federal city" being built on the Potomac River—Washington, D.C.

‡ Scrips in the Bank of the United States stock represented the opportunity to purchase $100 of stock in the bank and were offered for sale on July 4, 1791, at the price of $25 per unit. As noted above, the offering was sold out within forty-eight hours.

§ With the secretary of War's involvement, half of President Washington's cabinet—Hamilton and Knox—was involved in Hamilton's manufacturing scheme. Secretary of State Thomas Jefferson would actively oppose it, and Attorney General Edmund Randolph's position on it was unknown.

ston, Bank of New York and Bank of the United States director Nicholas Low, New Jersey congressman Elias Boudinot, leading New Jersey
businessmen Archibald Mercer and John Pintard, and New York City
merchants Herman LeRoy and Henry Livingston, a cousin to the jurist
and fellow investor with the same name.[1] It was a who's who of the
financial elite, the kind of men Hamilton had long considered suitable
to run the country.

With sufficient financial commitments poised to fill the coffers of
the SEUM, Hamilton next set his sights on securing a remarkably favorable charter for the corporation. Hamilton devised his charter with
a "crony capitalism" friendly state legislature and governor in mind. He
proposed that the society be granted a host of special privileges, including state and local tax exemptions and the ability to raise money from
lotteries.[2] The charter also allowed the federal government and state
governments to purchase stock in the company—with a minimum investment of $10,000.

Hamilton chose New Jersey as the state most likely to grant such
a privileged charter. It was close to financial investors in New York
City, was near enough to Philadelphia for him to easily monitor its
activities, and was controlled by politicians who shared his Federalist
philosophy. Hamilton was also very friendly with the new governor,
William Paterson.[*] They had served together at the Constitutional
Convention, and Paterson had been one of the most vocal supporters
of his entire program as one of New Jersey's representatives in the
First Congress.

In the fall of 1791, Hamilton made sure that word got out that a
favorable charter would soon be presented to a friendly New Jersey legislature. Soon subscriptions in the SEUM more than doubled.[3] In the
New Jersey legislature, opposition to the charter and proposed direct
investment by the state was fierce but ineffective.[4] The charter was
easily approved and the state invested $10,000 in the venture. With the

---

[*]. In 1793, President Washington appointed Paterson to serve on the Supreme Court as an associate justice, a position he held until his death in 1806.

blessings and support of the state secured, leading New Jersey private investors[5] followed in the footsteps of their political brethren and signed subscription agreements for the SEUM.

On December 5, 1791, two weeks after the SEUM triumph in New Jersey, Hamilton's *Report on Manufactures* was presented to the Second Congress. Over the next few weeks, individual members of Congress began to read Hamilton's report. Madison and his allies were shocked by what they found in it.

In the report, Hamilton argued the federal government should pay direct subsidies to specific favored companies that manufactured five products he personally considered important—coal, raw wool, sail-cloth, cotton products, and glass.[6] Hamilton suggested that Congress raise the existing tariffs on imported goods (first set at 5 percent by Congress in 1789, then increased to 8 percent in 1790) to a higher level.[7] The extra funds would then be paid directly into the bank accounts of these preferred manufacturing companies. With this proposal Hamilton became the first American public official to suggest that the government should pick winners and losers in a planned industrial economy.

Hamilton suggested that subsidy payments, which he called "bonuses" in the report, should be augmented by "premiums"—additional financial awards given by the federal government to manufacturers who produced particularly excellent products. Toward the end of the report, he specifically mentioned the SEUM as a potential beneficiary of the federal government's largesse.

Hamilton was supremely confident his arguments would prevail. Indeed, he anticipated the objection of Madison and Jefferson to the subsidy on constitutional grounds and addressed them in his report. His expansion of the "necessary and proper" clause had proved successful in the Bank of the United States battle. Now he turned to the "general welfare" clause to expand the claim of the federal government on its range of activities.

It had been less than four years since the two men had completed their successful collaboration on the Federalist Papers. Madison was now convinced that Hamilton's purpose in that effort had not been to support the national agreement described in the Constitution. Instead, Madison believed that Hamilton had cynically engaged his assistance in an effort to secure ratification, intending at the first opportunity to subvert its content.

Fortunately, Roger Sherman, who had supported Hamilton on the National Bank, agreed with Madison that subsidies for politically favored companies were unconstitutional. Sherman, the only man to have signed the Continental Association,* Declaration of Independence, Articles of Confederation, and the Constitution, pointed out that nowhere in the Constitution could he find that the federal government or Congress was granted the authority to make such a loan to a private enterprise.

On December 27, 1791, William Duer and Alexander McComb, another SEUM director, formed a new speculative partnership. Its original purposes were murky, but soon it became clear the partners intended to corner the markets on bank stocks (in particular the Bank of New York, which Hamilton himself had founded) and certain federal securities. They had no hesitation in using the SEUM's resources for that purpose.[8]

By late January, when the House turned its attention briefly to the *Report on Manufactures*, public opposition to Hamilton's plan for subsidies was beginning to mount. In a letter to the *Philadelphia General Advertiser* on the seventeenth, "The Anti-Monopolist" argued that

> [t]he "Jersey Manufacturing Company" . . . is an institution so opposed to the principles of a republican government that it could never have taken place in the free states of America . . . from any other motive than the avarice of speculation, and the ambition of our political leaders.[9]

In early March, prices for all financial paper began to fall. Duer had placed all his bets on a bull market. The Livingstons placed heavy bets

---

* Signed by members of the First Continental Congress in 1774.

on a bear market, and their stock sales, along with a general oversupply of financial paper, pushed prices further down. As the market fell, Duer's empire crashed along with it. The SEUM was but one of its casualties.

Heavily indebted, Duer scrambled to pay back his loans as prices continued to fall. He became desperate, taking money from small merchants and even a legendary New York City madam.[10] Soon Duer started to default on some of his debts.[11]

The public outcry and anger against Duer and his speculator friends—most of whom also served as directors of the SEUM—were so violent that some feared Duer would be lynched. It thus came as somewhat of a relief to Duer when he was thrown into debtors' prison on March 29. Soon most of the other SEUM directors would join him either in debtors' prison or in bankruptcy.[12]

The two years' worth of political capital that Hamilton had nurtured evaporated in the weeks of late March and early April 1792 as the sordid details of the speculative bubble caused by his friend became widely known. Mortally wounded by the dishonesty of its first directors and the violent public reaction against their blatant self-dealing, the SEUM limped along on life support for four more years, the only energy in the enterprise provided by the "ministerial interventions" of Alexander Hamilton.

Public anger at the self-dealing of the Hamiltonian elites, the $3 million in losses from the financial panic of the spring, and opposition to the manufacturing subsidy scheme powered the congressional elections in the fall of 1792. Jefferson's allies scored a dramatic victory in the House of Representatives. Their 32–40 deficit of the Second Congress transformed itself into a 55–50 majority in the Third Congress. The election results confirmed what Hamilton had feared for several months: the SEUM project was doomed. In early 1796, the directors mercifully decided to shut down all the manufacturing operations, sell what equipment they could, and lease out the buildings for whatever small rents they might bring in.[13]

Hamilton's attempt to institute crony capitalism had failed miserably. The special benefits of the SEUM had been squandered by

inexperienced and dishonest directors with no background in manufacturing but plenty of bad judgment. In short, they exhibited the same
qualities that would characterize every subsequent crony capitalism
project sponsored over the next two centuries by the federal government, from the Union Pacific Railroad to TARP, to the auto industry
bailouts, to the half a billion dollars in Obama administration stimulus
funds loaned by the Department of Energy to the politically connected,
but now bankrupt, Solyndra, manufacturer of solar panels.

Despite the failure of Hamilton's foray, the idea that the federal
government should provide direct financial assistance to certain politically connected private enterprises and not others remained popular
among an elite group of Federalist politicians, merchants, and speculators. During the first half of the nineteenth century, in one of those
improbable ironies of history, it would be championed by Henry Clay,
the Kentucky attorney and politician who had successfully defended
Hamilton's killer, Aaron Burr,* from charges of treason.

From the 1820s until his death in 1852, Clay took the core elements of Hamilton's mercantilist program and repackaged them into
what he called "the American System." It was this system upon which
the Whig political party, the successor to Hamilton's Federalist Party,
was formed. The program called for high tariffs to protect America's
"infant industries," a reintroduction of a national bank,† and subsidies
for "internal improvements," such as canals and roads.

During the 1820s and 1830s, Andrew Jackson carried on the
Jeffersonian-Madisonian tradition of opposition to Clay's Hamiltonian
scheme. He and his successors in the Democratic Party were largely successful at preventing the implementation of Clay's "American System."
Clay's Whig Party, which failed to address the pressing issue of slavery,
died an unmourned death in the 1850s, replaced by the vibrant new
Republican Party. Republicans abandoned the Whigs' reluctance to ad-

---

* Burr killed Hamilton in a duel in 1804.

† The Second National Bank, chartered in 1816, lost its federal charter in 1836, then went out
of business as a private entity in 1841.

dress the evils associated with the expansion of slavery, but they also embraced the "American System."

Railroads were the first big businesses in America, so it was to be expected that the next attempt to break the second promise of the Constitution would come in that industry. And this time the attempt would eventually succeed.

When Alexander Hamilton died in 1804, there was not a single mile of railroad track in the country. Two decades later America could boast of only one small cargo railroad, which had less than ten miles of track. The Mohawk & Hudson's sixteen miles represented almost 20 percent of the entire ninety-five miles of railroad track in the country in 1831. By 1840, that figure had grown to 2,800 miles.[14]

Within five years there were more than one hundred small local railroad companies, each operating single lines that varied in length from five to a hundred miles. The country still had only a little more than five thousand miles of railroad track, but it was beginning to become clear to the general population that steam locomotive–powered railroads would soon emerge from the status of "novelty" and become a reliable and efficient means of transporting passengers and freight across the entire country, not just short local hauls unconnected to the growing web of rail lines.[15]

Financing of these railroad companies had been haphazard at best. Most appear to have been privately financed, usually by a group of prominent local businessmen interested in expanding local markets. Profitability was a mixed bag and depended on the size of the markets the railroad connected on each end, and the comparative price and time advantage the railroad offered passenger and freight traffic over the local alternative—often a canal or public road traveled by wagon, carriage, or stagecoach.

Sometimes state or county governments* offered aid, usually in the form of a loan guaranteed by the assets of the railroad. At least one railroad, the Philadelphia & Columbia, was state owned and operated.

---

* The issuance of bonds by county legislatures was a feature most commonly seen in the less populated midwestern states, starting around 1850.

The vast majority of these early railroads, however, were private sector projects financed by local entrepreneurs.

In January 1845, Asa Whitney, a New England Yankee merchant who had made a fortune in the China trade, first proposed to Congress that it assist in the construction of a railroad that would connect the Atlantic coast to the Pacific. California, with 90,000 inhabitants, was still a territory of Mexico, though it had a large and growing American population.

Whitney's plan called for the construction of a railway from Lake Michigan to the Pacific. His method of financing was innovative. He asked that Congress sell him a strip of land that was sixty miles wide and 2,000 miles long (from Milwaukee to Portland or Milwaukee to San Francisco) at ten cents an acre. This amounted to an offer to purchase 78 million acres for $7.8 million. Whitney reasoned that by placing the railroad line in the center of this strip, he would increase trade and commerce along the way, and would be able to sell the land at prices significantly greater than ten cents an acre. The surplus would provide the capital to build the line along the way.[16]

For six years Whitney tirelessly promoted his Pacific railroad plan in Washington and throughout the country, until its final defeat in Congress in 1851.[17] Though his public proselytizing failed to secure support for his transcontinental railroad project, he succeeded in two arenas: First, he captured the public imagination around the romance of the idea of a grand railroad that connected the Pacific and Atlantic. Second, his novel idea was adopted of using federal land grants as a means of financing railroad construction in areas not blessed with sufficient population to support privately financed construction.

In 1851 a group of San Francisco investors decided to build the first railroad in the new state of California. Since no one in California knew how to build a railroad, they recruited Theodore Judah, a twenty-seven-year-old civil engineer with extensive experience surveying and constructing railroads, to build the line for them. He had been in the business for more than a decade, starting with the Albany & Schenectady line in his hometown and including his work in 1848 helping to build the famous Niagara Gorge Railroad.[18]

When the Sacramento Valley Railroad's short line was completed in 1856, no connecting lines emerged to help build profitable traffic. The company's investors did not receive an immediate return on their investment. The venture soured them and other potential local investors on the railroad business. To Judah's great disappointment, no one stepped forward to finance the building of additional lines in California.[19]

The timidity of California private investors persuaded Judah that the only way to finance such a project was to secure massive financing directly from the federal government. The engineer didn't puzzle the constitutional impediments to such a program. He was part of a breed of Americans who cared about getting the job done. He was honest, but he wasn't a constitutionalist. Efficiency, modernization, and the dream of connecting one end of the country to the other were his guiding principles, not the secular covenant of the Constitution.

Over the next four years, Judah made three separate trips from California to Washington to lobby on behalf of federal support for his Pacific Railroad dream.[20] In December 1859, acting as the official representative of the Pacific Railroad Convention, a group authorized by the state legislatures of California and Oregon, he met with the weak and overwhelmed President James Buchanan, who gave his general support for the project, though such words were largely symbolic.

The real work would be done in the committee of Iowa congressman Samuel R. Curtis, a former railroad executive. In 1856, Curtis was one of the first group of twenty congressmen elected to the House of Representatives under the banner of the new Republican Party.

The Republican Party had been formed largely as an antislavery party among supporters of "Free Labor and Free Soil"—small freehold farmers and industrial laborers who felt it was unfair that they should be forced to compete with slave labor. Mixed into the fire were some dying embers from Clay's old Whig Party.

When he met Theodore Judah in the spring of 1860, Curtis was comfortably serving his second term in Congress, supporting Lincoln's upstart candidacy for the presidency and confident of easy reelection in November. That March, the two crafted a bill that called for $60 million in government loans to the railroads selected to build the line.

The Curtis bill made it out of committee, but all attention turned to the looming presidential campaign. Consideration of the bill by the full House was tabled until after the election, when the second session of the 36th Congress would begin.[21] Judah headed back to California to await the outcome of the presidential election and to try to raise funds for his proposed Pacific Railroad.

Two months later, in May 1860, the Republicans convened at "the Wigwam" in Chicago to select a presidential nominee. Prior to the selection of Abraham Lincoln as the candidate, the convention unanimously adopted a party platform that included support for a transcontinental railroad:

> A railroad to the Pacific ocean is imperatively demanded by the interests of the whole country [and] . . . the federal government ought to render immediate and efficient aid in its construction.[22]

Though the northern Democrats and southern Democrats nominated different candidates and could not come to agreement on issues related to slavery, on the matter of a transcontinental railroad the platforms were almost identical. The northern Democrats pledged "such Constitutional Government aid as will insure the construction of a Railroad to the Pacific coast, at the earliest practicable period,"[23] while the southern Democrats pledged "to use every means in their power to secure the passage of some bill, to the extent of the constitutional authority of Congress, for the construction of a Pacific Railroad from the Mississippi River to the Pacific Ocean, at the earliest practicable moment."[24]

The Constitutional Union Party was silent on the matter of the Pacific Railroad, supporting the Constitution, the Union, and little else.

The failure of the Republican Party platform to couch the federal support for a transcontinental railroad in constitutional terms—and focus instead on "efficiency," a word not found in the Constitution—is indicative of the degree to which the party, at its core, embraced Hamiltonian conceptions of the role of the federal government.

With the election of Abraham Lincoln as president in November 1860, the sectional breakup of the Union became inevitable. Though he won a majority in the Electoral College with 180 votes in the eighteen states he carried, Lincoln won only 39 percent of the popular vote. This was, of course, misleading, since he received hardly a single vote in the eleven southern states, and received between 55 percent and 60 percent of the vote in every northern state.

In December 1860, when the 36th Congress met in its lame-duck second session, Curtis reintroduced his railroad bill.* The debate on the floor of the House was revealing. Congressman Muscoe Garnett of Virginia, a graduate of Jefferson's University of Virginia Law School, delivered a stinging rebuke that the Curtis bill was clearly unconstitutional in the eyes of almost every Virginian:

> [T]he people of Virginia—ninety nine in a hundred—believe this bill to be unconstitutional, and . . . though you may squander the public lands and attempt to increase the public debt, it is my solemn belief that the people of Virginia . . . will not hold themselves responsible for the first cent of these bonds and appropriations.[25]

Curtis and the infamous Dan Sickles† of New York argued that the railroad was a "military necessity" for the security of the Union. Their position brought loud guffaws from the bill's opponents. When the 36th Congress adjourned on March 4, 1861, Curtis's bill was but one of sev-

---

* Curtis resigned from Congress in 1861 to accept a commission as a brigadier general in the Union Army. He would go on to distinguish himself on the field of battle at Pea Ridge and Westport. In 1862 he was named in the first Pacific Railway Act as one of the 150 organizers of the Union Pacific Railroad, chartered in the bill by the federal government.

† Sickles was a legendarily corrupt member of the Democratic Tammany Hall machine in New York. He had a colorful personal history as well. A year earlier a jury in Washington, D.C., had found him not guilty of murdering his wife's lover (the son of Francis Scott Key), on grounds of temporary insanity. He was one of Lincoln's first political generals, and his insubordination at Gettysburg almost cost the Union a victory. He lived until 1913.

eral pieces of unfinished business that had yet to make it through both houses.

Back in California, Theodore Judah set about finding investors for his Pacific Railroad. As a last-ditch effort, he pitched San Francisco merchants Collis Huntington, Leland Stanford, Charles Crocker, and Mark Hopkins, who would soon be known as "the Big Four." They agreed to make enough of an investment to bring the new corporation to a sufficient level of capitalization to receive a California corporate charter.

When the Central Pacific Railroad was incorporated under this new California law in June 1861, the Big Four's $159,000 investment gave them control of a corporation whose total stock subscription was set at $8 million. Full subscription of that amount, however, would depend on how successfully the Central Pacific Railroad lobbied Congress. For that purpose they authorized Judah, a small shareholder now but also the company's chief engineer, to act as their agent in securing the maximum amount of federal aid for their new company.

When Judah arrived in Washington in December 1861, the 37th Congress had already been very busy—overwhelmed by the events related to the start of the Civil War. In April, the Confederacy had fired on Fort Sumter in South Carolina and the Civil War began. With the departure of the elected representatives from nine southern states, the Senate had only fifty members representing the twenty-four states that remained in the Union and two southern states whose three senators— future president Andrew Johnson of Tennessee and Waitman Willey and John Carlile, two Unionists from Virginia—refused to leave. The House had 178 members and 63 vacant seats.

Party affiliations were lopsidedly Republican. In the House, 107 Republicans and 25 Unionists easily outvoted the 44 Democrats. In the Senate, the 30 Republicans and 7 Unionists were almost three times as many as the 13 Democrats.

Before the first session ended in August, Congress had enacted the Revenue Act of 1861—the first income tax in American history. The session ended after a month, and the second session didn't begin until December, just as Judah arrived.

With the immediate requirements of kicking off the war effort behind it, Congress spent the revenue from the income tax and other financings on the expenses of war just as fast as it came into the federal coffers. Federal contracts to purchase ammunition, supplies, and other war materiel were quickly let, and unscrupulous businessmen reached for the profits from the federal cash with rapacious enthusiasm.

The smell of easy money was in the air, and it attracted a cast of unsavory characters. They knew that now, with a Republican majority, the $60 million loan that Samuel Curtis had promoted in the previous Congress as part of the transcontinental railroad legislation was likely to be part of similar legislation. With that much money on the line, everyone wanted a piece of the pie.

Those with open hands looking for their share included entrepreneurs with real and paper railroads, and the majority of the congressmen and senators. Agents of railroads looking for designation as recipients of loans and land grants swarmed the Capitol, handing out cash and stock in their railroads as if these presents were candy.

Over the next six months, Judah would prove to be a master politician, manipulating the landmark Pacific Railway Act to grant his new company and its obscure, untested ownership group unparalleled public largesse.

In addition to Judah's Central Pacific, another paper railroad, the San Francisco & San Jose, came from California. In Kansas there was the Leavenworth, Pawnee, & Western Railroad,[26] which had no track yet but did have land swindled from the Pawnee Indians. In Missouri two railroads wanted something from the government trough—the Missouri Pacific, which planned a line from St. Louis to Kansas City, and the Hannibal & St. Joseph, which had an actual operating railroad that ran across the north of the state, from Hannibal on the western banks of the Mississippi to St. Joseph on the eastern banks of the Missouri River.

Lincoln's old client from the Rock Island line, Thomas C. Durant, now operated the Mississippi & Missouri in Iowa. It had been intended as a line from Davenport on the western banks of the Mississippi to

Council Bluffs on the eastern banks of the Missouri, but was still only one-third complete.

Durant had hired Lincoln, the attorney, in 1856, when the Mississippi & Missouri's Government Bridge, connecting Rock Island, Illinois, to Davenport, Iowa—the first bridge across the Mississippi—was hit by a steamboat and his company was sued by the company that owned the steamboat. Lincoln won the case, and a personal and professional relationship developed between the two.

These and countless other aspiring railroad men from smaller operations with less political clout swarmed the Capitol like locusts. Instead of stripping the crops, they brought gifts of cash and stock in their railroads, which they spread liberally among congressmen and senators. It was the rare elected or appointed official in Washington who did not carry in his pocket some financial reward recently conferred upon him by a railroad interest.

Judah secured a room in the Capitol and opened what he called "the Pacific Railroad Museum" with maps of the projected route of the Central Pacific. War-weary congressmen and senators would receive a warm welcome from the enthusiastic Judah when they dropped by. He would explain to them his plans, and on more than one occasion drop into their hands some of the $100,000 worth of Central Pacific shares the Big Four had given him to sprinkle liberally around to the right connections in the Capitol.

On January 31, 1862, Aaron Augustus Sargent, a freshman congressman from California, rose in the House and argued the necessity of establishing a Pacific Railroad. His speech was well received. A House subcommittee was appointed, which Sargent chaired. Amazingly, Judah was named as the clerk. On the Senate side, California senator James A. McDougall, with whom Judah was friendly, was named the chairman of the Senate Pacific Railroad Committee. Even more improbably, Judah was also named secretary of this committee.[27]

Judah now played a central role in creating the legislative documents that would emerge from both houses. It was the first time in American history that an officer of a private company likely to benefit from pending federal legislation was given such a critical role in the creation of that very document.[28]

When the House debated the bill reported by the House Pacific Railroad Committee,[29] there was no Madison to suggest a constitutional alternative for the Pacific Railroad. Virginian Muscoe Garnett, who had brandished the sword of constitutionality in the previous Congress in opposition to the Curtis bill, was gone, serving not in the 37th Congress of the United States in Washington, D.C., but instead in the 1st Confederate Congress in Richmond, Virginia.

A few lonely defenders of the Constitution remained. Frederick Pike, a Republican from Maine, argued that, while he favored a transcontinental railroad, the massive expenditure—$60,000 per mile for 2,000 miles, half of which ($60 million) would be loaned by the government, the other half provided by the railroad companies—was inappropriate while the country was engaged in an expensive war for its very survival. Pike pointed out that the law allowed for only one company— the Central Pacific—to build in California, a key provision upon which Judah, the employee and shareholder in Central Pacific, had insisted. With no competition, Pike argued, the temptations of corruption and self-dealing would be irresistible.

Freshman congressman William Paine Sheffield,* who had been elected on the "Unionist" ballot, gave this critique of the proposed Pacific Railway Act:

> I believe involved in that scheme is the means of making this railroad, if it is ever constructed under this bill, one of the most stupendous swindling enterprises ever forced upon a people. . . . This great railroad enterprise involves, it may be, the integrity of this government. . . . I will vote for no bill involving so large an expenditure of money as this does, unless it is for the purpose of putting down the rebellion.[30]

---

* Like Frederick Pike, the Republican of Maine, Sheffield would serve only one term in Congress.

Illinois congressman Owen Lovejoy, a lonely Republican who opposed the bill, said in the floor debate that the Congress had become a railroad corporation.[31]

> My opposition to a bad bill is no ground to suppose that I am opposed to the building of a Pacific railroad. . . . I am for a Pacific railroad, although I am free to confess that I dislike the idea of converting Congress into a railroad company. We are not here as a railroad corporation.[32]

By now, the westernmost tip of the railroads in the center of the country was St. Joseph, Missouri, the traditional jumping-off point for westbound wagon trains; it was 1,600 miles from there to Folsom, California. Farther north, the trains ended at St. Paul, Minnesota, which was 1,700 miles east of Seattle. To the south the line terminated at Alleyton, Texas, about 120 miles east of San Antonio and 1,500 miles east of Los Angeles.

Development of the line segment by segment, aided by federal land grants but without massive loans, could easily have worked, though perhaps the spike-driving ceremony might have been five to ten years later than 1869. On the upside, the massive fraud and self-dealing that resulted from the act would have been avoided. Indeed, this would be precisely the strategy employed by entrepreneur James J. Hill two decades later, when he constructed the transcontinental Great Northern Railway without a dime of federal subsidies.[33]

But the 37th Congress was composed of men driven by political expediency and a hunger for personal profit, not by constitutional principle. Jefferson's warning of the corrupting nature of Hamilton's schemes upon members of Congress had been prophetic. Outright bribery by special interests of the sort that would have been condemned in the first few Congresses was, by the 36th and 37th Congresses, common practice.

When the vote was held in the House on May 6, it wasn't even close. The Pacific Railway Act passed 79–49. The opposition came from 18

Democrats (not quite a majority of the 44 Democrats), joined by 17 Republicans (15 percent of the 107 Republicans), including Pike and Lovejoy, as well as the 14 Unionists (a majority of the 23), including Sheffield.*

The bill sailed through the Senate the next month with little opposition on a 30–5 vote. On July 1, 1862, President Lincoln signed it into law. That same day he also signed the Revenue Act of 1862, which changed the previous year's 3 percent flat rate income tax (the first income tax in the country's history) to a two-tier progressive income tax that taxed income over $10,000 (equivalent to about $200,000 today) at the higher rate of 5 percent.

The final terms were extraordinarily favorable to the men who would control the Union Pacific and the Central Pacific. Each railroad would receive $16,000 in federal loans (maturing in thirty years, with an interest rate of 5 percent) for each mile of "easy grade" built, $32,000 for each mile of "high plains," and $48,000 for each mile of "mountainous terrain." In addition, massive land grants were given in patches of ten square miles adjacent to the rail lines that checkerboarded across the country. By the time the transcontinental railroad was completed, the federal government had granted 80 million acres to the two railroad companies.

As the crow flies, the distance from the eastern terminus to Sacramento would be 1,700 miles, but when feeder lines were added, more than 2,500 miles of rail lines were subsidized. By the end of the project, to which additional legislation added more subsidies, more than $100 million in federal loans had been given to the two companies.

The Union Pacific was, after Hamilton's First Bank of the United States and the now-defunct Second Bank of the United States, only the third federally chartered corporation in the nation's history. The law had listed a total of 158 "commissioners" who were authorized to organize

---

* There was a surprising geographic concentration to the opposition. The majority of the delegations in Kentucky, Indiana, and Illinois opposed the bill, with Republicans, Democrats, and Unionists in those areas in agreement.

the company (five of them were appointed by the federal government, with the remainder made up largely of friends and executives of the largest railroad companies in the country).

It soon became clear that it would be difficult to raise the initial $4 million of private capital required in the law, especially since the law prohibited any single individual from owning more than $20,000 worth of stock. Lincoln's former client, Thomas C. Durant, easily found a way around this legislative prohibition. He simply gave friends and associates the money to buy Union Pacific stock in their names. After the transactions were completed, they gave him their stock certificates. In this way he was able to gain control of nearly a majority of the stock in the Union Pacific, giving him control of both that railroad and the Mississippi & Missouri.

Predictions of corruption made by Owen Lovejoy and William P. Sheffield proved prophetic. By the time the golden spike was driven into the rail ties connecting the Central Pacific and Union Pacific at Promontory Point, Utah, in 1869, as much as a third of the $100 million in federal loans had been siphoned off into the private hands of Thomas C. Durant, at the Union Pacific, and the Big Four of the Central Pacific. So poor were the workmanship and quality of materials used during the mad dash across the country that within four years almost every inch of track from Council Bluffs to Sacramento had to be pulled up and rebuilt.

The extent of the corruption and self-dealing wouldn't be fully known until a decade after the bill's passage, but the man most responsible for the passage of the bill in its final form—Theodore Judah—soon realized what a monstrosity he had helped create. By January 1863 he was back in California, where he participated in the celebration that kicked off the beginning of construction. The Big Four asked him to sign an affidavit requesting the higher $48,000-per-mile loan for twenty-one miles of track that was flat as a pancake. By the terms of the law he had written, the company was due only the $16,000 "easy grade" loan. Judah refused to sign the false affidavit his partners submitted to the federal government, especially in light of the fact that his own previous surveys had shown that the stretch of land was neither "mountainous terrain" nor "high plains," but indeed "easy grade."[34]

Equally troubling to Judah was the clear pattern of self-dealing that had emerged. Charlie Crocker, one of the Big Four, had received the construction contract to build the railroad. Judah hadn't seen the invoices Crocker submitted for payment, but he correctly suspected that Crocker was double- and triple-charging the Central Pacific for materials, and that the other three members of the Big Four were also secret partners receiving payments from Crocker's construction company.

Unable to tolerate this illegal and unethical conduct, Judah resigned his position as chief engineer of the Central Pacific. He immediately went east, where he planned to secure financing to buy out the Big Four. But crossing Panama he contracted yellow fever, and he barely lived long enough to reach New York City, where he died on November 4, 1863, at the age of thirty-seven.[35]

As bad as things were with the Central Pacific, they were worse with the Union Pacific. A few weeks after Theodore Judah's death, President Lincoln met the Union Pacific's Thomas C. Durant in the White House. He gave Durant a handwritten note, announcing the decision much of the railroad community and country had been awaiting for over a year. Council Bluffs, Iowa—the western terminus of Durant's own Mississippi & Missouri—would be the eastern terminus of the transcontinental railroad.[36] The two other options—St. Joseph, Missouri, the western terminus of the Hannibal & St. Joseph Railroad, and Kansas City, the western terminus of the Leavenworth, Pawnee & Western, failed to make the cut, but both railroads received federal loans to build lines that would link to the Union Pacific. The law made sure that there was plenty of federal money to hand out, even to those railroad interests that didn't directly connect one coast to the other.

It was precisely the decision for which Durant had hoped and planned. Through agents he had been buying up land for himself around

Omaha, Nebraska,* the point across the Missouri River from which he planned on beginning construction. (Lincoln had set the terminus at Council Bluffs, hoping, perhaps, that Durant's Union Pacific would begin by building a bridge across the Missouri from Council Bluffs to Omaha, but Durant saw profit in starting construction immediately in Omaha.) For the next two years, Durant built his railroad in an oxbow around Omaha, most of its route along land he owned personally. The Union Pacific purchased this land from him at highly inflated prices. When the Civil War ended two years later, the Union Pacific had laid about one hundred miles of circuitous track, but the line extended only forty miles to the west of Omaha.

This was only the beginning of Durant's self-dealing. The previous year he had purchased controlling interest in a Pennsylvania company named Crédit Mobilier. The company was unique in having been formed under new rules of limited liability. In other words, the owners would not be held responsible for the liabilities of the company. Durant ensured that Crédit Mobilier was named the exclusive construction agent for Union Pacific.

Operating under the assumption that the Union Pacific was unlikely to be profitable as an operating entity, Durant followed the fine speculative tradition of William Duer. He decided to milk every possible dime he could out of the company.

His method was simple. Crédit Mobilier marked up its construction invoices by a factor of 5 or 6. Union Pacific would receive an invoice for $5,000 from Crédit Mobilier, when the latter's true costs—paying crews, foremen, and survey engineers; purchasing rail ties and steel gauge for the lines—were $1,000. The $4,000 in profits went right to the bottom line of Crédit Mobilier, which frequently paid extraordinarily high dividends to its shareholders, the largest of whom was Durant himself.

The wily Durant knew how to keep the goose laying golden eggs. He

---

* In the more populated areas, both railroads had to purchase land that was in private hands to run the line.

liberally sprinkled shares of stock in Crédit Mobilier among Republican members of Congress. His point man was Congressman Oakes Ames of Massachusetts.

Durant was aided in his efforts to secure favorable treatment of Union Pacific by Grenville Dodge. As a Union general in the Civil War,* Dodge had helped Durant create a fortune by smuggling contraband cotton. After the war, Durant named him chief engineer of the Union Pacific. In 1866, Dodge also ran for Congress as a Republican. He was elected from Iowa and served a single term, during which time he was also responsible for building the Union Pacific. He divided his time during these two years between Washington and Council Bluffs and points west along the growing rail line.

Dodge's sole purpose in Congress was to secure additional federal aid for the Union Pacific Railroad. While his conflict of interest was more blatant than other congressmen's, the nation's attention was focused on the challenges of Reconstruction and the romance of the technology that would soon allow one to go from one end of the country to the other in a matter of days.

In 1868, a year before the golden spike was driven at Promontory Point, a bitter and long-retired Asa Whitney reflected on how his original dream of a transcontinental railroad had been realized in such a corrupt and flawed manner:

> [Congress] never labored to bring forth a railroad to the Pacific till it was made a gambling, stock-jobbing Wall Street and Threadneedle [S]treet [in the London financial district] concern, backed by some hundreds of millions of Government bonds, with an annual subsidy from the Treasury to meet the expenses for its management, to be provided for by an enormous and burdensome tax upon the labor of the country to pay the European stockholder his rich dividends.[37]

---

* History buffs will recognize Dodge as the Union general who ordered the execution of Sam Davis, "the boy hero of the Confederacy," for spying in Pulaski, Tennessee, in 1862.

In the midst of much acclaim and self-congratulation, the two lines joined up at Promontory Point, Utah, on May 10, 1869. The Central Pacific had built 700 miles of track east from Sacramento, half of it through mountains. The Union Pacific had built 1,000 miles of track west from Omaha, most of it "easy grade" or "high plains."

Leland Stanford of the Central Pacific and Thomas Durant of the Union Pacific participated in the ceremonies. As a witness described it:

> When they came to drive the last spike, Governor Stanford, president of the Central Pacific, took the sledge, and the first time he struck he missed the spike and hit the rail. . . . Then Stanford tried it again and tapped the spike and the telegraph operators had fixed their instruments so that the tap was reported in all the offices east and west, and set bells to tapping in hundreds of towns and cities. . . . Then Vice President T. C. Durant of the Union Pacific took up the sledge and he missed the spike the first time. Then everybody slapped everybody else again and yelled, "He missed it too, yow!"[38]

The spike wasn't the only thing Durant missed. Virtually all the cash in the accounts of the Union Pacific was missing as well. Accountants estimated that as much as $23 million of the $50 million in government loans given to Union Pacific was distributed as Crédit Mobilier dividends.[39]

The full nature of the Crédit Mobilier scandal wasn't known until September 1872, when the *New York Herald* got wind of a lawsuit by a disgruntled Crédit Mobilier shareholder against Durant. Splashed across the front pages were the sordid details with names of the Republican congressmen to whom Oakes Ames had given stock.

In 1873 and 1874 the scandal became better known through Senate hearings and public disgust mounted. No one went to jail for the swindles, but Congressman Ames was censured; he retired to Massachusetts in disgrace. In the 1874 congressional elections, for the first time since the Civil War the Republicans lost control of the House to the resurgent Democrats.

The nation had its transcontinental railroad, and there were numerous benefits promoting economic growth and national unity related to that venture. But the costs of the methods used to create it were great.

The big winners were the handful of businessmen who had been favored by the law and knew how to manipulate it. Durant and Dodge became multimillionaires through Union Pacific and Crédit Mobilier. The Big Four—Stanford, Hopkins, Huntington, and Crocker—created fortunes so large they last to this day.

But the losers were innumerable, starting with the shareholders who bought stock in Union Pacific—the company went through several bankruptcies, the first in 1873, the last in 1892. American citizens who paid income taxes from 1862 to 1870, when the tax was finally ended, were also losers, as were the railroad entrepreneurs who could have and would have developed a transcontinental railroad that performed better. And the customers would have received better value in freight and passenger transport.

But the biggest loser of all was the future economy of America. The precedent of federal government involvement in the selection of winners and losers in business was established, and the bitter fruit of that tree has been with us now for a century and a half.

Chapter 5

WOODROW WILSON
AND THE DIVINE RIGHT
OF THE STATE

I n the aftermath of a bloody civil war, Hamiltonian policies were in the ascendant in America. The Republican Party's expansive federalism, so vital to success in that titanic struggle, was now applied to the economic realm. But after two decades watching the self-dealing that naturally accompanied such policies—seen so nakedly in the Crédit Mobilier scandal and graft surrounding protective tariffs—the voters of the reconstructed United States had had their fill of Republican corruption.

In 1884 they elected Grover Cleveland—the last constitutional Democrat—to the presidency in a close race, swung by the votes of 60,000 Republican "Mugwumps"* in New York who abandoned the party rather than stain their good names with a vote for the tainted James Blaine. It was the first time since the hapless James Buchanan that a Democrat occupied the White House.

No chief executive demonstrated greater fidelity to the constitutional principles of limited government than Cleveland during his two interrupted terms.

---

* The derisive name was given to the disaffected Republicans by a New York newspaper editor, who claimed the word was Algonquin Indian for "Big Chief."

Three issues defined his presidency. His actions in all three honored the Founders' originalism. In two of them he prevailed; in the third, his best efforts were not enough.

Cleveland kept the promise of following the plain meaning of a constitution when he vetoed a bill that would have had the federal government bailing out farmers in Texas who experienced a drought. He kept the promise of the fiscal constitution when he opposed the Republican Party's entitlement programs for the families of Civil War veterans. Finally, he supported the promise of free markets when he sought tariff reform. Only in this last effort did he fail.

In 1887, many areas of Texas experienced a serious drought, causing the farm crops to fail. The Texas farmers, lacking funds, couldn't afford to purchase seed grain, and the Democratic-controlled Congress passed a bill that specifically appropriated $10,000—not a large amount, even in those days—and authorized the commissioner of agriculture (it would be two years before Cleveland would sign the law elevating the Department of Agriculture to cabinet status) to purchase seed grain, which was to be distributed to farmers in the counties most affected by the drought.

Cleveland vetoed the bill, saying:

> I can find no warrant for such an appropriation in the Constitution; and I do not believe that the power and duty of the General Government ought to be extended to the relief of individual suffering which is in no manner properly related to the public service or benefit. . . . [T]he lesson should be constantly enforced that, though the people support the Government, the Government should not support the people.[1]

Cleveland's next battle was much larger, and his principled stand in opposition to unnecessary spending cost him the presidential election of 1888.

The Grand Army of the Republic—an organization of Union Civil War veterans—wanted more generous pensions for their members from the federal government, and they lobbied Congress and Cleveland vigorously for such a program.* As with most entitlement programs, Union veteran pension programs started small, but they soon got out of control. In 1887 Republicans in the Senate passed a Dependent Pension Bill, which would have dramatically increased pension payments even further—by making dependents of Union veterans eligible to receive pension payments and by granting pensions to anyone who had served as few as ninety days in the Union Army during the Civil War. The Republican minority in the House of Representatives enlisted the assistance of the Grand Army of the Republic to pressure Democrats in the House, and they too passed the bill.

But President Cleveland would have none of it. He vetoed the bill on the grounds that it would encourage fraudulent pension claims.[2] Events would prove Cleveland entirely justified in his veto, but neither the Republican Party nor the Grand Army of the Republic saw it that way. Angered, they turned Cleveland out in 1888, replacing him with their own Benjamin Harrison.

In 1890, Harrison and the Republican-dominated "Billion Dollar Congress" passed the Dependent Pension Act of 1890, which gave Union veterans who had served for a minimum of ninety days—regardless of whether they had been in combat or not—and their dependents a pension from the government. Harrison signed the bill into law, and the first massive entitlement program in American history was put in place. Three years later, more than one million Americans were receiving checks from the federal government. The strain on the federal budget was enormous: by 1893, 41 percent of all the expenditures in the federal budget were for these Republican-supported entitlement payments.[3]

The Republicans' profligacy and their support for the highly protectionist McKinley Tariff helped sweep Cleveland back into the White House in 1892.

---

* Confederate veterans received pensions from their state governments, not the federal government, on the theory that they had been in rebellion against the federal government and were therefore not eligible to receive benefits from it.

High tariff rates had long been part of the Republican platform—an extension of the Hamiltonian concept of protecting "infant industries." The consequences of such tariffs were higher-priced imported goods, for which there was a lesser demand, and simultaneously higher-priced domestically produced competing goods, for which there was also a lesser demand.

With an electoral mandate to reduce the unpopular McKinley Tariffs, Cleveland went to work in 1893. His efforts, however, were hampered by the combination of a severe economic downturn and the manipulation of political leaders by special interests. The tariff bill they finally passed—the infamous Wilson-Gorman Tariff Act—was so riddled with special benefits (particularly for the sugar industry) that Cleveland let it become law without his signature.

As Cleveland struggled with special interests and a flagging economy, a young former congressman from Nebraska was at work advancing a new vision for the Democratic Party. Cloaked in tributes to Jeffersonian traditions, William Jennings Bryan championed a muscular federal interventionism based on his deeply held Christian majoritarian view of governance.

It was the birth of liberal populism—not in the tradition of the conservative "leave me alone" populism of Jacksonian democracy. Bryan believed in a kind of egalitarianism that played well in the small agricultural communities of the American Midwest and South. These communities were homogeneous, their residents living in modest economic circumstances and sharing common religious affiliations.

Bryan had tried to jump from Congress to the Senate in 1894, but failed, in part due to the unicameral Nebraska legislature's discomfort with his populism (U.S. senators were still appointed by state legislators at the time). Unfazed, he accepted a position as editor of the *Omaha World-Herald* but spent much of his time spellbinding crowds in the Chautauqua shows and assemblies that had sprung up around the country in the prior decade.

Despite his flowery tributes to Jefferson, Bryan's economic program was more a tribute to Gerrard Winstanley's Christian socialism* than to the economic policies of the Sage of Monticello.

Bryan's political philosophy can be understood as indistinguishable from his religious worldview, one shaped in a Presbyterian fundamentalism of America's Third Great Awakening. Where the Second Great Awakening had replaced the dour predeterminism of Calvinism with Arminian free will, the Third Great Awakening† of the last half of the nineteenth century introduced a new vision of millennialism. The lord Jesus Christ was coming again, it held, but only after Christians on earth perfected our social and governmental institutions. This sparked the same sort of social activism that powered the Social Gospel, and in Bryan it brought out a kind of domineering majoritarianism that subjected the will of the individual to what he persuaded the majority of his fellow Christians any individual's conduct ought to be.

Unlike Cromwell, who sought to impose his view of Christian conduct upon others at the point of the sword, Bryan sought to impose his views on others through the power of the ballot box. Cromwell sought a Bible-state where order was kept by the threat of violence. Bryan sought a premillennial Bible-state where order was kept by the tyranny of the majority.

This explained his lifelong commitment to support of four key constitutional amendments: for the income tax, the direct election of United States senators, women's suffrage, and the prohibition of the sale of alcohol, the last of which would turn out to be a disaster.

In only women's suffrage would he have secured the support of a Jefferson come back to life. Jefferson, the Deist with a reverence for the scientific method, would have reacted in horror to most of Bryan's prescriptions, especially as they evidenced themselves in the latter part

---

* During the Leveller Movement of 1647–1649 in England, Winstanley and a few hundred followers formed a Christian socialist group known as the "Diggers" who squatted on unoccupied farmland before Cromwell rousted them out of their few settlements.

† Not all scholars formally recognize this movement as constituting a Third Great Awakening.

of his life, when he played the villain to Clarence Darrow's hero as described by H. L. Mencken's contemporary reports of the famous Scopes "Monkey" Trial of 1925.

To say that Bryan misappropriated Jefferson would be the kindest description of his true Jeffersonian apostasy. In his age, Jefferson decried the "Norman yoke" of one hundred and sixty thousand Parliamentary electors in England. Had he lived in the era of Cleveland and Bryan, he would have decried Bryan's policies as the seedlings upon which the wood of the "Collectivist yoke" would later be constructed by Woodrow Wilson, Franklin Roosevelt, and the pantheon of Democratic leaders of the late twentieth and early twenty-first centuries.

But Bryan had certain talents more suited to the modern age than Cleveland's, and with energy and purpose he took his twisted Jeffersonianism across the lands to the Chautauqua theaters where small-town Americans of a Christian inclination gathered for summer entertainment. After two years and thousands of such events, he was able to steal the Democratic nomination for president away from Cleveland and his allies, mixing religion and politics once more with his inflation-promoting "cross of gold" speech.

When all the votes were counted in the presidential election of 1896, it was a decisive victory for McKinley and the Republicans, who won 51 percent of the popular vote and 276 Electoral College votes to Bryan's 171 (27 of which came to him from the Populist Party line, whose nomination he also obtained). Though Bryan lost the presidency, he and his allies took over the Democratic Party.

Bryan would never gain the presidency. His subsequent campaigns in 1900 and 1908 also failed, but his control of the machinery of the Democratic Party set the stage for another Presbyterian president with similar sensibilities—Woodrow Wilson.

As the nineteenth century turned to the twentieth, the United States saw a revitalized Republican Party championing the Hamiltonian view of an increasingly expansionist federal government, and a Democratic Party following Bryan's lead, abandoning the limited government constitutionalism of Jefferson, Madison, Jackson, and Cleveland. Both came to agree on the need for ever-increasing federal regulation of personal and business conduct.

As was the case for Bryan, Wilson's politics were molded by his religious views. Though they were both Presbyterians, Wilson adhered to the Mosaic covenant instead of Bryan's Christian majoritarianism. Just as Moses led the Jewish people out of Egypt to the Promised Land in fulfillment of his covenant with God, Wilson saw himself as the chosen one to lead the American people out of their "outdated" inefficient constitutional governance into a Promised Land of the modern efficiency of a "living constitution," driven by a powerful and magnanimous elected executive. For Wilson, the pre-Wilsonian "constitutional wilderness" was grounded in the outdated Newtonian worldview of the Founders; in contrast, the Wilsonian "Promised Land" was grounded in the superior Darwinian worldview.

When the Civil War began in 1861, four-year-old Woodrow Wilson's father was the Presbyterian minister in Augusta, Georgia. Woodrow's self-righteousness was firmly rooted in his father's southern Presbyterian covenant theology. It was a worldview the younger Wilson wholeheartedly embraced.

Wilson came from a family of Presbyterian ministers. His father, Joseph Ruggles Wilson, born in Ohio from Scotch-Irish stock and educated at Jefferson College, had been called to serve as minister to a Presbyterian church in Staunton, Virginia, when his son Woodrow was born in 1856. His mother's father, Thomas Woodrow, and brother, James Woodrow, were prominent, nationally regarded Presbyterians ministers. Educated at Princeton and recipient of a Ph.D. from Germany's prestigious Heidelberg University, James Woodrow would become as important in the development of Woodrow Wilson's worldview as his father.[4]

Deeply imbued within six generations of Wilson preachers who preceded Woodrow were the theological viewpoints of Protestant Reformation theologian and theocrat John Calvin. It was his Geneva Republic in Switzerland—the same place that gave shelter to the exiles from England who wrote the Geneva Bible in the 1560s—that provided a model of biblical civil governance and leadership that influenced Wilson throughout his life.

From his earliest childhood, the Southern Presbyterian covenant theology of James Thornwell, his father, and his uncle defined Wilson's worldview. He was raised to believe his political life's purpose was to fulfill God's plan here on earth, the elements of which he, as an academic well trained in the study of both the Bible and comparative government, was uniquely capable of discerning.

The covenant theology that prompted Wilson's father to join other prominent Presbyterian ministers and theologians in 1861 to break from the national body and form the Southern Presbyterian synod was self-righteous enough to rationalize the institution of slavery as part of God's covenant with man. Wilson's maternal grandfather, Thomas Woodrow, saw it otherwise, and he remained loyal to the national body, staying in Ohio throughout the war.[5]

That December, as the Presbyterian Church in the Confederate States of America convened in Joseph Wilson's church for the first time, young Woodrow Wilson's father and uncle were in attendance as Thornwell laid out the group's position on slavery:[6]

> We have no right, as a church, to enjoin [slavery] as a duty or to
> condemn it as a sin. Our business is with the duties which spring
> from the relation; the duties of the masters, on the one hand, and
> of the slaves, on the other . . . the general operation of the system
> is kindly and benevolent; it is a real and effective discipline, and,
> without it, we are profoundly persuaded that the African race in
> the midst of us can never be elevated in the scale of being. As long
> as that race, in its comparative degradation, coexists, side by side
> with the white, bondage is its normal condition.[7]

It's easy to extrapolate this viewpoint to the racist segregationist policies Wilson implemented during the first year of his first term as president of the United States. His later embrace of "Darwinian" principles and their application from the scientific to the civil realm is also consistent with this.

But of equal importance to the development of Wilson's political philosophy was Thornwell's statement of the idea that God has a plan for everyone's station in life:

> The truth is, the education of the human race for liberty and virtue is a vast providential scheme, and God assigns to every man, by a wise and holy degree, the precise place he is to occupy in the great moral school of humanity. The scholars are distributed into classes according to their competency and progress. For God is in history.[8]

Wilson's own station, he believed, was that of leader of the American people, and his election to the presidency merely confirmed that providential appointment. He had a very different view of the type of covenant that bound him, and though it was exercised in a secular arena, it was entirely providential in his mind. It was the "anointed leader" model of covenant—of Moses and John Calvin—that guided his action. The members of his congregation—the citizens and voters of the United States—periodically selected leaders, hoping they would achieve the greatness of Moses and Calvin. Since Lincoln, Wilson would argue, the leaders had failed to live up to their part of the covenant, because they had failed to lead with vigor. For Wilson, the legitimacy of action came not from the secular covenant of the Constitution but from the "plebiscitary" election of 1912 that placed him in the position of America's leader.

On the campaign trail in the fall of 1912 as the Democratic Party's presidential nominee, the now fifty-five-year-old Wilson made it clear to the entire country that he was not bound by the secular covenant of the Constitution. Indeed, the concept that the Constitution was a secular covenant that bound the federal government, the states, and the people into a compact whose terms were described in the plain meaning of the words of the document was one he had rejected many decades earlier.

> [T]he Constitution of the United States had been made under the dominion of the Newtonian Theory. . . . The trouble with the theory

is that government is not a machine, but a living thing. It falls, not
under the theory of the universe, but under the theory of organic
life. It is accountable to Darwin, not to Newton. . . . Living political constitutions must be Darwinian in structure and in practice.
Society is a living organism and must obey the laws of life, not of
mechanics. . . . All that progressives ask or desire is permission . . .
to interpret the Constitution according to the Darwinian principle;
all they ask is recognition of the fact that a nation is a living thing
and not a machine.[9]

Twenty-eight years earlier, in October 1884, on the eve of Cleveland's election as the first Democratic president after the Civil War,
Wilson had been a supremely self confident twenty-seven-year-old graduate student at Johns Hopkins University. Though still two years away
from receiving his Ph.D., he had submitted a manuscript, of which he
was quite proud, to a New York publishing house. *Congressional Governance* was accepted, and published in book form in January 1885.

Wilson argued that we should throw out our constitutional system
of checks and balances. Congress, he said, was an ineffective but overly
powerful collection of political fiefdoms, and should be replaced by the
British Parliamentary system. It was an audacious claim, especially con-
sidering that Wilson had never set foot in the Capitol Building in Washington, nor would he do so for more than another decade.

He formed his opinion based not upon painstaking research, but
from his reading of English scholar Walter Bagehot's 1867 book, *The
English Constitution*, which set forth the concept of the superiority of
England's "living constitution." The British Parliamentary system, led
by a strong national leader, meshed with Wilson's Southern Presbyterian covenant theology far better than our American constitutional
system did.

The date of publication of his first work coincided with another influential event—the trial of his uncle, James Woodrow, by the Southern Presbyterian Council on charges of heresy for his teaching of the
Darwinian theory of evolution at the Columbia Seminary, the South

Carolina institution that had employed him as a professor of natural theology for more than two decades. Woodrow, who attempted to teach that Darwin's theory of evolution was not inconsistent with a proper understanding of the Bible, was convicted, and immediately fired from his job.

Woodrow recovered professionally very quickly, ending up as the president of the University of South Carolina, but his intellectual journey—from the Southern Presbyterian concept of a theologically just war used in the defense of the institution of slavery and Confederate secession during the Civil War, to support of Darwinian evolution—mirrored the journey of his nephew, Woodrow Wilson, who idolized him. Wilson applied Woodrow's concept of the preeminence of the Darwinian paradigm of evolution to the political environment. Both were strongly influenced by the German Hegelian school of historicism—the inevitable progress of man toward perfection.

James Woodrow had been influenced by his graduate studies three decades earlier at the University of Heidelberg, and in turn influenced his nephew Woodrow Wilson. Wilson was also influenced by the numerous German historicist scholars at Johns Hopkins University who encouraged him to learn German (which he did) and study the great German thinkers in the school of historicism led by Hegel.

Wilson followed this up with an essay the following year, "The Study of Administration," in which he argued that government bureaucrats ought to pay attention to public opinion on large matters but ignore it on small matters.

In 1912, almost a century before the election of Barack Obama, Wilson set out to become a transformative president, and he wasn't afraid to trample upon the traditions of the Constitution. Forty-two percent of Americans agreed with him that year. Due to a split between the William Howard Taft Republicans and the Theodore Roosevelt Bull Moose Progressives, that was enough to make Wilson president. He was the first Democrat elected to that office in the twentieth century, and only the second since the Civil War.

He succeeded spectacularly, helped in large part by the Democratic majority he enjoyed in both houses in the 63rd Congress, which met from 1913 to 1915. It was only the third Congress since the Civil War where Democrats controlled both houses. It was also the only time in which the Democratic Party maintained control of both houses in successive Congresses. Wilson Democrats maintained a majority in both houses in the next two Congresses—the 64th Congress, which met from 1915 to 1917, and the 65th Congress, which met from 1917 to 1919. For six years Wilson enjoyed governing under conditions that offered the nearest proximity to the British Parliamentary system possible under the American Constitution.

His legislative accomplishments during this period significantly expanded the role and powers of the federal government.

The Federal Reserve Act, which established the Federal Reserve Board; the Revenue Act of 1913, which enacted a national income tax after the passage of the Sixteenth Amendment, which made the income tax constitutional; and the Clayton Anti-Trust Act and the Federal Trade Commission Act, both of which increased federal regulatory control over business, easily sailed through Congress.

During his administration, half of the amendments to the Constitution passed since 1800 were ratified—in addition to the Sixteenth Amendment there were the Seventeenth, which changed the method of election of United States senators from the state legislatures to direct popular vote; the Eighteenth, which authorized Congress to prohibit the sale of alcohol (which it did in the Volstead Act that same year); and the Nineteenth, which gave women the right to vote. Though he vetoed the Volstead Act, the Christian majoritarians behind it echoed his own views.

The Democratic congressional majorities he enjoyed during his first six years provided Wilson with the opportunity to exercise the muscular executive leadership he had so long advocated in his academic works. A few years earlier, in 1908, he had described his ideal role of a president in his book *Constitutional Government of the United States*, in which he argued that a strong executive "will be as big as and as influential as the man who occupies it."[10] The president who acted on behalf of the people, a "plebiscitary president," was authorized by the vote of the people to enact certain policies administratively without any congressional support through executive orders, and in those where broader support from Congress was required, he would lead the legislative charge.

Unlike its counterpart a century earlier, the opposition party had no Jefferson-like advocate of limited government to oppose Wilson's expansion of centralized power. Instead it offered Wilson's centralized power with a few twists.

The presidential executive order offered Wilson another opportunity to exercise the kind of leadership he envisioned. Benjamin Harrison had issued four, Cleveland seventy-seven, and McKinley fifty-one. TR increased McKinley's twenty-fold, with 1,006.[11]

Wilson broke all of TR's records. TR's successor, William Howard Taft, issued only 600 executive orders, but Wilson issued a total of 1,791 throughout his two terms.[12]

Wilson's domestic policies in his first administration—the laws passed and enacted, the executive orders signed and implemented—were but a prelude to the more drastic centralization of power that he engineered in response to the crisis of America's engagement in World War I. A century later, President Obama's then chief of staff Rahm Emanuel's statement that "you never want a serious crisis to go to waste" could easily have been modeled after Wilson's action in the immediate aftermath of Congress's declaration of war on Germany in April 1917. Indeed, historian Paul Johnson has argued that it was the dramatic expansion of centralized government powers initiated in the ensuing months that generated a continuum stretching from Wilson to Hoover to Roosevelt to Lyndon Johnson and culminating in the establishment of the welfare state of the Great Society.

The regulatory authorities and agencies empowered with new and extraordinary powers by Congress in the next few months became "the kindergartens" of bureaucratic learning that sowed the seeds for the ranks of the New Deal and Great Society brain trusts.[13] It was through these agencies that Woodrow Wilson's concept of the divine right of the state entered the bloodstream of the republic. Soon variants of all sorts began to spread. Within a century, the mere existence of the state's bureaucracy was the source of that "divinity."

Four agencies soon to be created—the Food Administration, the Fuel Administration, the War Industries Board, and the Railroad Administration—in particular proved to be the training ground for key players in the development and implementation of policies that would further expand the powers of the federal government over the next several decades. The men who ran or helped run these agencies represented a new breed of American bureaucrats, driven more by the desire to acquire and use power than by specific ideologies. The ideologies of one political party or another seemed to be mere window dressing to that core desire.

Just as Lincoln had responded to the occasion of war by consolidating and centralizing federal power, so too did Wilson. But Wilson was determined not to "make the mistakes that he did,"[14] which in Wilson's mind centered on Lincoln's failure to sufficiently centralize power around himself as president, and in particular to tolerate the establishment of a congressional committee charged with oversight of the war efforts.[15]

Lost on Wilson, apparently, were the numerous instances of Lincoln's executive overreach, as well as the use of the "national emergency of war" as a justification for the massive financial assistance the federal government provided to the politically connected private corporations selected to build the transcontinental railroad.

World War I, of course, was a different sort of war from the Civil War. All the battles took place on the European continent, and its major combatants—England, France, and Italy for the Allies, Germany and Austro-Hungary for the Axis—had been engaged for the past three years in a brutal display of the type of slaughter that twentieth-century technology brought about when combined with nineteenth-century tactics. For much of those three years, the United States had been a source of credit and supplies—war materiel and food—for the Allies. Now drawn into the war, the United States knew that its contribution to victory would not only be manpower—it would be the continuation of the supply of war materiel and food. Of the two, food loomed as the largest strategic need.

Hostilities had cut off the flow of wheat exports from Russia and Romania to the rest of Europe. As a consequence, the European allies went to America to purchase wheat. Higher demand increased wheat prices worldwide and domestically. American wheat exports tripled from the "average" level of 54 million bushels in 1913 to 186 million bushels in 1917. Prices increased from $1.46 per bushel in the fall of 1916 to $3.25 per bushel in May 1917, a month after the United States entered the war. Beef and dairy product prices had also increased during this time, but not as significantly.[16] Though prices had risen significantly for all food products in this nine-month period, American consumers did not experience shortages. So long as they were willing to pay the higher market prices, there was abundant supply.

Wilson understood the strategic importance of food, and he knew exactly how he wanted to proceed. Within days of the declaration of war, he sent up legislation to Congress that would give him virtually dictatorial authority in food, fuel, transportation, and communication. To run the food side of things, he had just the right man in mind, forty-three-year-old Herbert Hoover. It would be four months before Wilson's legislative proposals would be enacted into law in the Lever Act of 1917,* but neither Wilson nor Hoover worried about the formality of assuming power.

Hoover was already somewhat of a legend. Orphaned at the age of ten, he had talked his way into the first class at Stanford University, where he graduated with an engineering degree. While a student, he not only met the Central Pacific's Leland Stanford, but also experienced what he called "his first touch with greatness" when he met former president Benjamin Harrison at a school function. His business career as a mining engineer had been dramatic and spectacularly successful, taking him from Australia to China and points around the world. Hoover had become wealthy. When World War I broke out he found himself in

---

* Also known as the Food and Fuel Control Act.

London. There he put his organizational and engineering skills to work, first organizing the evacuation of Americans from Europe, then coordinating food relief efforts in Belgium and other parts of Europe.

Hoover's knowledge about world food supplies as well as distribution problems throughout Europe made him Wilson's hands-down pick to lead the Food Administration, which was awaiting congressional authorization. Hoover was ready for the challenge but refused to take the job unless he could report directly to the president and was granted extraordinary powers in his position. He left London in late April and arrived in early May in New York City, where he set out his terms for "Colonel" Edward House, President Wilson's aide, in a meeting held on May 3, 1917.[17]

First and foremost, Hoover wanted to be independent. The additional powers he sought included the power to license distributors, ration goods if necessary, have exclusive authority and responsibility for all food exports, and punish those he defined as "profiteers" or "hoarders." House assured him that most of those elements were already in the bill, and those that weren't would be added before it became law.

The next day, Hoover paid a courtesy call to Secretary of Agriculture David F. Houston, and secured his consent to a direct reporting relationship between himself—when named coordinator of the proposed Food Administration—and the president. Later that week, on May 7, Hoover testified in secret before Congressman Asbury Lever and the House Committee on Agriculture and outlined all the powers he wanted assigned to the coordinator of the Food Administration in the new law.[18]

Hoover proposed that the administrative apparatus of the new Food Administration be centralized in decision making but extremely decentralized in implementation. Local enforcement of the "voluntary" price controls not specifically authorized in the proposed Lever Act of 1917 but assumed on a de facto basis by Hoover regardless of legislative authority, as well as "voluntary" rationing, would be managed at the county level, with an intervening state level of administrative control. Thus Hoover proposed forty-eight state food administrators and roughly 4,500 county food administrators, all operating on a volunteer basis.

Hoover issued a press release in late May, more than two months before Congress approved the enabling law, that outlined his vision for the Food Administration. The basic points: The food problem was one that required "wise administration." He insisted he be called "administrator," not "dictator." The administration of food could be carried out through existing relationships between producers and consumers. Communities should be organized to voluntarily conserve. All administrators should be volunteers. He would report directly to the president, not the secretary of agriculture.[19]

By the time Congress finally passed the Lever Act of 1917 and President Wilson signed it into law on August 10, 1917, Hoover had effectively already been on the job for more than two months. The law itself didn't actually establish the Food Administration and name Hoover the administrator—that not insignificant detail was handled by President Wilson, who immediately issued an executive order to administer the law through the Food Administration created by the executive order, with Hoover at its head.

Hoover got right down to business, immediately setting up the forty-eight state food administrators, setting prices, and issuing press releases filled with colorful slogans. Each state food administrator was charged with setting up the county food administrators. Among the oft-repeated slogans of the new program: "Food Will Win the War, Don't Waste It" and "By All Means Save the Beans." A few seemed oddly out of touch with Hoover's supposed "voluntarism," among them this classic, alluding to the famous book by Oliver Wendell Holmes Sr.: "Herbert Hoover, the Autocrat of the Breakfast Table."[20]

Two days after the Lever Act of 1917 was signed into law, Hoover issued a press release that left many free market proponents slack-jawed. Though he had no statutory authority to do so, he told the entire country that he would soon be setting the price of wheat.[21] He softened the blow with his now obligatory emphasis upon the "voluntary" nature of the program. Ominously, however, Hoover warned that "[t]he small minority who refuse to cooperate should not be allowed to defeat the nation's necessities."

The "voluntary arrangements" trumpeted by Hoover were often implemented at the county level with the threat of legal punishment. One Monday in Indiana's Switzerland County, where the county's thirty-six grocers gathered with County Food Administrator J. W. Smith every week to report the amount of flour and sugar their customers had purchased, grocer representative E. P. Downey had some news for them about their level of "voluntary" cooperation. State Administrator H. E. Barnard had told Downey that, as a historian of the county program wrote, the "Switzerland County Grocers would be allowed a few more weeks in which to compel their customers to use less foods, and if they failed, then the stores would be taken over by the government and a government man would superintend the distribution of food in the county."[22]

In Porter County, Indiana, County Food Administrator Charles Link "was obliged to issue repeated warnings to hoarders and war profiteers, and at times the law had to be invoked to successfully enforce the food administration laws."[23]

In Oregon, one farmer, irritated by mandatory substitute ingredients in bread, complained that "[p]eople wondered if they could live eating the bread that many of them had to eat. They thought that they might as well go over in the fields of France and be killed in an honorable and heroic way."[24]

In Madison County, New York, "[s]ome 100 investigations were made upon complaints . . . [but] only four convictions were necessary in the entire county for food violations during the war."[25]

In the fall of 1917, Hoover set the price of wheat at $2.20 per bushel. By January 1918, Hoover's program of voluntary conservation, increased production, and price controls had created domestic food shortages around the country.

Instead of eliminating the shortages by allowing prices to rise to market levels, thereby setting an equilibrium for supply and demand, Hoover and Wilson set upon a strategy of forced voluntary rationing.

The thin veneer of Hoover's volunteerism was peeling away badly. In Burt County, Nebraska, one history recounts:

> Food conservation was a measure that affected every home, they did not fully understand the import of the orders for wheatless and meatless days, or the rationing of flour, sugar and other commodities, neither did they take kindly at first to the food cards, they did not know exactly what was expected of them. Later when it became understood, most everyone gladly joined the conservation propaganda and tried to make themselves believe they liked it whether they did or not.[26]

Around the country, newspaper notices began to spring up announcing schedules from the local county food administrator that applied to private homes, hotels, and restaurants alike for wheatless Mondays, meatless Tuesdays, wheatless Wednesdays, meatless breakfast and wheatless supper on Thursdays and Fridays, porkless Saturdays, and not even a day of rest on Sundays, when breakfasts were meatless and supper was wheatless.[27]

By February 1918, the populist Democratic senator from wheat-growing Oklahoma, Thomas Gore, the so-called Blind Cowboy,[*] was sick of Hoover's dictatorial command-and-control approach. Consumers were experiencing unnecessary shortages, and farmers couldn't make any money. Gore proposed legislation that would raise the price of wheat from $2.20 a bushel to $2.50 a bushel.

Debate raged on the Senate floor. Senator James A. Reed of Missouri, a supporter of Gore's proposal, asserted that the Lever Act contained no authority "to fix the price of a single foodstuff" and that any man who did so was a "lawbreaker."[28]

The bill passed, but Wilson vetoed the price hike. It would, he argued, be inflationary and might harm the British ability to purchase more wheat from America.

---

[*] Senator Gore was the maternal grandfather of novelist Gore Vidal.

Farmers in wheat-growing states were furious, and the anger spread to tomato-growing states like New Jersey, Maryland, and Delaware, when Hoover imposed price controls of $21 per ton on that product. Missouri's Reed couldn't restrain himself from issuing a public "I told you so" to his colleagues from these states:

> I told you so . . . I warned you that the Lever Act would be used "to fix the price of the farmer's products." I told you "not to turn the prosperity of the great agricultural portion of our population over to a man ignorant alike of farming, stock raising, and of American conditions."[29]

In February 1918, Hoover issued a rule prohibiting the killing of hen chickens. Farmers had reacted to the various across-the-board market-restricting price regulations by selling hen chickens for slaughter, since it was the best way for them to make a profit. The unintended consequence for Hoover was that the country's poultry stock was largely being depleted, and eggs were becoming scarce. Soon a new set of newspaper notices with more rules began appearing around the country:

> You are forbidden to buy hens at any time for killing purposes. You are not permitted to sell any laying hens from now until May 1 and produce-men are prohibited from buying hens of any kind from now until May. If you sell any hens at all, they must be sold to other poultry raisers.[30]

By the time World War I mercifully came to a halt in November 1918, domestic agricultural markets were in chaos. Hoover claimed victory, but farmers continued to resent his imperious interventions in the free market.

The mess was even greater in fuel and railroads. Wilson chose Harry Garfield, his former colleague at Princeton and now the president of Williams College, to head up the new Fuel Administration authorized by the Lever Act of 1917. Despite his presidential pedigree (his father,

James Garfield, had been elected president in 1880, and assassinated a year later), Garfield did not have the same knack for public relations and self-promotion enjoyed by Hoover.

He shared with Hoover, however, a sense of his own judgments as superior to the free marketplace. Like Hoover in agriculture, Garfield exercised complete control of the coal industry. In January 1918, frustrated that ships lay idle in East Coast ports because they didn't have enough fuel, Garfield ordered all factories east of the Mississippi closed for five days. The theory was this would free up coal and other fuels for use in the idle ships. The imperious action infuriated every factory owner in twenty eastern states, and Garfield's reputation was severely damaged.

Government control of the railroads was equally disastrous. At the outbreak of war, Wilson set up a Railroad War Board to handle the movement of men and goods to ports on the Atlantic coast from the inland. Working with the Interstate Commerce Commission, this group set up a system of prioritizing freight cars, which soon led to bottlenecked congestion all over the country. With a failed system, Wilson seized complete control of the railroads, and the federal government ran them until March 1920.[31]

Wilson established the U.S. Railroad Administration in December 1917 and named Secretary of the Treasury William McAdoo (also his new son-in-law) as its head. Despite the even greater government control—in fact, most likely because of it—the situation did not improve.

Government controls were disastrous. Government losses exceeded $1 billion over two years. Many railroads were hurt so badly they simply went out of business. It would be decades before the railroad system fully recovered.[32]

The War Industries Board, established at the start of the war, was eventually headed by financier Bernard Baruch, who was assisted by journalist Herbert Bayard Swope and former general Hugh Johnson, whose deputy, Gerard Swope, Herbert's brother, just a few years after the war would be named president of General Electric. In 1924, Gerard Swope instigated the Phoebus Cartel, GE's highly effective plan to control the international lightbulb market, and in 1931 he proposed the radical Swope Plan for industrial recovery.

The war brought federal expenditures to unparalleled levels, rising from $730 million in 1916 to $2 billion in 1917, then skyrocketing to $12.7 billion in 1918, and $18.5 billion in 1919. Revenue for the war came from increased income taxes, borrowing, and inflation prompted by the printing of money by the federal government.[33]

The Allied victory that accompanied the armistice in November 1918 should have resulted in a political boon for Wilson and the Democrats, but the massively intrusive and ubiquitous government regulations he had implemented, which interrupted virtually every aspect of civilian life, did not sit well with the voters. Democrats lost their majority in both houses that month but Wilson, politically tone deaf to the will of the people, pushed his League of Nations proposal. A stroke virtually incapacitated him in early 1919 and he limped through the remainder of his term.

Woodrow Wilson died in 1924, but his legacy of constitutional usurpation and expanded federal control and intrusiveness into private lives and economic action has grown over the nine decades since his passing. Though he never used the phrase "divine right of the state" to describe his philosophy of government, that, in essence, describes how Wilsonian covenant theology was applied to governance under his administration. Those who tasted the power associated with that philosophy remembered the thrill they experienced when they exercised it. While they didn't share Wilson's covenant theology, they held to the premise that actions of the state, because they were of the state, and the state was the people, were de facto "divine."

After the war, all of Wilson's wartime agencies eventually wound down. But the damage had been done. The principle of the divine right of the state had been established, though it was ostensibly reserved for exercise in national emergencies. The people had begun to become more timid in the assertion of their individual liberties, accepting the superior call of the state to determine their actions (one obvious example was the support for and acceptance of Prohibition).

Equally important, the exercise of power by the elite corporate and government bureaucrats had whetted their appetite for more. Soon these elites would find an excuse to exercise those emergency powers during times of peace.

The men who had exercised unparalleled power in these administrative agencies during World War I found they enjoyed it. They wanted more. They were, after all, uniquely qualified by virtue of their education, training, and accomplishments to make those decisions that had previously been left to the individual. Opportunities—new kinds of emergencies—would soon arise for them to exercise that power once more. When that happened, they were ready and eager to do so.

Chapter 6

REPUBLICANS
FAIL TO OFFER
AN ALTERNATIVE

I f Herbert Hoover believed in the Constitution during his public
career before his election to the presidency in 1928, it was only as a
subordinate appendage to his own engineering "efficiency." Perhaps
he saw it as a meaningless creed to be recited on occasion as a form of
political ritual. Or perhaps he considered it an archaic relic of an ancient age that preceded modernity. Whatever his views of the Constitution, it was not the document that gave him sustenance.

Like his mentor in public service, Woodrow Wilson, Hoover saw himself at the head of the inevitable march of history. Unlike Wilson, who was
guided by the intellectually engaged God of the Southern Presbyterian
General Assembly, Hoover was guided by the God of Scientific Management. The brainchild of Frederick Winslow Taylor, an "efficiency" expert
famous for his time and motion studies, this top-down system of business
management broke down tasks to their fundamental components and
held employees to increasingly higher standards of performance.

In 1922, at the height of his popularity while serving as secretary of
commerce, Hoover published a short book titled *American Individualism*. Not one of its 13,000 words referenced the Constitution, an odd
omission for a sitting cabinet member.

In 1934, a year out of office, he wrote a lengthy article for the *Saturday Evening Post*, "The Challenge to Liberty," which was later turned into another small book, of the same name. "Out of our philosophy," Hoover wrote in the *Post* article, "grew the American Constitutional system, where the obligation to promote the common welfare was mandatory."[1]

Article I, Section 8 of the Constitution grants Congress the power to provide for the general welfare, but despite Hoover's claim, this is not "mandatory." The Constitution states, "The Congress shall have Power To . . . provide for the common Defence and general Welfare of the United States."

Hoover's reasoning was similar to that of Hamilton, who used "the general welfare" clause as a rationale to promote the ill-fated Society for Establishing Useful Manufactures. Ever since, a multitude of governmental excesses have been justified by invoking this false claim.

Hoover's views on the Constitution mattered greatly, because for sixteen years, from 1917 to 1933, he was at the center of power in Washington. For the last twelve of those years—eight as commerce secretary and four as president—he was arguably the most significant shaper of the federal government's domestic economic policies.

Despite the infringements on liberty he inflicted on the public in his role as Wilson's food administrator, he emerged from World War I with his reputation relatively unscathed. This mostly just reflected his skill at public relations and communications, in contrast to the highly unpopular Harry Garfield, administrator of the equally unpopular Fuel Administration.

In 1920, several leaders in both parties wanted Hoover to run for president. Wilson, in particular, considered him a suitable successor. Hoover's future nemesis, Franklin Roosevelt, also considered him presidential material. FDR had also served in Wilson's administration, for eight years as assistant secretary of the navy, and also like Hoover, he admired Wilson's progressivism.

But Hoover threw in his lot with the Republicans, knowing that Wilson's policies had been so unpopular it was certain to be a Republican landslide. But his campaign gained little support among the rank and file. When the affable Warren G. Harding won the nomination, Hoover pledged his support and campaigned aggressively. Harding was impressed with Hoover, calling him "the smartest gink I know."

Harding scored a smashing victory in the general election, thumping the Democratic ticket of James M. Cox and Franklin Roosevelt by a whopping 60–34 percent margin in the popular vote, and an equally impressive 404–127 Electoral College victory. Hoover had called it right. The voters were sick of Wilson and his policies. When Harding named him secretary of commerce, Hoover had an opportunity to continue to implement those policies with his own twist.

Hoover took the job at Commerce, until then a veritable backwater of power, and transformed the department into a powerhouse. He plunged in with typical enthusiasm, promoting "voluntarism" and cooperation between big business and government. Hoover called this "associationalism." He set about helping industries establish standards, improve efficiencies, and increase foreign exports. He also built his empire at Commerce, adding numerous independent agencies to his department, persuading Congress to dramatically increase his staff, and inserting his opinion into virtually every aspect of federal operations, earning the enmity of other members of the cabinet, especially Henry C. Wallace at Agriculture. Wallace was still mad at Hoover for what he saw as the destruction of farm profitability wrought by the Food Administration's price controls and regulations.

Hoover's energy and ambition were a force of nature, and during the 1920s he won virtually every battle he undertook. It was common knowledge—especially after his first attempt in 1920—that his drive had but one purpose professionally—the presidency.

Hoover described his philosophy in the misleadingly titled *American Individualism*:

Today business organization is moving strongly toward cooperation. There are in the cooperative great hopes that we can even gain in individuality, equality of opportunity, and an enlarged field for initiative, and at the same time reduce many of the great wastes of over-reckless competition in production and distribution.[2]

Many who dealt with Hoover found him unbearably autocratic. At Commerce, just as at the Food Administration, his concept of "voluntarism" was persuading others to accept his ideas. When persuasion, bullying, or threats failed, Hoover often brought in the heavy hand of governmental authority.

At Commerce, Hoover's concept of "associationalism" was an expansive one. He was particularly interested in sharing research and information collected by the federal government with large private corporations and associations to advance the rationalization and efficiencies of industry. This was a natural extension of the World War I practices of the War Industries Board.[3]

Even more troubling than Hoover's desire to create what were essentially government-sanctioned cartels was his cavalier attitude toward private property, one of the sacrosanct cornerstones of the Constitution. He described his views on property in *American Individualism*:

> Private property is not a fetich in America. The crushing of the liquor trade without a cent of compensation, with scarcely even a discussion of it, does not bear out the notion that we give property rights any headway over human rights.

> Our development of individualism shows an increasing tendency to regard right of property not as an object in itself, but in the light of a useful and necessary instrument in the stimulation of initiative to the individual; not only stimulation to him that he may gain personal comfort, security in life, protection to his family, but also because individual accumulation and ownership is a basis of selection to leadership in administration of the tools of industry and commerce. It is where dominant private property is assembled in the hands of the groups who control the state that the individual begins to feel capital as an oppression.[4]

At Commerce, Hoover promoted his unique brand of public-private partnerships, working largely with executives of large corporations in the design of standards to improve industry efficiency. The fact that the Constitution had nothing to say about the federal government's role in industry efficiency bothered Hoover not at all. He was a man driven by an overwhelming confidence in his own capabilities and the benefits of rationalization.

One of the many initiatives Hoover undertook was in the housing arena. With typical public relations flair, he worked cooperatively with several industry groups—the Home Modernizing Bureau, the Architects' Small House Service Bureau, and various other real estate, savings and loan, and home building groups—to launch a program called "Own Your Own Home." A key component was the introduction and promotion of long-term home mortgages, which were intended to increase new home construction.

At the time, mortgages were entirely a private banking matter. The typical mortgage required 50 percent down and had a five-year term to pay the entire principal. By lengthening the term of each mortgage to fifteen or thirty years and reducing down payments from 50 percent to 10 or 20 percent, the long-term mortgages Hoover promoted had a major unintended consequence.

Prior to the acceptance of the concept of long-term mortgages like this, most monthly mortgage payments were primarily to reduce the principal, rather than to pay interest on the principal. As long-term mortgages proliferated, this ratio changed. Now, especially in the early years of a mortgage, interest payments were a far greater component of the typical mortgage payment than reduction of principal.

This meant that the interest deductibility element of the less than a decade old income tax became a far more important feature. It was, as one scholar recently wrote, an accidental deduction, probably not intended by Congress when the income tax had been enacted a decade earlier, but once established, it became a sacrosanct, untouchable deduction. It remains so nine decades later.

Despite these machinations, the new long-term mortgages did little to increase home ownership rates in the country. In 1900, before the establishment of the income tax, home ownership was 45 percent, a rate that remained steady for the next two decades. After long-term mortgages became more popular, home ownership rates increased slightly, from 45 percent in 1920 to 47 percent a decade later. The big jump toward today's 67 percent home ownership rate wouldn't happen until after World War II.[5]

Hoover's version of "American individualism" was not the libertarian vision of individual liberty that had been the core of Anglo-American constitutional principles since the days of Lilburne, the Glorious Revolution, the Declaration of Independence, and the Constitution. Hoover was much more Hamiltonian—in the sense that he supported a sort of hierarchical meritocracy. For Hoover, every American started life with equality of opportunity. During the course of his life, by dint of hard work, education, good decision making, and dedication to principles of efficiency, the "best and the brightest" emerged at the top of the economic and corporate ladder.

"Our individualism," he said, "differs from all others because it embraces these great ideals: that while we build our society upon the attainment of the individual, we shall safeguard to every individual an equality of opportunity to take that position in the community to which his intelligence, character, ability, and ambition entitle him."[6]

Once at the top, these individuals had the right and the responsibility to lead the rest of us by voluntary persuasion. Part of that right was to enforce their ideas of social fairness upon the rest of society. When Hoover spoke of American individualism he was not speaking of our traditional individual liberties. He was instead referring to a kind of collectivist pressure imposed upon individual liberties by peers who had climbed the ladder of economic and political power.[7]

Having rejected the traditional constitutional understanding of property rights, Hoover took the next step and rejected the principle of free markets:

> In our individualism we have long since abandoned the laissez faire
> of the 18th Century—the notion that it is "every man for himself

and the devil take the hindmost." . . . [W]e have learned that it is the hindmost who throws the bricks at our social edifice, in part because we have learned that the foremost are not always the best nor the hindmost the worst—and in part because we have learned that social injustice is the destruction of justice itself. . . . We have also learned that fair division can only be obtained by certain restrictions on the strong and the dominant.[8]

Hoover never understood or accepted the idea of "second order" effects that Henry Hazlitt would describe so brilliantly in his 1946 classic, *Economics in One Lesson*. If Hoover ever learned this lesson, it was long after he was in a position to do anything about it from a position of political power.

Hoover's rejection of free market capitalism, combined with his willingness to subvert private property rights, would, during the critical period of 1921–1927, become the most important reason our country adopted a "natural monopoly" model of oligopolistic control of the radio and television airways, regulated and controlled by the federal government.

Like Wilson, Hoover saw the role of government as driving the march toward social perfection. It was a march that, of course, would be led by enlightened leaders such as himself:

But no civilization could be built or can endure solely upon the groundwork of unrestrained and unintelligent self-interest. The problem of the world is to restrain the destructive instincts while strengthening and enlarging those of altruistic character and constructive impulse—for this we build the future.[9]

Hoover's natural human tendency, like that of the entire group of bureaucrats who had populated Wilson's executive agencies during World War I, was to establish his personal dominance at the top of the power chain—the desire to acquire and exercise power to control the behavior of his fellow Americans. At Commerce this inclination was allowed to run wild. His only limitation was not his ambition, which was boundless, nor his physical capability to work, which by all accounts was also virtually boundless, but his internal sense of where the line was that he would not cross.

Unfortunately, Hoover did not consistently apply this sense. He had written that the United States should not to be like the Kaiser's German government, in which the state and its bureaucracy used the coercive power of force and specific detailed regulations to tell citizens what they could or could not do.

In no sector was there a better example of Hoover's unique brand of autocratic governmental cooperation with big business, cloaked in a thin veneer of "volunteerism," than in the emerging radio industry.

The dramatic advances in technology that characterized the American economy in the last half of the nineteenth century and first decades of the twentieth presented expansionist federal government proponents with unlimited opportunities for intervention.

Congress first addressed the matter in the last year of the Taft administration, with the Radio Act of 1912, which simply authorized licensing of amateur radio operations for anyone who applied. When World War I broke out, however, the federal government—most notably the navy under Secretary Josephus Daniels and his assistant secretary, Franklin Roosevelt—wanted complete control of the technology.

In April 1917, at the outbreak of World War I, President Wilson exercised the authority granted him in the 1912 act and completely took over the industry. Amateurs were kicked off the air and the ownership of virtually all of the 127 prototype "commercial" stations was transferred to the navy, which operated them for exclusively military purposes.[10]

Not wanting to give up control completely, the navy formed and organized a private company, the Radio Corporation of America (RCA), that would own and operate all the existing radio stations owned by the navy and would have cross-licensing agreements of all existing radio patents through what was known as the Radio Trust, which included RCA, General Electric, Westinghouse, and United Fruit (the monopoly owner of virtually all the wireless radio stations in Central America). To make the radio industry even more closely held, GE owned a controlling interest in RCA. In essence, the navy sanctioned a natural monopoly of the manufacture of radio equipment and the operation of wireless radio stations.[11]

One approach Hoover had used to manage the spectrum was to grant licenses that limited the time of day for operation. For instance, Hoover granted the Zenith Radio Corporation an extremely limited license. They could use a wavelength of 332.4 meters, but only for two hours a week—every Thursday from 10 p.m. to midnight—and during those two hours only if the GE licensee who had also been licensed the 332.4-meter wavelength wasn't using it.

Not surprisingly, Zenith found these terms far too constraining, and regularly violated them. Hoover was not amused. Soon he brought criminal charges against Zenith and its officers.

When a federal appeals court ruled in April 1926 that Hoover had once again exceeded his statutory authority under the Radio Act of 1912, he knew that he needed to finally secure legislative authority for his regulatory actions, and so he began formulating such a scheme to sell to Congress.[12]

With every control Hoover had attempted to exert over the industry now removed by the courts, applications and issuance of commercial radio licenses exploded. Within a year, another two hundred stations were operating legally.[13]

In the midst of all this growth and chaos, RCA had been taking steps to consolidate its position in the industry. In 1923, for instance, they purchased WJZ from Westinghouse, changed the call letters to WABC, and moved it from Newark, New Jersey, to New York City. As long as their friend and ally served as secretary of commerce, they could be assured that their licensing requests would receive the most favorable treatment. Hoover's associationalism philosophy naturally favored large corporations whose executives he knew, rather than small start-up companies whose owners had not proved that they belonged, like Hoover and the executives at GE and RCA, at the top of the meritocratic Darwinian elite. For RCA and its owner, General Electric, unpredictable court cases that limited the authority of the secretary of commerce were a real threat to their business interests.

Hoover now intensively began his preparations to persuade Congress that only the federal government could control and regulate this "natural monopoly." His efforts became even more important to him when it became clear that the natural process of litigation and court decisions was creating a common law solution to the market problem caused by rapid advances in radio technology. Court decisions were establishing the concept that entrepreneurs who had applied for radio licenses had created their own private property rights in the frequency of the spectrum they had been assigned by their effective use of that frequency. Through programming and broadcasts unique to their frequency, they had developed a listening audience. In essence, the courts had decided that "homesteading" of frequencies in the spectrum had as much legal authority to the establishment of property rights to those frequencies as "homesteading" of farms had in establishing property rights to land.

In November 1926, an Illinois state court ruled in *Tribune Co. v. Oak Leaves Broadcasting Station* that the *Chicago Daily Tribune's* station, WGN (World's Greatest Newspaper), had "'created and carried out for itself a particular right or easement in and to the use of' its customary wave length, and that outsiders should not be able to deprive them of that right. . . . The court concluded," Carl Watner writes, "that 'priority of time creates a superiority in right' in the property of a commercial broadcaster."[14]

Over the next two months, Hoover, GE, Westinghouse, and RCA lobbied Congress furiously to head off the establishment of homesteading property rights in the broadcast spectrum for anyone with sufficient pluck and capital to have secured a radio license and to have operated it long enough to have secured a following.

When the Federal Radio Act of 1927 passed, the concept of statist corporate control over small operating homesteading rights was firmly established. The newly created Federal Radio Commission was granted exclusive authority to grant broadcasting licenses. The airwaves were the property of the government of the United States, and broadcasters were merely granted the privilege to use them, at the discretion of the government.[15]

Many modern-day libertarians, encouraged by Ronald Reagan's admiration for him, have pointed to President Calvin Coolidge, who was serving in the White House at this time, as the ideal "limited government" president. Yet throughout his administration, Coolidge did little to resist Hoover's aggressive statist policies. Indeed, he signed the Federal Radio Act of 1927, which codified Hoover's philosophies, on the same day it came to him from Congress. Therein lies the conundrum for Coolidge fans. He didn't like Hoover, thought his efforts were far too intrusive, yet did little to thwart his ambitions as secretary of commerce when, as president of the United States, Coolidge clearly had the power and authority to do so.

With legal authority in hand, Hoover went to work to create the kind of "ordered" market that reflected his associationalist views. One of the first things Hoover did was create a spectrum that allocated sixteen gigantic 50,000-watt stations across the country. He licensed these stations to GE, Westinghouse, and a few other powerful manufacturing interests. This meant that large corporations were essentially given valuable spectrum rights, upon which great fortunes were made.

The specific mechanism for accomplishing this was General Order 40, which Hoover issued on November 11, 1928, a week after he was elected president. Local stations were authorized to operate at 250 watts and below, limiting their range to fifty miles or so. Regional stations were authorized to operate at 1,000 watts, giving them a regional range of a few hundred miles. Clear channel stations were given the largest prize of all. Initially they were authorized to operate at 5,000 watts, but within a few years this power was increased to 50,000 watts.

A clear channel license was, in essence, a license to print money because each clear channel station could, in the evenings, reach up to half the geographical territory of the United States. Each station, then, could reach well over 50 million listeners, and advertisers were more than willing to pay top dollar to reach those listeners, provided of course that the programming was halfway decent.

It was easy to see how RCA, by providing programming to these stations, was able in 1927 to create the National Broadcasting Company, which operated two separate programming networks—the Red Channel, which ultimately became today's NBC; and the Blue Channel, which became today's ABC.

When President Coolidge announced he would not seek reelection in 1928, all eyes moved to Hoover, the logical successor. Hoover easily won the Republican nomination and swept to a landslide victory in November 1928, winning the popular vote by a 58–40 percent margin, and stomping his Democratic opponent, New York governor Al Smith, in the Electoral College, 404–58. Hoover even won three southern states— Tennessee, Kentucky, and Florida.

Hoover's landslide victory was expected. Why shouldn't people vote for him? The 1920s had been spectacular economically, and Hoover had been part of the Republican administration that had presided over the growth.

Inaugurated in March 1929, Hoover came in fresh from what he considered a major triumph of "associationalism" in the radio industry. He quickly undertook the kind of expansive progressive policies that had characterized his years at the Food Administration and the Department of Commerce.

One of his first legislative programs was the Agricultural Marketing Act of 1929, which authorized the government to intervene in the market prices of agricultural products through government lending to agricultural entities and government purchase and sale of agricultural products. The effort was a failure, as the Federal Farm Board authorized to make the purchases soon ran out of authorized funds. Prices of agricultural products, which had been on a downward slide, continued to sink.

Despite this setback, Hoover remained popular. In October 1929 he was cheered heartily by the fans when he appeared for the fifth game of the World Series in the home stadium of the Philadelphia Athletics. When he showed up in the same stadium for the 1931 Series, which the Athletics had also reached, he was showered with boos.

The intervening two years had seen the collapse of the economy and the general failure of his associationalist progressive policies. It had begun literally while he was at the ballpark, with the stock market crash of October 1929. Unemployment, which had been only 5 percent in November of that year, jumped to 9 percent in December, the highest point in decades.[16]

As 1930 began, the unemployment rate fell in the first few months, reaching a low of 6 percent in June, still uncomfortably high for a country used to the booming economy of the 1920s.[17] Hoover for his part continued to promote his "progressive" and "associationalist" policies, which, as it turned out, were a prescription for reversing the natural corrections taking place in the marketplace.

By June 1930, the end of his first full fiscal year as president, Hoover could report that despite a reduction of gross domestic product from $108 billion in 1929 to $91 billion in 1930, federal expenditures of $3.3 billion represented only 3.4 percent of the GDP. With revenues at $4 billion, the country had a surplus of over $700 million.[18]

Hoover and the Republican majority in both houses simply couldn't resist their interventionist tendencies. High protective tariffs had long been an article of faith among the leadership of the Republican Party. Indeed, a proposed increase in tariffs purportedly to protect farmers had been included as a plank in the 1928 party platform. Work to honor that promise had begun in the early months of 1929. By June 1930, the bill that emerged—the Smoot-Hawley Tariff Act—increased tariffs dramatically. As the economist Thomas Sowell describes the situation, the bill passed "against the advice of literally a thousand economists, who took out newspaper ads warning against it."[19]

The results were disastrous. By November 1930, unemployment had shot up to 11.6 percent; in December it was 14.4 percent.[20] That fall, Murray Rothbard writes, "Hoover established an Emergency Committee for Employment . . . headed by Colonel Arthur Woods. Woods was a trustee of the Rockefeller Foundation and of Rockefeller's General Education Board. The Committee strongly recommended increased expenditures for public works at all levels of government."[21] Hoover agreed with the commission and began to undertake public works projects, not on the grand scale of the New Deal, but nevertheless at what were then unprecedented levels for the federal government.

Hoover's other policies compounded the problem. Convinced that the economy could only improve so long as workers maintained their purchasing power, Hoover persuaded virtually all major manufacturers to voluntarily maintain their wage rates. Whereas in a normal downturn wage rates had been cut, and profits and employment had ultimately recovered, Hoover's policy, as adopted by industry, had the opposite effect. Employers, stuck with the higher wage rates they had promised, simply stopped new hiring.

The economy tumbled drastically in 1931. The GDP fell from $91 billion to $76 billion.[22] When the fiscal year ended in June 1931, the federal budget was in a deficit for the first time since World War I; revenues had dropped to $3.1 billion, and spending had increased to $3.5 billion, putting spending as a percentage of GDP at 4.3 percent.[23]

By October 1931 unemployment had climbed to a record 16.7 percent.[24] The wise men who a year earlier had advised Hoover to undertake public works suggested that though he had followed their advice and ramped up public works, his efforts in the subsequent year had not been bold enough. That fall, Rothbard writes, the newspaper tycoon William Randolph Hearst organized a conference of "31 leading economists . . . [who] recommended a $5 billion public works program. It was to be financed by a bond issue. The economists emphasized that a rise in Federal public works outlay during 1931 had been offset by a decline in state and local construction, so that overall public construction was less than in the previous year. They urged a bold program, accompanied by credit expansion, and conducted in the good old spirit of a wartime emergency."[25]

There was now widespread support at the highest levels of corporate and political America for expansionist governmental policies that would break the promise of the fiscal constitution. More public works were needed, they argued, and Hoover agreed.

The gun was primed, the trigger was ready, and Hoover was poised to pull it.

Chapter 9

HOOVER, FDR, AND THE BROKEN PROMISE OF THE FISCAL CONSTITUTION

Herbert Hoover broke the third promise of the secular covenant of the Constitution—that the federal government would honor the customs, traditions, and principles of the "fiscal constitution"—on December 11, 1931. Desperate to "do something" as unemployment climbed to 14 percent and GDP plunged by 20 percent for the second consecutive year, President Hoover played Santa Claus in his Christmas message to Congress and called for massive increases in federal expenditures for public works, subsidies, and loans. Congress's quick approval signaled the first time in American history that federal expenditures had been authorized without any source of revenue to pay for them during a time when we were not at war.

For the preceding 142 years American political leaders had uniformly observed the principle that the finances of the federal government should be managed by the same "norms for prudent conduct"[1] as the finances of private families. As the economists James M. Buchanan and Richard E. Wagner have written, "Barring extraordinary circumstances, public expenditures were supposed to be financed by taxation, just as private spending was supposed to be financed from income."[2]

Fifteen months later, on March 20, 1933, newly elected president Franklin Roosevelt restored the promise of the "fiscal constitution" when he signed the Economy Act of 1933. That bill, passed by a Democrat-controlled Congress at Roosevelt's insistence a mere eleven days after his inauguration, fulfilled his campaign promise to cut spending by 25 percent. On the stump during the 1932 presidential campaign, Roosevelt had railed against the profligacy of Hoover's last budget, in which a $2.6 billion deficit accompanied federal expenditures that had jumped to a peacetime high of 8 percent of GDP.

The restoration was short-lived.

Four days later, on March 24, 1933, Roosevelt shocked fiscal conservatives around the nation, as well as his new head of the Bureau of the Budget, Lewis Williams Douglas, when he repudiated that promise. There would be two budgets, he proclaimed to the hundred reporters who crowded into the Oval Office for the sixth press conference of his new administration. The "regular" budget would be balanced under the terms of the bill he had signed just days earlier. But the "emergency" budget would not be balanced. In his first year in office, Roosevelt ran up deficits far greater than those of Hoover. It was a pattern that would continue for the remaining twelve years he served as president.

Roosevelt's artifice of a dual budget in permanent deficit—a balanced "regular" budget and a dramatically unbalanced "emergency" budget—broke the promise of the fiscal constitution that had been made by every Founding Father, Framer of the Constitution, and delegate to the state ratification conventions that were held in 1788 and 1789. Even Hamilton, Jefferson, and Madison, who so bitterly disagreed over the promise of the plain meaning of the words of the Constitution, were unified in their views about the fiscal constitution. The federal government ought to conduct its business in the same manner as the family. Nothing could be spent without a source of revenue to support the expenditure, and that source was almost always taxation.

While the Constitution has no language specifically prohibiting annual deficits or the accumulation of national debt above a certain limit, the customs and traditions of financial management of the day were so widely practiced that, as economists Buchanan and Wagner have written,

> it was, nonetheless, almost universally accepted. And its importance lay in its influence in constraining the profligacy of all persons, members of the public along with the politicians who acted for them. Because expenditures were expected to be financed from taxation, there was less temptation for dominant political coalitions to use the political process to implement direct income transfers among groups.[3]

This widespread acceptance of the unwritten fiscal constitution was shared by virtually every group that formed the secular covenant of the Constitution. The Framers, the delegates to the state ratification conventions, the state legislators who ratified the Bill of Rights, and the voters who elected them stood shoulder to shoulder on these principles. With the exception of times of war, this fiscal constitution constrained the conduct of politicians (whose natural inclinations are to pander to those groups responsible for their election) so effectively between 1789 and 1931 that federal expenditures as a percentage of GDP had remained steadily within the 2–4 percent range for the entire string of those 142 years during years of peacetime.

The origins of the fiscal constitution that first Hoover and then Roosevelt so readily rejected could be traced to the traditions of Scottish parsimony, which were first set forward in the context of public finance by the most famous frugal Scotsman of all, the economist Adam Smith. In 1776 Smith wrote in *The Wealth of Nations* that "[w]hat is prudence in the conduct of every private family, can scarce be folly in that of a great kingdom."[4]

Two and a half decades later, Alexander Hamilton, himself the son of a Scotsman, affirmed the principle on which the third promise of the Constitution was based when he delivered his Report on Public Credit to the First Congress in January 1790: "States, like individuals, who observe their engagements are respected and trusted, while the reverse is the fate of those who pursue an opposite conduct."[5]

Hamilton's problem was determining how to handle the debts racked up by the federal government and the separate states to finance the American Revolution. By persuading the Congress that the federal government should not only pay its debt, but also assume the war-related debts of the states as well, Hamilton established the financial principle that wars could be financed by debt, and that after the wars were over, the interest on the debt must be paid, and the principal be paid off over time.

In his last act as secretary of the Treasury in January 1795, Hamilton again made this "government as family" budgeting point when he argued in Congress on behalf of establishment of a sinking fund to pay down the national debt:

> [There is a] danger to every government from a progressive accumulation of debt. A tendency to it is perhaps the natural disease of all governments; and it is not easy to conceive anything more likely than this to lead to great convulsive revolutions of empires. . . . There is a general propensity in those who administer the affairs of government, founded in the constitution of man, to shift off the burden from the present to a future day; a propensity which may be expected to be strong in proportion as the form of the state is popular. . . . To extinguish a debt which exists, and to avoid contracting more, are ideas almost always favored by public feelings and opinion; but to pay taxes for the one or the other purpose, which are the only means to avoid the evil, is always more or less unpopular.[6]

It's important here to make the distinction between the "unwritten fiscal constitution" of customs, traditions, and principles subordinate to the written words of the Constitution, but in harmony with their intent, and the concept of a living constitution, in which any number of unenumerated powers are "implied" to have been intended to be given to the government by the Founders.

When questions arise as to what is proper and what is not, the written words of the Constitution have a superior claim. While we reject the concept of a living constitution, one in which subsequent judicial decisions are considered superior to the actual words of the Constitution, another concept—that tradition and custom can form a constitutional framework when that framework is consistent with the words of the Constitution—is appropriate when we consider the fiscal constitution whose rupture constituted the third broken promise of our federal government.

The Constitution's guarantees of individual liberty, however, support this fiscal constitution. The individual liberties of future generations are as protected under the Constitution as the individual liberties of current generations. Long-term debt, designed to pay for current programs, and especially current transfer payments, essentially forces future generations to transfer income to current generations. In the case of wars designed to save the republic, this is clearly defensible. But when the funds are merely designed to add to the current income of current generations, no such defense can be made.[7]

Another great economist born with penurious Scottish sensibilities was Nobel Prize winner James M. Buchanan. He and his coauthor, Richard E. Wagner, wrote in the 1977 masterpiece *Democracy in Deficit*:

Until the advent of the "Keynesian revolution" in the middle years of this century, the fiscal conduct of the American Republic was informed by this Smithian principle of fiscal responsibility: Government should not spend without imposing taxes; and government should not place future generations in bondage by deficit financing of public outlays designed to provide temporary and short-lived benefits.[8]

It was no surprise that Buchanan came from a family with a strong Scotch-Irish heritage and was steeped in that culture's traditions of wild, natural liberty. Born on a small Tennessee farm in 1919, Buchanan grew up strongly influenced by his grandfather, John Price Buchanan, who had served one term as the Democratic-Populist governor of Tennessee in the early 1890s. James believed fiercely in the financial management principles of the fiscal constitution.

As a child, young Buchanan scoured through the attic of his grandfather's farm and read all the political literature from his grandfather's heyday. He quickly absorbed the lessons of prudent public finance his grandfather practiced. When he was a teenager, those lessons were reinforced when he paid for college tuition with money he earned with farmwork and bicycled fourteen miles a day round-trip to his classes.

Buchanan bicycled because he didn't have a source of income to pay for a car. The thought of borrowing money that he could not pay back to buy a car was as foreign to his penny-pinching Scotch-Irish heritage as the idea then being practiced by the Roosevelt administration that the government should borrow money to pay for current income transfer payments, or anything other than to fund wartime expenditures. His was a decidedly pre–World War I view.

But in World War I, as Buchanan would later argue, the new generation of leaders had come to enjoy the power associated with unlimited federal spending and incessant interference in private markets. They relinquished those powers reluctantly. When, a decade later, the Depression gave rise to a national economic, as opposed to military, emergency, they were only too eager to volunteer to grasp those powers once more.

Softened by acquiescence to the calls to patriotically accept massive government spending and control of the economy during the military emergency of World War I, little more than a decade later a majority of the population was vulnerable to elements of the corporate and political elite who promised a resolution to this economic, not military, crisis with more of the same—increased government spending and extraordinary government control of the workings of the marketplace.

It would be left to Lewis Williams Douglas, another political leader of Scotch heritage, to mount the last futile battle to defend the principles of the fiscal constitution. The thirty-eight-year-old Douglas had left a promising career in the House of Representatives, where he had served as Arizona's at-large congressman since 1927, to serve as Roosevelt's budget director. He had known when he took the position that the program of budget cuts he would implement would end his career, but he accepted Roosevelt's offer to run the Bureau of the Budget because he believed the country needed him. Roosevelt insisted on elevating the position to cabinet status, so from the onset, Douglas was part of the inner circle.

Thirteen years younger than FDR, Douglas in appearance somewhat resembled FDR before the polio had put him in a wheelchair a decade earlier. Both were tall, lanky, handsome, charismatic, and privileged. Both came from money, and had been educated at exclusive eastern universities—Roosevelt at Harvard, Douglas at Amherst.

Roosevelt came from old money. On the Roosevelt side, his Dutch family had been in New York's financial community since the seventeenth century. His great-great-grandfather, Isaac Roosevelt, had cofounded the Bank of New York with Alexander Hamilton in the 1780s. Wealthy as the Roosevelts were, the Delanos on his mother's side— from hardy French Huguenot stock—were even wealthier. She had doted on Franklin, her only son, his entire life.

Douglas, in contrast, came from new money. His grandfather, a Canadian-born son of a Scotch physician, ended up managing a prosperous copper mine in the isolated community of Bisbee, Arizona. Mining made him rich, and his son, Lewis's father, expanded the fortune, buying up copper mines throughout the state and earning a well-deserved reputation as a no-nonsense, iron-willed labor union buster. They were laissez-faire limited government Grover Cleveland Democrat patriarchs who presided over their region of Arizona in much the same way the Roosevelts presided over their part of the Hudson River valley.

In Congress, Douglas had established a reputation as an independent budget hawk who voted as often with the conservative Republicans as he did with his own party. Not surprisingly, for one of such a fixed laissez-faire philosophy, he found Herbert Hoover's policies inconsistent and troubling. He brought with him to Congress his thrifty Scotch heritage and his family's rough-and-tumble, independent approach to business. Along with that came an unwavering commitment to the fiscal constitution.

When he arrived in Calvin Coolidge's Washington as a freshman member of the 70th Congress in the spring of 1927, the idea that the federal budget should be balanced in the same way as family budgets had been an unwritten but widely accepted element of the Constitution in each of the sixty-nine previous Congresses. The consecutive streak reached all the way back to the very first Congress, which had convened in New York City in March 1789. Coolidge's 70th Congress continued that streak. During fiscal 1928 and 1929, federal expenditures as a percent of GDP remained in the 2–4 percent range, with 3 percent the consistent "trend line." Douglas had no reason to believe that these sound policies would ever change.

Reelected in 1928 during the Hoover landslide, Douglas found himself in opposition to many of Hoover's policies. Though both men owed their fortune to the mining industry, the similarities between the two ended there. Douglas aligned more with the independent, states' rights policies of conservative Democrats like Maryland's governor, Albert Ritchie, who resisted Harding, Coolidge, and Hoover administration efforts to force his state to comply with federal standards, particularly in the area of enforcement of the Eighteenth Amendment and the Volstead Act, which Ritchie refused to enforce.

When the stock market crashed in October 1929, Hoover's reaction was to immediately propose $600 million of public works projects, a concept that did not sit well with Douglas. The next eight months that finished out Hoover's first fiscal year saw revenues rise from the $3.8 billion of Coolidge's last fiscal year to $4 billion. Expenditures also rose slightly, by $200 million—almost all of it in public works—closing out at $3.3 billion, leaving the federal government with a $738 million surplus in Hoover's first year, almost identical to the surplus in Coolidge's last year.

But the downward trend of the American GDP after the crash—it had plunged from $108 billion in 1929 to $76 billion in 1931—cut federal revenues dramatically. The trend was ominously downward.

All the other indicators were bad as well. Unemployment, 5 percent the month of the crash, had risen to 16 percent, and there was no relief in sight.

From the fall of 1929 through 1930 and 1931, Hoover held steady on his policies. He continued to urge large corporations to maintain their wage rates, which they did with increasing reluctance.

"Nice work, if you can get it"—the phrase made popular in a Depression-era song described the situation well. Those who had jobs actually saw their real income increase as prices fell. But because companies didn't want to add to their expenses by taking on employees at wages that were being kept higher by government pressure, fewer and fewer new jobs were being created. The normal ebb and flow of employment hiring and firing ceased. Layoffs and firings continued, but hiring came to a standstill.

During his first two years as president, Hoover's budgets were within the 2 percent to 4 percent of GDP that had been the peacetime "fiscal constitution" for the prior 140 years—3.4 percent in 1930, and 4.3 percent in 1931. In contrast to his first two years, when he enjoyed large Republican majorities in both houses, in the November 1930 elections the unpopularity of his policies combined with continued economic decline resulted in dramatic losses. In the House, a GOP loss of fifty-two seats put the Democrats back in control by a slim margin for the first time since World War I. And in the Senate, a 48–48 tie* gave the Republicans a majority only by the constitutional stipulation that allowed the vice president to break ties.

Though the new Congress let stand the despised Smoot-Hawley Tariff Act, most members of Congress, like Hoover, were prepared to abandon the fiscal constitution that had guided the country's leaders for 140 years. Cries for dramatic federal intervention arose from all corners, and Herbert Hoover was prepared to respond.

By the time Hoover began acting as Santa Claus, when he sent his list of Christmas treats to Congress in December 1931, he was increas-

---

* There were forty-seven Democratic senators and one Farm Labor senator.

ingly unconnected with not only the situation on the ground, but also the principles of the fiscal constitution. On the one hand, he mouthed the words of support for a balanced budget. On the other hand, he readily proposed another $1 billion in federal expenditures at a time when the deficit for the year was already well in excess of $500 million and revenues were plunging dramatically because of continued economic contraction.

Over the next two fiscal years, 1932 and 1933, Hoover dramatically increased spending by 25 percent. As a result, federal expenditures as a percentage of GDP increased to 6.7 percent and 8 percent, respectively, the highest peacetime levels in American history.

The increased spending did nothing to halt the economy's decline in the spring of 1932, and now Hoover compounded his strategic errors. Having spent more than double his revenues to no good effect, he decided it was now necessary to raise taxes to fund the expenditures that had already been made. This was imprudence at its worst. A prudent chief executive would have first ascertained a possible source of taxation before undertaking dramatically increased spending. Given the failing economy, however, it was clear to many that any kind of tax increase—income, excise, or tariffs—would merely stall recovery.

Despite this obvious flaw, Hoover stuck to his course. His Revenue Act of 1932, signed into law in June of that year, increased income taxes by as much as 25 percent in the upper brackets. Predictably, the tax increase had virtually no impact on revenues—fiscal 1933 revenues of $1.9 billion were actually flat from the previous year. The tax did, however, have the effect of reducing business investment and slowing economic growth.

It was in the midst of these economic calamities and political errors that the presidential campaign of 1932 was launched. Both Hoover and Roosevelt would display the same kind of dexterity with the truth for which politicians are justly disdained. Each gave his allegiance to a balanced budget while at the same time calling for increased federal activism. Hoover had the disadvantage of a record that proved his call for a balanced budget was insincere.

The Republicans held their convention first, in Kansas City, Missouri, from June 14 to June 16, and Hoover's political operatives ran the event with an iron fist. He was renominated with 98 percent of the vote on the first ballot.

The budget must be balanced, Hoover had said throughout his administration, but Douglas, the Democrat budget hawk, noted that Hoover proceeded to increase expenditures as revenues tumbled. Public works skyrocketed to $700 million during the last two years of his administration, quadruple the rate of Coolidge's last budget. Add another $700 million in agricultural subsidies and corporate loans, plus another $150 million in public handouts, and his last two budgets—fiscal years 1932 and 1933—combined to make Hoover's "the greatest spending administration in peacetime in all of history,"[9] as his 1932 presidential opponent Franklin Delano Roosevelt rightly charged.

Hoover's big spending was one of the key issues of the 1932 campaign, which was dominated by finding blame for the dramatic economic downturn of the Depression. Hoover was on the defensive. Nothing he had tried had worked. Roosevelt, in contrast, had the advantage of being able to offer the hope that his ideas—as vague and inconsistent as they were during the campaign—were no worse than Hoover's and just might be better.

Roosevelt embraced the fiscal conservatism of the Democratic Party platform, adopted at the Chicago convention in late June and early July:

> We advocate an immediate and drastic reduction of governmental expenditures by abolishing useless commissions and offices, consolidating departments and bureaus, and eliminating extravagance to accomplish a saving of not less than twenty-five per cent in the cost of the Federal Government. And we call upon the Democratic Party in the states to make a zealous effort to achieve a proportionate result.

> We favor maintenance of the national credit by a federal budget annually balanced on the basis of accurate executive estimates

within revenues, raised by a system of taxation levied on the principle of ability to pay.[10]

Like Hoover, Roosevelt paid homage to the concept of a balanced budget, using it like a sword to strike at Hoover's weak underbelly—a record of unparalleled peacetime spending and deficits. But, like Hoover, Roosevelt also championed the countervailing theme of federal activism to "solve the crisis."

On the campaign trail, Roosevelt heard cheers and approval when he pointed out, as he often did, that Hoover was guilty of "reckless and extravagant spending."[11] Roosevelt knew that the public agreed with him when he made this charge.

In October, Roosevelt's running mate, Speaker of the House John Nance Garner, sharply criticized Hoover for breaking the promise of the fiscal constitution. Garner employed the metaphor of the family budget. "Their failure to balance the budget of a family of 120,000,000 people is at the very bottom of the economic troubles from which we are suffering," he said.[12]

Roosevelt piled on further. Hoover spent too much and taxed too much. He had increased the national debt and forced millions into the ranks of the unemployed. Worse yet, Roosevelt said, Hoover believed "that we ought to center control of everything in Washington as rapidly as possible."[13]

In November, Roosevelt trounced Hoover, winning the popular vote 58–40 percent and the Electoral College by 472 to 59 votes. Democratic Party successes in Congress were equally dramatic. The Senate was now 60–36 Democratic, and in the House, a Democratic majority of a few votes had ballooned to 311–116. It appeared that come inauguration in March, Roosevelt would be able to put through pretty much any program he set forward.

In February, Roosevelt invited Douglas to visit him in Hyde Park. Though Douglas was his second choice, Roosevelt offered him the position of head of Bureau of the Budget. He also wanted Douglas to draft the Economy Act of 1933—it would be one of the first acts of his administration, Roosevelt told Douglas, and he wanted Douglas to lead the charge. He said he intended to honor his campaign pledge to cut the budget by 25 percent.

Douglas's views on spending, so far as he knew when he accepted the appointment to head the Bureau of the Budget, were in line not only with the Founding Fathers, but also with Roosevelt himself. As Adam Cohen recently wrote:

> When Roosevelt took office his views were, [fellow New Dealer Raymond] Moley later said "as frostily thrifty" as those of Calvin Coolidge. In the 1932 campaign, he had embraced the Democratic Party platform, which called for cutting the federal budget by 25 percent. In a major address in Pittsburgh, he had railed against President Hoover's budget deficits, calling them a "veritable cancer in the body politic and economic." Now, he was about to introduce the Economy Act, a bill to slash federal spending. If there had not been a banking crisis when he took office, the Economy Act would have been Roosevelt's first legislative initiative.[14]

The law Douglas drafted contained many reduced expenditures for the "regular" budget—salaries of federal employees and veteran pensions were cut. In what is one of the biggest ironies of history, the bill also cut the pension for Supreme Court justices in half. Recently retired associate justice Oliver Wendell Holmes Jr. complained rather bitterly about this to his colleagues who remained on the Court, and as a result, two of its most conservative members, George Sutherland and Willis Van Devanter, chose not to retire, depriving Roosevelt of two key votes on the Court. With Pierce Butler and James McReynolds they formed "the Four Horsemen" who led the way in declaring most of Roosevelt's New Deal unconstitutional in 1934, 1935, and 1936. Van Devanter would not retire until 1937, when Congress restored full-salary pension benefits to retiring Supreme Court justices. Sutherland followed in 1938.

Most of the $500 million in savings in the Economy Act of 1933 came from cuts in the salaries and pensions of government employees, and cuts in pensions for veterans.

The bill passed in Congress on March 14. Even with FDR's great popularity, it made it through the House by only a 266–138 margin, requiring 69 Republican votes to succeed. Roosevelt craftily scheduled the Senate vote for immediately after the one on the Cullen-Harrison Act, which legalized beverages with 3.2 percent or lower alcohol content. (Later in the year the complete repeal of the Volstead Act was achieved with ratification and enactment of the Twenty-First Amendment.) "Let's have a beer!" said Roosevelt, and the prospects of downing a few now-legal glasses of 3.2 percent beer made the penny-pinching of the Economy Act easier to take for the Senate. FDR signed the Economy Act into law on March 20.[15]

Not everyone was comfortable with the powers given to Roosevelt in the law. The *New York Times* declared nervously that it would give Roosevelt "more arbitrary authority than any American statesman has had since the Constitution was framed."[16]

For four days, Douglas and Roosevelt basked in the glow of the political victory.[17] To any outside observer, Douglas was FDR's favored protégé. During the first months of the New Deal, he and fellow New Dealer Raymond Moley were the only two members of what was called Roosevelt's "Breakfast Cabinet." Every morning the two would meet with Roosevelt as he had breakfast in his bedroom. As author Cohen observed: "Douglas's future looked bright. Roosevelt told Moley that one day Douglas would make 'an excellent candidate for President.' It was the only time, Moley said, that he had ever heard Roosevelt mention a possible successor."[18]

Roosevelt's March 24, 1933, press conference announcing the "dual budget" approach was quickly followed by successful legislative proposals that added $3 billion to the appropriations for the "emergency budget" that were paid for not by debt and an expanded money supply but by taxation. This $3 billion included expenditures for public works that eclipsed Hoover's own; make-work jobs; increased veteran benefits; and direct federal relief expenditures.

Blindsided by Roosevelt's pronouncement, Budget Director Douglas wrote a bitter memo to the new president: "Why should we steel ourselves to the heart-breaking task of saving a billion dollars of ordinary expenditures, when, with a prodigal hand, we scatter over seven billions upon extraordinary expenditures?"[19] The idea of dual budgets, he argued, was a political fabrication that "fools no one."[20]

But the new president remembered his World War I experience as assistant secretary of the navy, and, as unemployment climbed to 25 percent during his first month in office, he was more than willing to declare that federal expenditures "that relate to keeping human beings from starving in this emergency"[21] ought not to be limited. It was a line straight from Herbert Hoover's days heading Woodrow Wilson's new Food Administration. Hoover and Wilson had undertaken great powers and spent extraordinary amounts of federal funds in the military emergency of World War I, and now Roosevelt, following Hoover's lead, agreed that economic emergencies justified similar levels of federal attention. It was a dramatic departure from the fiscal constitution.

Hoover had been the first to break what economists Buchanan and Wagner called "the expenditure-taxation nexus."[22] FDR had campaigned on the promise that he would restore that nexus, and for four brief days he had done just that. But once he was in power, it was easy for him to break the promise again. Once it was broken, the opportunities for transferring income to special interest groups and political coalitions were endless.[23]

Douglas could have saved himself a year and a half of misery had he resigned on the spot. Instead he loyally undertook the role of Sisyphus, rolling the boulder of budget cuts up the hill, only to have it roll back down bigger and grander, with more unpaid-for expenditures each time.

Over the next two months, a flurry of expenditures for the "emergency budget" were proposed by Roosevelt and approved by Congress. Before the end of March, the Civilian Conservation Corps was established, appropriating well over $100 million for 250,000 jobs that put young men to work in various make-work projects shoveling, raking, planting trees, and grading roads, needed and unneeded.[24] In early May,

the Federal Relief Act appropriated $500 million for immediate distri-
bution of food and other supplies to the unemployed. That same month,
Congress passed the Agricultural Adjustment Act, which paid farmers
to cut production, loaned them money to meet their mortgages, and
"authorized the president to inflate the currency by devaluating its gold
content or the free coinage of silver and issue $3 billion in paper cur-
rency."[25]

That same month, Congress passed the Tennessee Valley Authority
Act, which over the course of the next decade would require hundreds
of millions of federal dollars for the construction and operation of six
dams in six southeastern states. The dams were used for flood control
and to sell electricity, competing with private companies doing the same
thing.[26]

In June, Congress passed the National Industrial Recovery Act,
which gave the government the power to compel industries to form
price-setting cartels, but also set up the Public Works Administration,
which was funded over several years to the tune of $3.3 billion.[27]

As Roosevelt and Congress piled on the spending for the "emergency
budget," Douglas set about successfully cutting the "regular budget" expenditures for fiscal year 1934 by the promised 25 percent. Hoover's
$4.6 billion in fiscal 1933 was Roosevelt's "regular budget" of $3.4 billion in fiscal 1934. Had there been no "emergency budget," revenues
of $2.9 billion in fiscal 1934 would have brought only a $500 million
deficit—a dramatic improvement from Hoover's $2.7 billion deficit.

In December 1933, midway through his first fiscal year (fiscal 1934),
Roosevelt joked with reporters about his budget philosophy. He explained that he was trying to balance two extremes. On the one hand,
there was Lewis Williams Douglas, who wanted "to spend nothing."[28]
On the other side were "the people who want to spend ten billions additional on public works, [which] we will get somewhere."[29] Roosevelt
felt his dual budget, which combined Douglas's budget cutting with an
"emergency budget" whose "unpaid-for" appropriations quickly skyrocketed to $3 billion, set just the right tone. This dual budget brought fed-
eral expenditures to a record $6.5 billion and a record peacetime deficit

of $3.6 billion. At 10 percent of GDP, Roosevelt's profligate budget set a new record for federal extravagance, beyond the 8 percent mark set by Hoover the previous year.

From the beginning, Douglas suspected that Roosevelt never intended that the "emergency budget" would be temporary. He saw it for what it was—a political sleight of hand that conveniently allowed coalitions and special interest groups to persuade politicians to violate the prudent principles of the fiscal constitution. Roosevelt had used the language of emergency to enable congressmen to exercise their natural tendencies to spend without constraint. Previous presidents had been unwilling or unable to conjure up the concepts of nonmilitary emergencies to justify such expenditures, but the combination of the severity of the Depression and the desire of the elite to exercise the control they had so briefly enjoyed during World War I gave Roosevelt the opening to sell the concept politically.

The majority of Democrats in the House and Senate needed little coaxing and in fact would prove even more profligate than Roosevelt. The traditional conservative Democrats, however, were a different matter entirely. They believed in the 142-year tradition of the fiscal constitution. Deficit financing through public debt and expanded money supply could be justified only in times of war. Otherwise, in times of peace, the rule of the fiscal constitution applied by which federal expenditures could be authorized only if the funds came from taxation.

Roosevelt undermined Douglas's budget-cutting program in small ways as well as large. In addition to the enormous unfunded "emergency budget" expenditures, Roosevelt steadily chipped away at the cuts included in the Economy Act of 1933. In June he restored $50 million of veteran pension cuts,[30] and in January 1934 he added back another $21 million.[31]

Roosevelt was not alone in his fiscal constitution apostasy. In March 1934, at Douglas's insistence, Roosevelt vetoed the Independent Offices Appropriations Bill, which restored $90 million in veteran pension cuts and $120 million in salary cuts to federal government employees.[32] Douglas's suspicions that FDR cried crocodile tears when the Democrat-dominated Congress overrode his veto were confirmed that June, when he discovered Roosevelt intended to go back to Congress to request another special appropriation for $600 million to fund social programs.

Disgusted, Douglas resigned. Roosevelt pleaded with him to hold on until after the midterm elections, but Douglas was adamant. He had to leave, he told Roosevelt, because it was tearing him up to be part of an administration whose conduct destroyed the fiscal constitution.

With Douglas gone, FDR, lacking anyone in the executive branch willing to exercise constraint on his natural tendencies to spend and pander, set down an even more reckless financial path. Douglas had managed to keep fiscal year 1935 expenditures at the same level as fiscal 1934—about $6.5 billion. Subsequent years saw big increases.

The intellectual vacuum left by Douglas's departure was never filled. With Douglas's exit, any constraints on Roosevelt's spending habits left, too. A Treasury official, Daniel Bell, was named to replace him as director of the Bureau of the Budget, but Bell was a pencil pusher without any independence of thought, and certainly little loyalty to the century-and-a-half tradition of the fiscal constitution.

It was Bell's former boss, Secretary of the Treasury Henry Morgenthau Jr., who would eventually become the voice of opposition to FDR's spending sprees, but that opposition came far too late in the New Deal for it to have any effect. For most of the New Deal, Morgenthau bought into FDR's faux concept of a dual budget.

Morgenthau had two chief qualifications for the position when he was named by FDR to serve as secretary of the Treasury in January 1934. In the first place, his father, Henry Morgenthau Sr., was an immensely wealthy real estate investor. By all accounts, young Henry was a prudent and conservative steward of the fortune he inherited. More significantly, he was FDR's neighbor and loyal friend. Indeed, as the years went on, Morgenthau arguably became FDR's closest friend.

Forty-three years old when he took over at Treasury, he was nine years younger than Roosevelt, whom he adulated and sought to please, at times to the point of embarrassment. He didn't have much record of accomplishment. As a child he had struggled to graduate from Exeter, the elite prep school in New Hampshire. At seventeen, he enrolled at Cornell University, but, despite the private tutor hired by his parents, he failed to graduate, leaving in 1913.[33]

That same year, Morgenthau and his father purchased a 1,000-acre farm in Dutchess County, New York, just miles from Roosevelt's Hyde Park, and a close friendship between the two families began.[34] Roosevelt had already experienced great political success—elected to the New York State Senate in 1910, he had been named assistant secretary of the navy by President Wilson in 1913 and spent much of his time in Washington.

The two were an odd match. Morgenthau was Jewish, and so conscious of popular stereotypes of adherents to his faith that he had, since boarding school, consciously developed a reserved and friendly style that no one would be able to call "pushy." In Roosevelt he found the epitome of the wealthy WASP patrician—self-confident to the point of arrogance, but friendly and ebullient. Like Morgenthau, Roosevelt was a financially dependent adult child of a wealthy parent. In Roosevelt's case, the money purse was held by his wealthy widowed mother, Sara Delano Roosevelt.

Morgenthau fancied himself a farmer, and though he never made money on his farm (it was, in truth, an expensive hobby), he was passionate about agricultural issues. In 1922 he purchased a money-losing agricultural magazine, the *American Agriculturalist*, which grew under his ownership but continued to lose money.

When FDR was struck with infantile paralysis in 1922, it was Morgenthau who kept his spirits up, visiting and playing cards with him for hours. In 1928, when the Democratic presidential candidate and New York governor Al Smith persuaded Roosevelt to run for governor to improve the party's ticket, Morgenthau served as Roosevelt's unpaid advance man, driving around upstate New York in his Buick with Roosevelt as he pitched reluctant Republican farmers. When Roosevelt squeaked to victory with a margin of 24,000 votes, he named Morgenthau to head up an Agriculture Commission, whose mission was to help the state's farmers.

Like his father, Henry Morgenthau Sr., whose support for Woodrow Wilson was rewarded not with the cabinet position he coveted, but
instead with a position as ambassador to Turkey, Henry Jr. was at first
disappointed when he was not immediately offered a cabinet position
when FDR won the presidency. Instead he accepted an appointment as
the head of the Federal Farm Board, a position at which he proved his
administrative merit in a few short months.

When Douglas left the fold of the Roosevelt administration, Morgenthau was eight months into what would prove to be eleven years
of service as the secretary of the Treasury. His position within the
administration was the firmest of all cabinet members', though he
himself always feared that Roosevelt, despite their friendship, might
dismiss him any day. This lack of confidence in Roosevelt's trust was
perhaps more a sign of Morgenthau's own insecurities than it was
a true reflection of Roosevelt's thoughts—most observers considered Morgenthau to be Roosevelt's most valued and trusted cabinet
member. At cabinet meetings the two close friends constantly joked
with each other, passing notes back and forth, exchanging knowing
glances as other members of the cabinet set forth reports or proposals
of various degrees of merit.

Douglas left just a few months into fiscal year 1935, but his efforts
had some effect. Spending and deficits were at the same record level
that year as in the prior year, but they had not increased. But with his
departure and Morgenthau's acceptance of the dual budget premise he
despised, the financial floodgates opened. In fiscal year 1936 spending
rocketed to $8.2 billion. On revenues of $3.9 billion, this put the country in the precarious position of the highest peacetime deficit ever—
$4.3 billion. Once again, federal expenditures as a percentage of GDP
exceeded 10 percent.

It is often claimed that Roosevelt's part in this broken promise
was inspired by his adherence to the new economic theories of John
Maynard Keynes, but this is not true. Roosevelt, like Hoover but to a
greater degree, merely followed the tawdry path of least resistance in a
democracy where a great number of the people wanted the government

"to do something" in response to an economic crisis. In times past, all politicians honored the tradition that a program couldn't be undertaken unless a means to finance it had been secured.

Nineteen thirty-six was, of course, an election year, and Roosevelt himself was smarting from a series of Supreme Court decisions that had declared much of his New Deal program unconstitutional. In May 1935, the Court struck down the National Industrial Recovery Act in the *Schechter Poultry* case, and the Agricultural Adjustment Act was struck down in the following year in *United States v. Butler*.

Despite these judicial rebuffs, Roosevelt's "fiscal constitution"– busting spending met with significant popular support. The increased public works and relief expenditures, as well as the new Social Security program, contributed to an even greater landslide for him over the hapless Alf Landon in the 1936 presidential election.

Roosevelt had gone to the people, and they appeared to agree with him.

But his 1936 reelection saw Roosevelt at the apex of his domestic popularity. His egocentric tendencies got the better of him, and he overreached.

During the entire New Deal era (1933–1940), in the years before World War II, federal expenditures as a percent of GDP ranged from 8 percent to 10.5 percent, which was from two to four times higher than the 140 years of peacetime government expenditures during the period in which the fiscal constitution was observed.

Neither Roosevelt nor his Secretary of the Treasury Morgenthau could fully bring themselves to admit and acknowledge that the old-time fiscal religion and fiscal constitution had been abandoned by the New Deal policies. Indeed, as we have seen, Roosevelt insisted on maintaining the fiction that there were actually two budgets—the "regular" budget, which was bound by the traditional fiscal constitution; and the "emergency" budget, which was for the one-time-only purpose of spending emergency federal funds to put people to work and keep them from starving. In theory, Roosevelt intended to end the emergency budget when the economy improved, but Keynes's concepts provided him a convenient intellectual basis for continuing them long thereafter.

John Maynard Keynes was not a Jeffersonian Democrat eager to advance the power of the common man in the conduct of governmental policies. He was an English upper-class elitist who believed that government decisions ought to be made by leading aristocrats operating out of the pure best interests of the country. In his idealized conception of the application of Keynesian principles, government deficit spending would be conducted not to feed the political appetites of special interest groups but rather to "prime the pump" equally and across the board, for all the players in an economic system.

Keynes's philosophy of government spending and high deficits to "prime the pump" was well known in academic circles but had not been broadly accepted by politicians, in part because it would be three years before Keynes would publish his famous "General Theory." Nonetheless, FDR's brain trust was filled with academics who knew of and supported Keynes's philosophy, including FDR's general "fix-it" guy, Harry Hopkins.

As had been the case in previous American administrations in times of economic recession, with government revenues down, temporary annual deficits were inevitable. FDR's response to this recession, however, was different. Instead of cutting back government expenditures when revenues were down, FDR decided to increase government expenditures dramatically.

Of course, before this could all be played out domestically, World War II intervened, and the question became not merely improving the economy but saving Western civilization first, and the American republic itself as part of that.

The years 1937 and 1938 represented a spending anomaly in the New Deal. Federal expenditures were cut each successive year, by more than $600 million in 1937 (from $8.2 billion in 1936 to $7.6 billion in 1937) and by another $800 million in 1938 (from $7.6 billion in 1937 to $6.8 billion in 1938). These cuts were so dramatic that in 1938, the federal budget was almost balanced—the deficit shrank to a mere $89 million.

By the spring of 1939, Morgenthau had come to an awful realization. The unbalanced "emergency budget" concept that FDR had been
following for six consecutive years was neither temporary nor effective.
With his natural conservatism when it came to financial stewardship,
he had seen enough.

In private testimony recorded by his secretary on May 9, 1939,
before Robert Lee Doughton, the powerful North Carolina Democrat
who chaired the House Ways and Means Committee, Morgenthau
pitched his plan to raise taxes and cut spending to balance the budget.
He began by admitting that six years of Roosevelt administration spending and two years of Hoover administration spending had failed to restore the economy:

> Now gentlemen, we have tried spending money. We are spend-
> ing more than we have ever spent before and it does not work. And
> I have just one interest, and if I am wrong, as far as I am concerned,
> somebody else can have my job. I want to see this country prosper-
> ous. I want to see people get a job. I want to see people get enough
> to eat.
>
> We have never made good on our promises. We have never tak-
> en care of them. We have said we would give everybody a job that
> wanted it. We have never taken care of people through your moun-
> tains . . . who get $30 or $40 a year income. There are 4 million
> that don't have that much income. We have never done anything for
> them. I want to see those people taken care of.
>
> We have never begun to tax the people in this country the way
> they should be. We took this program to the President showing how
> to raise another $2 billion and how to balance the budget, and we
> had it in October of this year. 2 billion!
>
> We have never begun to tax the people. I don't pay what I
> should. People of my class don't. People who have it should pay. We
> have not changed. We have been absolutely consistent for two or
> three years. It's never a good year to have a tax bill, but I think it's
> a darn good year to begin to balance the budget. This statement I

made yesterday about the $380 million over and above the budget, I asked him before I made that. . . .

But what are we going to do about it? The biggest deterrent of all, I think, is that the country does not know when the end is in sight and this un-balancing of the budget, that's the biggest deterrent of all and that's what frightens people.

[A]fter eight years if we can't make a success somebody else is going to claim the right to make it and he's got the right to make the trial. I say after eight years of this Administration we have just as much unemployment as when we started.[35]

Chairman Doughton interrupted his statement, exclaiming, "And an enormous debt to boot!"

It was a point with which Morgenthau emphatically agreed.

"And an enormous debt to boot!" he concurred. "We are just sitting here and fiddling and I am just wearing myself out and getting sick. Because why? I can't see any daylight. I want it for my people, for my children, and your children. I want to see some daylight and I don't see it."[36]

Morgenthau's epiphany came six years too late. Fiscal year 1939 was closing out with a $2.8 billion deficit on revenues of $6.2 billion and expenditures of $9.1 billion.[37] The economy, with a GDP of $92 billion, was still $16 billion less than the $108 billion of 1929. Unemployment, at 19 percent,[38] was lower than the 25 percent of FDR's first month in office, but the same as in Hoover's last full year, 1932. And the debt, which had been less than 20 percent of the GDP in 1929, had climbed to 50 percent of the GDP by 1940.[39]

As for the daylight Morgenthau yearned to see, it never came, at least not in the form he thought it might. Soon the United States was involved in another wartime emergency. World War II began in Europe in September 1939, and American involvement was almost inevitable. By the time Pearl Harbor pushed America to declare its entry into the

war on December 7, 1941, the economy had been on an emergency foot-
ing already for some time.

With the new war came the resurrection of the top-down economic
controls and federal expenditures that had whetted the bureaucratic appetite in World War I. When the country finally emerged victorious in
1945, the new president, Harry Truman, began to think even more seriously of new kinds of social and economic emergencies that could be
used to justify increased federal expenditures even beyond the record
levels set by Franklin Roosevelt during the New Deal.

Morgenthau retired from public life a few months after FDR's death
in April 1945 and Harry Truman's elevation to the presidency. He devoted the rest of his life to Jewish charities. When he died in 1967,
he had still not seen the fiscal daylight he sought back in 1939. FDR's
eager protégé, the former Texas congressman and New Deal supporter
Lyndon Baines Johnson, by this time president himself and busy sweeping in his "Great Society," had elevated the welfare state leviathan to
such breadth and width that it blocked any sunlight that might have
emanated from the old fiscal constitution. What remained was but the
memory of its promise, the faint, distant light of a star already extin-
guished thirty years in the past.

Chapter 8

FDR'S ASSAULT
ON FREE MARKETS AND
THE CONSTITUTION

Herbert Hoover did more than set the stage for FDR's policies that broke the promise of the fiscal constitution. He also
carefully teed up FDR's successful attacks on the first and
second promise of the Constitution.

Where Wilson thought the Constitution outdated, and Hoover considered it an impediment to efficiency, Roosevelt took a much more
Hamiltonian approach. Just as Hamilton sought to make the Constitution an instrument of his personal will, so too did Roosevelt. Like Hamilton, who used the "necessary and proper" and "general welfare" clauses
as convenient covers for his actions, Roosevelt plowed new ground by
advocating an interpretation of the commerce clause that allowed his
administration to do virtually anything it wanted. Once more, it was
Article I, Section 8. This time it was clause 3, which granted Congress
the power "to regulate commerce with foreign nations, and among the
several states, and with the Indian tribes."

Roosevelt's legislative agenda in his first term boldly assaulted this
clause. When virtually every element of his First New Deal was ruled
unconstitutional by a perturbed Supreme Court, Roosevelt launched
a political attack upon the Court, which, though it backfired initially,

ultimately paved the way for a more compliant Court, one that by his third term affirmed virtually every aspect of FDR's Second New Deal.

The linchpin was their ultimate acceptance of his wildly expansive interpretation of the commerce clause.

FDR's economic policies were but the next logical step in the associationalism Hoover had spent most of his public career promoting. But where Hoover stopped short of the last step toward economic fascism, Roosevelt boldly took it. Herbert Hoover's falling-out with some of the major leaders in the business community in the last two years of his administration was the natural consequence of decisions he was forced into by his strong political support of Prohibition during the presidential campaign of 1928.

But Hoover was a man who thought it fitting that the community could establish standards of behavior for all, and he made it clear that, if elected, he would vigorously enforce the Volstead Act. Despite his Quaker heritage, Hoover was a creature of the communitarian standards and ordered liberty of the Puritan view of the world.

Warren Harding and Calvin Coolidge, having a more practical understanding of human nature, understood the folly of this particular temporary law of the land. While they did not shirk from their constitutional duties to enforce the law, neither did they seek out opportunities to force the community to observe its letter as well as its spirit.

Hoover, who hadn't paid much attention to the Constitution at any earlier point in his career, decided that as chief executive he would hang his hat on the enforcement of the Eighteenth Amendment—Prohibition. Support for Prohibition had been an important element in his campaign against the Catholic Al Smith in 1928. Hoover was a "dry," Smith a "wet."

Once elected, however, Hoover was faced with a dilemma. Having campaigned to vigorously enforce the Volstead Act, he now needed an attorney general capable of doing so. The logical pick, William Donovan (who later headed up the Office of Strategic Services, predecessor of the Central Intelligence Agency, in World War II), was a well-known "wet" and therefore automatically disqualified. After a considerable search for the right talent, Hoover found his man—Minnesota's attorney general, William DeWitt Mitchell.

When Hoover offered him the position, Mitchell accepted, on the condition that he, as attorney general, was empowered to enforce all laws as vigorously as he did the Volstead Act. Hoover, glad to finally find a qualified "dry" attorney general, readily agreed. The president didn't fully anticipate the consequences this promise would have on his own relationship with the business community.

Mitchell believed Coolidge's Department of Justice had been lax in the enforcement of both the Sherman and the Clayton Antitrust Acts and that the Federal Trade Commission had overstepped its statutory authority by providing advisory opinions in advance of mergers, essentially giving them the sanction of governmental approval. Similarly, the FTC had also approved industry codes and practice. In essence they were sanctioning what amounted to organized price-fixing. Mitchell told them to cease all such practices immediately.

On October 25, 1929, Mitchell articulated the Justice Department's new get-tough policy at a dinner in New York City. It was the first public renunciation of Calvin Coolidge's policies and it surprised and perplexed the business community.[1] The following day's *Wall Street Journal* noted that Mitchell promised to "deal vigorously with every violation of the Sherman Anti-Trust Act which comes to its [the department's] attention."[2]

Many officials at the FTC, as well as leaders in the business community, were shocked.[3] Was this the same Herbert Hoover, they asked, who for eight years had been promoting the very practices his Department of Justice was now declaring illegal?

FTC officials weren't the only ones asking that question as they read newspaper accounts of Mitchell's speech the next day. In Schenectady, New York, Owen D. Young, the chairman of General Electric, and Gerard Swope, the company's president, were scratching their heads, too. Hoover's attorney general was acting in ways completely at odds with Hoover's own conduct toward corporations in general during the dozen years they had known him.

Young and Swope correctly feared that Mitchell's speech signaled a complete reversal of course on the part of Hoover's administration with regard to the GE-RCA relationship. Six months later their fears were confirmed when Mitchell's Department of Justice filed a lawsuit against RCA and its owners, GE and Westinghouse, charging that the "patent pool was in restraint of trade."[4]

Young, an attorney, took great pride in the legal craftsmanship he had displayed when he had established RCA back in 1919, working closely with then assistant secretary of the navy Franklin Roosevelt on the project.

Swope, an engineer like Hoover, took the lawsuit just as personally as Young did. Swope had also been there in the heady World War I days of bureaucratic control and close cooperation between Wilson's federal government and large corporations. He had worked at the War Industries Board as the director of purchasing for the army. It was there that he got to know and became friends with Bernard Baruch, the famous Wall Street financier, and Hugh Johnson, the admirer of fascism who would become the first director of Franklin Roosevelt's National Recovery Administration.[5]

Swope's subsequent rise to the top at General Electric had coincided with Hoover's rise in government—first at Commerce, then to the pinnacle of the presidency itself. For most of this period, Hoover's promotion of associationalism had been completely aligned with GE's corporate interests. He had supported the cozy post–World War I deal that had granted RCA, controlled by General Electric and Westinghouse, an effective monopoly of the radio industry, then had maneuvered through Congress the Radio Act of 1927, which had not only strengthened the RCA radio monopoly but also extended it across the nascent radio broadcasting industry.

Over the next year, as the RCA lawsuit hung over their heads, Swope and Young found themselves preoccupied with issues relating to conducting a proper defense, all the while stewing over Hoover's reversal of course. Meanwhile, as the economic decline of the Depression worsened, other leaders of the business community began to question Hoover's more aggressive antitrust policy as well.

As the RCA lawsuit dragged on for more than a year, Swope began to develop an economic plan of centralized government control that echoed his War Industries Board experience, but went even further. In the ultimate irony, he used the National Electrical Manufacturers Association, a trade association formed with the encouragement and blessing of Hoover himself only a few years earlier, as the forum in which to announce a sweeping and radical plan of government-authorized cartels, which would soon be known as "the Swope Plan."[6]

The policies suggested by Swope that day gained adherence among those at the highest levels of American industry. Soon the U.S. Chamber of Commerce was on board. In 1931, Chamber official Henry I. Harriman, also CEO of New England Power, issued a report that stated: "A freedom of action which might have been justified in the relatively simple life of the last century cannot be tolerated today. . . . We have left the period of extreme individualism."[7]

Later that year, Harriman was asked how the government and industry association that would form a Chamber-proposed National Economic Council should respond to those businessmen who didn't want to play ball. "They'll be treated like any maverick," he responded. "They'll be roped, branded, and made to run with the herd."[8]

Hoover, for his part, finally reached the end of his associationalism rope. As for the Swope Plan, in David Hart's words he "would have none of it. Coercion made the plan a step toward European fascism—the most gigantic proposal of monopoly ever made in history rather than the realization of enlightened American individualism."[9]

A week after FDR's decisive victory over Hoover in November 1932, both Hoover's Department of Justice and General Electric decided it was time to finish their antitrust lawsuit in a settlement.

Within the Roosevelt administration, the "Brain Trust"—the group of Columbia University academic advisors organized at FDR's direction by law professor Raymond Moley—put plans in motion to turn the Swope Plan into legislation that would be enacted within the first hundred days of FDR's inauguration.

The responsibility for developing the legislation fell upon Moley, whose background in criminal law left him unprepared for the assignment. Nonetheless, filled with academic certitude and warmed by Roosevelt's electoral glow, Moley undertook the project with confidence in its success. Inexperienced in economic policy, Moley would later remark that FDR himself was governed by no economic philosophy other than expediency:

> But to look upon [FDR's] policies as the result of a unified plan was to believe that the accumulation of stuffed snakes, baseball pictures, school flags, old tennis shoes, carpenter's tools, geometry books and chemistry sets in a boy's bedroom could have been put there by an interior decorator.[10]

Unlike his mentor, Woodrow Wilson, who had a clear ideology and a belief in himself as a Mosaic prophet fulfilling a Christian messianic mission, Roosevelt had no ideology other than the simple desire that his will—whatever it might be—be followed by others. Among political leaders, this was not an unusual desire. What was unusual about FDR is that he came to power in a time when the usual constraints upon political pandering were extraordinarily weakened.

In late April 1933, a month into his assignment to put together a national industrial policy law, Moley bumped into Hugh Johnson, Bernard Baruch's former lieutenant in the War Industries Board. Would Johnson take the lead on putting the law together? Moley wondered. Johnson jumped at the opportunity.

If ever there was a man in America eager to assert his dominance over his fellow Americans, it was Hugh Johnson. A native Kansan, he had graduated from the U.S. Military Academy in 1903, along with Douglas MacArthur. He served with Pershing in Mexico before becoming Baruch's lieutenant at the infamous War Industries Board during World War I.[11]

The fifty-one-year-old Johnson brought with him a reputation for hard drinking, tough talking, and profanity-laced bullying. He would work at an endeavor feverishly for months, then, to blow off steam, would disappear for days on alcohol-fueled benders. Once he had deter-mined that a course of action was correct, he would follow it regardless of what anyone else told him. He was stubborn, and abusive to anyone who got in his way. He sat in his office and barked out commands as he chain-smoked Old Golds. He had a face, one observer noted, "like 40 miles of rough road." As a complete package, he was dominating, intense, and intimidating.

Johnson had come to admire fascism. He was an enthusiastic propo-nent of fascist economic policies, particularly as described in *The Struc-ture of the Corporate State*, a pamphlet written by Raffaello Viglione. Sir Oswald Mosley, a former member of Parliament and member of the highest class of English society, had formed the British Fascist Party in 1931, and had Viglione's work translated into and published in English in 1933. Johnson treated the document with the same reverence some of the Founding Fathers had for Thomas Paine's *Common Sense*.[12]

The fascist economic program outlined in *The Structure of the Cor-porate State* resonated with Johnson in part because it brought back memories of his glory days with Baruch during World War I at the War Industries Board, where existing laws were ignored in order to "get the job done." As he recalled in his memoir,

> We did not repeal the Anti-Trust Acts. We simply ignored them. Competitors pooled their resources, their trade secrets, their facili-ties. Industries organized themselves into groups and figures with the speed and almost the precision of a highly drilled chorus on a musical comedy stage and government took charge of both produc-tion and consumption and to a large extent, prices.[13]

His idea of American individualism was a watered-down version not dissimilar from Herbert Hoover's:

> "Let-us-alone" and unhampered individualism worked well enough during the formative days of individual pioneering—nothing else would have worked—but it did not work when we had to meet the

war crisis and after-the-war reorganization of trade and industry. It had become a relic of old days and, as things turned out, a very dangerous one.[14]

Johnson cared little about ideas of "class warfare" upon which the Italian fascists obsessed. His focus was on eliminating "ruinous competition within industry."[15]

It was in this mind-set that in May and early June 1933 Johnson set about finalizing the legislative proposal that would soon become the National Industrial Recovery Act. The bill that Congress passed and Roosevelt signed on June 16, 1933,[16] gave Johnson everything he wanted. The victory was especially sweet for him. Not only were his ideas codified into law, but Roosevelt had named him to head the new agency that would administer that law. It was the fulfillment of Herbert Hoover's associationalist dreams, and then some. It gave the president and his authorized agent, Johnson, tremendous unencumbered executive power to force codes of conduct upon industries, even without their consent.[17]

Hoover had used the power of public propaganda to persuade individual citizens and businesses to "voluntarily" comply with rules and regulations. Like Hoover in his Food Administration press releases, Johnson emphasized the patriotic nature of compliance at every opportunity. But unlike Hoover, Johnson did not attempt to hide the heavy hand of government-enforced compliance. Where Hoover wanted to create the impression that compliance was always voluntary, Johnson gloried in the public exercise of power. "Dare to defy me," he seemed to say, "and I will crush you."

Johnson began his job as director of the National Recovery Administration with his trademark frenetic action. He dived right in on the first of his five hundred industry codes. Work began early each day, and ran late. In typical hard-driving, hard-drinking fashion, he ran over anyone who stood in his way.

The early days of the NRA were dominated by the cult of personality. There were two personalities that mattered—the mercurial Johnson, and the egocentric Roosevelt. Giving Johnson, whose naturally unstable personality was difficult to deal with on its own, the virtually unbridled power to control 85 percent of American industry added gasoline to a brightly burning fire. The constitutionally authorized executive power of Roosevelt flowed directly to Johnson, and from Johnson to his twenty-six-year-old assistant, the beautiful and ambitious Frances "Robbie" Robinson.

A petite woman, five feet tall and barely one hundred pounds, Robinson was working as a secretary at the Democratic National Committee when Johnson discovered her. She had worked previously for RCA, and was said to have good recommendations, but beyond that her past was mysterious. There was no college pedigree to claim, and little was known of her family.

She quickly moved from a position in the secretarial pool to become Johnson's personal assistant. The two were inseparable, it seemed, working twenty-hour days during the months when the first industry codes were written. During the next year they traveled more than forty thousand miles by air together, attended dinners, went to business conferences at the White House, and engaged in diplomatic missions.[18]

Time magazine wrote that Robinson "is a power in NRA. . . . [S]he trots in and out of offices on her high heels, sometimes dropping a wink to those in her favor, giving curt directions in a slightly strident voice, popping from telephone to telephone to give orders to captains of industry and Cabinet officers. . . . Newshawks play up to her because her word is law."[19]

Their professional relationship quickly became personal, and an affair was widely suspected. This unusual pairing merely added to the peculiarly political and personal conduct of the NRA. The fawning sycophants and courtesans who had circulated in the sphere of the great corrupt kings of Europe found a new home in FDR's New Deal.

Taking a page from the successful use of symbols and imagery deployed so effectively by the Italian fascist regime, Johnson called in Charles T. Coiner, one of the country's top ad agency art directors, to help work with him on an idea. Johnson wanted to draw upon concepts of American patriotism but also inspire average citizens by the power of the new NRA program.

The resulting image of a Blue Eagle was used in advertising around the country to promote the National Recovery Act. Placards bearing the Blue Eagle were posted in every business that complied with the code.

The image itself was evocative of the powerful eagles of the German Reich and Italy's fascist regime. Johnson's "Blue Eagle" held a clutch of lightning bolts in one claw and a manufacturing cog in the other.[20] The lightning bolts mimicked the bundle of Roman sticks—*fasces*—held by the eagles that adorned the uniforms of Mussolini's Italian army. Johnson was so pleased with the image and the program it represented that he warned critics, "May God have mercy on the man or group of men who attempt to trifle with this bird."[21]

Johnson took another page from the Nazis and fascists by promoting the program in massive public parades, the most significant of which took place in New York in September 1933. More than a quarter million people participated, and another million people watched.[22]

The historian Arthur Schlesinger, noting the mass participation in such events, said Johnson had succeeded in "transforming a government agency into a religious experience."[23]

Most large businesses embraced the NRA codes emphatically, but they were less popular among small businesses. Indeed, the various codes were most often considered by the independents as sledgehammers to force them into a compliance that was not in their own economic interests. Most codes adopted the higher pricing policies of large businesses, penalizing small businesses that survived by offering the same product or service for a lower price.[24]

Johnson trumpeted this policy as preserving rather than destroying the business community:

> It is black on the record that the unchecked competitive plan under the Anti-Trust Acts was destroying small enterprise of every kind at a most astonishing rate. It is a shorter record but equally certain the NRA has exactly reversed this killing process.[25]

More than 500 industry codes were developed over the first few months and then implemented under the authority of law, with local industry association enforcers chosen from local businesses that wanted to crush their local competitors. In recognition of the sway of the program, Henry Luce's *Time* magazine named Johnson the Man of the Year on January 1, 1934. The cover photo shows Johnson with a menacing frown on his face, sitting at his desk, reviewing documents, presumably industry codes awaiting his approval or rejection.[26]

But the number of inequities and lawsuits began to pile up in early 1934. The NRA was less than a year old but it was already under assault. Whether Johnson was *Time's* Man of the Year or not, his desire to compel submission throughout the country began running into opposition.

Johnson had built an unwieldy and cumbersome bureaucracy populated by eager sycophants. The 4,500 workers housed at the Department of Commerce building and distributed across the country had created more than just the 546 "codes of fair competition," as well as over 11,000 orders to interpret the code. In addition, they proposed seventy executive orders, which President Roosevelt signed, all related to the implementation of the National Industrial Recovery Act.[27]

Given this vast array of rules, regulations, and bureaucratic paperwork, it was not surprising to find that the agency was soon the defendant in innumerable lawsuits.[28]

In the spring of 1934, famed attorney Clarence Darrow, almost eighty years old, was named to head up a formal NRA Review Board, which was designed to investigate the problems of the NRA.[29] Johnson had reluctantly agreed to the formation of the board and invited Darrow to call upon him at the NRA offices in the Commerce building. When Darrow showed up, Johnson offered him the use of NRA staff to compile his report.

"But supposing," Darrow asked, "we find out the codes are not all right?"[30]

Johnson told Darrow that all he needed to do was to report those findings to him, because, he said, "I am the big cheese here."[31]

Darrow had other ideas. His final report went to President Roosevelt in June 1934. Among other things, the report found that "in virtually all of the 34 codes examined 'one condition has been persistent, undeniable and apparent to any impartial observation. It is this, that the code has offered an opportunity for the more powerful and more profitable interests to seize control of an industry or to augment and extend a control already obtained.'"[32]

The NRA's record of prosecuting "the little guy" who competed against larger companies in his industry by cutting expenses and prices was well documented. Like any bully, the NRA code enforcers enjoyed picking on those small businessmen least able to defend themselves.

Such was the case in Jersey City, New Jersey, where Abraham Traube, the local authority responsible for administering the NRA Cleaners and Dyers codes, decided to make an example of Jacob Maged, an immigrant tailor who had been able to stay in business in one of the less attractive parts of town for twenty-two years by offering lower prices to his customers.

The NRA code for Cleaners and Dyers, as developed by Johnson, his assistant Robinson, and various owners of dry-cleaning establishments and "consumers" during the summer of 1933, was finalized in the fall of that year. Among the elements of the code was the establishment of a minimum price point for pressing a suit. The makers of the code determined that it should be 40 cents.

Jacob Maged thought differently. He had stayed in business so long by offering lower prices, and he intended to continue to do so. The code might have set the price at 40 cents, but for his business, the right price was 35 cents. And besides, he hadn't been one of those businesses that had signed up to be part of the Blue Eagle program. No Blue Eagle placard was displayed in his shop window. Instead there was a sign that said "Suits pressed for 35 cents."

Maged was an unsuspecting maverick who wouldn't run with the herd. And so the local NRA official decided it was time to rope and brand him. He would be made to run with the herd by force of law.

The initial foray didn't go very well. Maged intended to keep the price to press a suit at 35 cents. "You can't tell me how to run my business," he told the NRA man who came to enforce the 40 cent code.

The NRA responded by having Maged arrested. He was convicted of violating the NRA code, sentenced to three months in jail, and fined one hundred dollars. He was released only when he agreed to raise his prices and place the Blue Eagle placard in his store window. He spent the remaining five years of his life struggling to survive in his small tailor shop and cleaning business. He died of cancer at the age of fifty-four in 1939, never quite understanding why his own government had jailed him and made it harder for him to make a living in his small business.[33]

Having successfully intimidated an immigrant tailor in New Jersey into compliance with the law, the NRA began casting about for other small businessmen to crush. They found their next victim in York, Pennsylvania. His name was Fred Perkins, and he owned a small company that made "wet batteries," primarily used to provide power for electrical lights on farms.

The "wet battery code" had been written by several of his larger competitors, and it specified 40 cents per hour as the standard minimum wage. Perkins had ten employees and couldn't afford 40 cents per hour. He had been paying them 20 cents an hour. After running the numbers on the business, from which he could afford to take out only $2,500 a year—just barely enough to support him, his wife, and their two children—Perkins concluded that the most he could afford to pay his employees while still staying in business was 25 cents an hour.

The code came down hard on him, threatening to put him in jail. His friend, an attorney, suggested he write a letter to NRA administrator Hugh Johnson and request a small business waiver. The letter undoubtedly went through Johnson's young gatekeeper "Robbie" Robinson, who herself was drawing a government salary of $5,800 per year, more than double what Perkins himself was taking home.

Johnson rejected Perkins's request. Soon thereafter, Perkins was brought to trial and convicted. Because he couldn't raise the bail, he was sent straight to jail. He ran his business out of the jail cell. Finally, a successful and wealthy businessman in town, who had never met Perkins before, read about his imprisonment and put up the bail money to free him.[34]

At his trial, after experts had testified to the need for a battery code that would force Perkins to pay his employees higher wages, the government rested its case. Most observers agreed that Perkins's lawyer, Harold Beitler, simply wanted to hurry the case up to a higher court before opening constitutional fire on the NRA. The jury obliged him with a prompt verdict of guilty.[35]

The stage was set for a showdown at the Supreme Court, but Hugh Johnson and Franklin Roosevelt thought another, less sympathetic defendant would make a better test case for their side.

They found their victims in Brooklyn, New York, where four Jewish brothers operated a live poultry business. Joseph, Martin, Alex, and Aaron Schechter had a thriving business, with several retail outlets that provided live chickens to kosher butchers in the area. In early 1934, when the NRA targeted them, the Schechters were competing successfully against three local businesses backed by union bosses.[36]

In June of that year, they were charged with violating about sixty NRA rules. In November they were convicted in federal court, and all four brothers served some time in jail. But rather than accept the verdict, which had already had the effect of dramatically lowering their revenues, they proceeded with a legal appeal. They were convinced they had done nothing wrong and that much of the motivation in the case came from their local competitors.

It was a brave but costly decision for them. Though their business, at the time the NRA came after them, was doing about $20,000 per month in revenues, they weren't wealthy. Joseph, the oldest brother and the main owner of the business, had about $20,000 in savings at the time, and he deployed it all to hire attorneys for their appeal.

In May 1935, when the case reached the Supreme Court, their local attorney, Jacob Heller, called in Frederick Wood, a white-shoe attorney from the most expensive law firm in Manhattan (today it is known as Cravath, Swaine & Moore) to make the argument before the justices. Roosevelt's Department of Justice thought the Schechters could be defeated because one of the charges brought against them was that they had sold "sick chickens."

The Schechters were charged with violating the NRA's "straight killing" rule. Under this rule, customers were not allowed to select the specific live chicken they wanted from among a group in a pen. "Straight killing" required that the customer accept a chicken randomly selected from a pen and given to them by the business operators. When this rule was explained to the Supreme Court, its arbitrary silliness left several of the justices howling with laughter.

The Court announced a unanimous ruling in favor of the Schechter brothers on May 27, 1935. The NRA had been struck down. The court "held the National Recovery Act invalid because it unconstitutionally regulated intrastate commerce and it was an impermissible delegation of legislative authority to the president."[37]

But for the Schechter brothers it was a pyrrhic victory. By the time of the decision, the business was already ruined. Monthly revenues had declined from $20,000 to $2,000, in part due to the general decline of economic activity, and in part due to the local Blue Eagle–inspired product boycott of them. Also, the brothers were preoccupied—each having spent time in jail, and then assisting in their own legal defense. The $20,000 spent on legal fees wiped out the family's savings. They still owed an additional $40,000 to their lawyers.

Schechter Poultry went bankrupt within weeks, and all four brothers were out of a job. Their last retail shop was boarded up and sold to the highest bidder. The father's house, where two of the brothers lived, was foreclosed upon. Three of the brothers found employment, but Joe, the proprietor, was still out of work a year later. When his wife, Lillian, was interviewed by the *Brooklyn Eagle* about the Supreme Court case later that year, she said that she wanted "to forget it all. I wish everybody would stop talking about it."[38]

Joe finally found work in the local poultry industry, going from job to job, working at a time for another brother, Sam. When without work in the poultry industry, he would travel outside New York for something else.

In the 1940s, Joe and Lillian lost their house in the Brighton Beach section of Brooklyn, but stayed on in a part of the house made into an apartment. Their daughter Estelle was born in 1936, the year after the *Schechter* decision. She recalls her family being very poor during her childhood. She was embarrassed by their circumstances.

"My father was a realist. He didn't talk very much about the Supreme Court case, but I know he felt that he was in the right," she said. "Though it wasn't all bad, I don't have a lot of pleasant memories of growing up. My mother was lonely. I know that, and when my father traveled, it was tough on her."[39]

One courageous small businessman had paid a very high price to make a stand for liberty. Against the overwhelming power of the federal government, he had exhausted his resources in a difficult and lonely battle. Though he won a legal victory for the nation, his best shot at personal business success was ruined by the effort. He was still a poor man when he died in 1966.

President Roosevelt, however, was undeterred. In early June, Roosevelt bitterly attacked the Court's decision. "We have been relegated to the horse-and-buggy definition of interstate commerce,"[40] he said. He called on Congress to renew the NRA (its original two-year term would have ended in June 1935, regardless of the outcome of the Supreme Court case), but his plea gained no traction.

Buoyed by the victory over the New Deal's NRA in the Supreme Court, FDR's opponents rushed to find a test case to do the same thing to the Agricultural Adjustment Act. They found it in *Butler v. United States*. By January 1936, the case reached the Supreme Court, and much to the delight of FDR's enemies, the agricultural act was ruled unconstitutional. Roosevelt's New Deal was going down in judicial flames.

In the spring of 1936, Roosevelt's opponents had reason to be optimistic about their chances of defeating him in the presidential election that November. The economy had improved little since 1933, and the Supreme Court's invalidation of the New Deal's mainstays left Roosevelt angry and frustrated.

Though the NRA had become politically unpopular as well as of-

ficially unconstitutional, another Roosevelt program was viewed very favorably by the public. The Social Security program, which had become
law in 1935, was extraordinarily popular. It had three key components:
immediate direct payments to the poor elderly, withholding of payroll
taxes for the payment in the future of old-age Social Security benefits,
and withholding of payroll taxes for unemployment insurance, such
payments being made to the unemployed. Though Supreme Court challenges were likely, not everyone thought the Court would rule these
programs unconstitutional.

As the arena of battle switched from the courts to the polls, the
country prepared for the November election. Roosevelt's challenger was
Alf Landon, the moderate Republican governor of Kansas. Landon had
become a millionaire in the oil industry in Kansas before becoming
governor, but he was no free market champion. He was a progressive
Republican in the tradition of Teddy Roosevelt.

In October, the *Literary Digest*, which had correctly called every
presidential election since 1916, predicted that Alf Landon would win
at least 370 electoral votes and defeat Roosevelt.

Political opposition to Roosevelt came from the left and the right.
On the left, the "Share the Wealth" populism of Louisiana senator
Huey Long, fanned by the radio broadcasts of the anti-Semitic Father
Coughlin, ended when Long was assassinated in 1935.

On the right was the American Liberty League, founded in August
1934 by a group of wealthy industrialists, primarily from the Democratic Party, who despised the New Deal. Their leader was John Jakob
Raskob, an executive at General Motors and DuPont who had served as
chairman of the Democratic National Committee from 1928 to 1932.

A top-down organization, the league was anything but populist. Its
budget of over $1 million was provided by a handful of wealthy business
leaders and was used to "educate" the public on nonpartisan constitutional issues through pamphlets sent through the mail.

The squeamish Republican Party distanced itself as far as possible
from the Liberty League.

In the end, it didn't make much difference. Despite the *Literary*

Digest's prediction, Roosevelt defeated Landon in one of the most lop-
sided political victories in American history. He took the popular vote
by a 60–37 percent margin. Poor Alf Landon won only the states of
Maine and Vermont, prompting FDR's sharp-tongued campaign man-
ager, Jim Farley, to coin the famous saying "As Maine goes, so goes
Vermont."

Reeling from the Supreme Court rulings by which virtually his
entire New Deal program was declared unconstitutional, FDR took his
landslide victory in 1936 as an indication the public would support any
action he undertook. So he chose to attack his opponents on the Supreme Court. In his March 1937 fireside chat, days after his second
inauguration, he outlined a scheme to add six new justices to the Supreme Court:

> In the last four years the sound rule of giving statutes the benefit
> of all reasonable doubt has been cast aside. The Court has been
> acting not as a judicial body, but as a policymaking body. . . . Dur-
> ing the past half-century the balance of power between the three
> great branches of the federal government has been tipped out of
> balance by the courts in direct contradiction of the high purposes
> of the framers of the Constitution. It is my purpose to restore that
> balance.[41]

The idea of changing the number of justices on the Supreme Court
was not on its face unconstitutional. The Constitution, in fact, makes
no mention of the number of justices who should serve on the court.
The first Court had only six justices, and the number nine had been arrived at only in the 1850s.

Still, Roosevelt's intent was clearly far beyond the tradition of the
separation of powers, a naked attempt to change the outcome of Supreme Court decisions by adding six new justices who would vote the
way he wanted—in favor of his policies.

For a while, it looked as if Roosevelt might succeed in this, yet another usurpation. Senate Majority Leader Joe Robinson of Arkansas

was firmly on his side, and the Court-packing legislation was given a fair chance of succeeding. Two events prevented it from happening.

The first came within weeks of the president's fireside chat announcing the plan. Unexpectedly, the Court announced a decision in his favor. "A switch in time saves nine" was the quip used to describe the vote of Justice Owen Roberts in the Supreme Court decision in *West Coast Hotel Co. v. Parrish*, announced in March 1937. Justice Roberts, who had usually sided with the "Four Horsemen" who had opposed FDR in most other decisions of the Supreme Court, sided with the pro-Roosevelt justices in this case, who declared Washington state's minimum wage law constitutional. All subsequent Supreme Court decisions would rule in favor of the New Deal, while all prior decisions had ruled in opposition to it.

The second event that ended the Court-packing plan was the unexpected death of its only real proponent in Congress. In the summer of 1937, Senate Majority Leader Robinson died of a heart attack. Roosevelt's scheme died with him.

Whether there was a direct connection between Roosevelt's Court-packing attempt and the sudden change in the Court's decisions about New Deal programs has been a matter of debate ever since. Conventional wisdom holds that, somewhere deep in his inner psyche, Justice Roberts's switch was probably influenced by Roosevelt's political pressure. That change, plus the retirement of a number of the more conservative justices, gave Roosevelt a chance to place justices on the Court who were friendly to the New Deal.

In May 1937, the court announced three case decisions that held Social Security to be constitutional, the most prominent of which was *Helvering v. Davis*. In the following Congress, Roosevelt made corrections to his First New Deal legislation in ways that were to make his new programs more acceptable to the Supreme Court. Most notable of these changes was the Agricultural Adjustment Act of 1938.

One element of this act mandated the amount of particular crops that farmers could grow on their land. It was an allotment that Ohio wheat farmer Roscoe Filburn considered silly, and which he knowingly violated. In 1940, his allotment for growing wheat was set at 11 acres. Filburn decided to plant 23 acres instead. When he harvested the wheat in 1941, he sold none of it on the open market, feeding it instead to his chickens.

In *Wickard v. Filburn* the Supreme Court unanimously made the most expansive interpretation of the commerce clause (Article I, Section 8, which gives Congress the power "to regulate commerce with foreign nations, and among the several states, and with Indian tribes") in history, when it ordered Filburn to pay a fine for exceeding his allotment by twelve acres.

The Court reasoned that by not buying wheat for his chickens on the open market because he had grown more wheat than he was allotted, Filburn had affected the international price of wheat.

It was a silly argument, one entirely void of any supporting economic data. Wheat, as most economists will tell you, is a commodity, and the microscopic amount of wheat Filburn hadn't bought had no impact on the price of wheat.

Nonetheless, the die was cast. There was now far less limitation, at least as far as Supreme Court precedent went, to the powers of Congress under the commerce clause.

Chapter 9

LBJ, RICHARD NIXON, AND THE FINAL DESTRUCTION OF THE THREE PROMISES

On November 23, 1963, Walter Heller, chairman of the Council of Economic Advisers, walked into the Oval Office and gave new president Lyndon Johnson a proposal for what became known as the War on Poverty.

It was time, Heller said, for the federal government to undertake massive social expenditures to end poverty in America. Poverty had actually been on the decline for well over a decade, but both Heller and Johnson thrilled at the idea of having a "problem" the federal government could solve.

It would cost money, Heller told Johnson, but the benefits of the programs would be significant. The government needed to eliminate the causes of poverty, he argued, not just its symptoms. That meant government programs to educate poor children earlier in life, feed them, train their parents in jobs, give their parents jobs.

Johnson, who had cut his teeth as the youngest state administrator ever in the New Deal's National Youth Administration, liked what he heard.

"That's my kind of program," he told Heller. "I'll find money for it one way or another."[1]

No politician in America during the New Deal had tied himself to Franklin Roosevelt more closely than Lyndon Baines Johnson. Born in the poor hill country of Texas, Johnson had unbounded ambitions and ego. He came from a poor family, steeped in Democratic populist politics. His father, Sam Johnson Jr., had served in the lower house of the Texas legislature. In 1906, the highlight of Sam's courtship of Lyndon's mother, Rebekah Baines, "was a date to hear the famed William Jennings Bryan address the state legislature. Both were entranced by the great orator."[2] When Lyndon was born two years later, he would grow up in a household steeped in reverence for Bryan's brand of populist government interventionism. Guests at the Johnson residence were often treated to the sounds of Bryan's speeches, played on the family's Victrola.[3]

After getting a teaching degree at Southwest Texas Teachers College in 1930, Johnson landed a job at a high school in Houston. Snapped up by a scion of Texas's powerful King family, Richard Kleberg, Johnson worked on Kleberg's successful congressional campaign as Kleberg's administrative assistant. For two years, driven by ambition, he ran Kleberg's office with an iron fist. In 1935, when the chance came to run Roosevelt's Texas NYA program, he pulled every string he could to get the job.

Given federal money to hire teenagers, but no tasks to assign them, Johnson hit on the idea of building roadside rest stops. Over two years, he built more than 4,000 of them across Texas, giving unemployed young Texans a working wage along the way.

It was there that his conception that the role of government was to "give things to the people" solidified.

Johnson's view of the relationship between the individual and the state was exactly opposite that of his nineteenth-century Democratic predecessor Grover Cleveland. Where Cleveland made it clear that "though the people support the Government, the Government should not support the people,"[4] Johnson wanted the people to view the government as the Divine Father who provided for all their needs. Government, LBJ believed, should support the people.

It was a clear and natural evolution of thought, from William Jennings Bryan to Woodrow Wilson to Franklin Delano Roosevelt. Johnson was much more like Roosevelt than either Bryan or Wilson, who at least could claim to be driven by a political agenda they saw as based on their Christian faith.

Johnson and Roosevelt, in contrast, were flat-out power-hungry political panderers from whom the restraints of the fiscal constitution had been removed. In Roosevelt's case, he paid lip service to the fiction of a "dual budget" in which the extra social programs were only "temporary" to get through the current economic crisis.

Where Roosevelt never fully embraced the Keynesian economic model, for LBJ it was a godsend, the perfect justification provided by the academic eggheads whom he so deeply mistrusted, to allow him to dole out ever-increasing subsidies to those special interest groups who would continue to vote for his party.

The excuse of a wartime or economic emergency having proved an excellent selling point for Woodrow Wilson and Franklin Roosevelt, Johnson hit upon the idea of using the symbolism of "war" to sell his program. Hence a laundry list of government subsidies were packaged together and called the "War on Poverty." It was the linchpin of the "Great Society."

Federal expenditures as a percentage of GDP had declined from a World War II high of 44 percent in 1944, to 14 percent in 1951, Democrat Harry Truman's last full year. In 1952, with the Korean War in full swing, spending jumped to 19 percent. Under President Eisenhower, we successfully exited the Korean entanglement, but by his last full year, spending as a percentage of GDP had not returned to the peacetime level under Truman. Instead, in 1960 it was 17.8 percent.[5]

Eisenhower consolidated and institutionalized the New Deal programs of Roosevelt and Truman in the federal government, just as Herbert Hoover, the last Republican president before him, had expanded upon the structure of government interventionism established by

Woodrow Wilson. The pattern of the twentieth century was clear—
and would be repeated again: Democratic administrations expanded
government, and Republican administrations confirmed the expansion,
despite political rhetoric to the contrary.

During the three years of John F. Kennedy's presidency, federal
spending went up slightly—to 18.6 percent in 1963. Johnson considered
Kennedy "too conservative to suit my taste"[6] and spent more. By 1968,
spending on his Great Society and the war in Vietnam increased federal
expenditures as a percentage of GDP a full 2 percent—to 20.5 percent.[7]

Early in 1964, Congress enacted the tax cut program Kennedy had
proposed before his death. The resulting increase in economic growth
and federal revenues, confirming as it did the supply-side policies that
Reagan would support sixteen years later, was squandered by Johnson's
unwise simultaneous pursuit of guns and butter. Indeed, the architect
of the tax cut and the War on Poverty, economist Walter Heller, was so
disgusted by Johnson's inconsistencies on the matter that by year's end
he had resigned from the Council of Economic Advisers and returned
to academia.

Legislatively, 1964 would prove to be a tremendously productive
year for the expansive Johnson agenda. In March the president delivered a special message to Congress, submitting a budget request for his
full War on Poverty program in the Economic Opportunity Act of 1964.
Congress should pass the bill, Johnson told them, "because it is right,
because it is wise, and because, for the first time in our history, it is
possible to conquer poverty."[8]

He outlined five new areas of federal expenditures: to provide "basic
opportunities" to underprivileged young Americans to develop job skills;
to provide every community a (vague) "opportunity to develop a com-
prehensive plan to fight its own poverty"; to offer a program to encourage volunteer help; to offer subsidies to low-income workers, as well as
farmers; and to set up a bureaucratic empire, the Office of Economic
Opportunity, to supervise the entire package.[9]

In short, it was a laundry list of programs designed to subsidize
voting blocs that would be loyal to the Democratic Party. Little in the

way of measurable results in reducing poverty came from the original programs, or their descendants.

Despite the booming economy, Johnson's across-the-board spending increases extended the string of consecutive federal budget deficits—from Hoover's 1931 budget to his own 1969 budget—to thirty-eight years. Johnson institutionalized such deficits and blessed them with Keynesianism.

Johnson also broke the constitutional promise of plain meaning in dramatic fashion. All twentieth-century presidents had followed a policy of paying lip service to the Constitution but violating it when they thought it necessary to do so. Johnson's administration brought presidential disregard for plain meaning to the highest (or lowest, one might say) level yet.

One of the fundamental powers reserved to Congress in the Constitution is the ability to declare war. Yet in Vietnam we engaged in an undeclared war during the 1960s and '70s that killed more than 50,000 American soldiers. The War of 1812, the Mexican-American War, the Civil War, the Spanish-American War, World War I, and World War II had all required such congressional declarations. No such declaration was requested by President Truman in Korea during the 1950s, when a "police action" that was really a war also cost us the lives of 50,000 soldiers. That bad precedent could in theory be excused by President Truman's argument that we were obligated to intervene as a condition of our UN membership when North Korea invaded the South. In any case, in Vietnam Johnson maneuvered us into an undeclared war by cleverly manipulating the Congress to pass the Gulf of Tonkin Resolution in August 1964.

That act, not a declaration of war, was supposed to be limited to a specific reaction to an alleged incident that may or may not have happened as it was described by Johnson to Congress. Regardless, Johnson never troubled himself to secure a formal declaration of war against North Vietnam, and Constitutional originalists around the land who knew that Article I, Section 8 granted the power to declare war to Congress, not the president, marveled at his audacity.

Richard Nixon, the Republican who succeeded Johnson and was so greatly reviled by Democrats, turned out to be responsible for consolidating Johnson's expansive government policies even more significantly than Eisenhower had done for Truman and Roosevelt.

Nixon brought spending down slightly, but only to JFK's 1963 levels—18.6 percent of GDP. Social spending ballooned under Nixon. In 1970, Nixon's first year, it was only $55 billion, or 28 percent of the federal budget, slightly higher than Johnson's previous year. By Nixon's last budget year, 1975, it had skyrocketed to $132 billion—40 percent of the federal budget.

It was Nixon, not Johnson, who officially declared Keynesianism to be the policy of the American government. The acknowledgment had been brewing for some time.

On December 31, 1965, *Time* magazine ran a cover story with the title "The Economy: We Are All Keynesians Now."* The editors explained:

In 1965 [the U.S. government's economic managers] skillfully applied Keynes's ideas—together with a number of their own invention—to lift the nation through the fifth, and best, consecutive year of the most sizable, prolonged and widely distributed prosperity in history. . . . [They] scaled these heights by their adherence to Keynes's central theme: the modern capitalist economy does not automatically work at top efficiency, but can be raised to that level by the intervention and influence of the government.[10]

In the article, *Time* attributed the phrase "we are all Keynesians now" to the free market economist Milton Friedman, who had been Barry Goldwater's economic advisor in 1964. About a month later, in February 1966, Friedman wrote a letter to the editor complaining that his quote had been taken completely out of context:

---

* In February 2009, *Newsweek* would echo this headline with a poorly timed and incorrect headline: "We Are All Socialists Now." The Tea Party movement quickly disproved this assertion.

You quote me as saying: "We are all Keynesians now." The quotation is correct, but taken out of context. As best I can recall it, the context was: "In one sense, we are all Keynesians now; in another, nobody is any longer a Keynesian." The second half is at least as important as the first.[11]

Friedman was no adherent of Keynesianism. He was, instead, merely recognizing the obvious—the widespread acceptance of Keynes's economic theories among many academics and Democratic and Republican politicians simply meant that economists of all persuasions had to communicate in the language of Keynes to either discredit or favor his policies.

Five years later, in 1971, after taking the United States off the gold standard, Nixon was quoted as saying, "I am now a Keynesian in economics." As used by political leaders from Johnson to Carter, however, acceptance of Keynesianism merely offered cover for their political pandering to interest groups and their violation of the fiscal constitution.

It was a similar story with regulations. The Federal Register (which prints all new federal regulations) grew in size by only 19 percent during Johnson's six years, but jumped 121 percent in Nixon's five years.[12] This was a consequence of the introduction of a slew of new regulatory agencies, not the least of which was the Environmental Protection Agency, which was formally established in 1969. The Washington that had hummed with the hyperactivity of imperious bureaucrats and overeager attorneys during the early days of the New Deal now experienced the influx of a new generation of bureaucrats for the Great Society and beyond.

Johnson also broke the third promise of the Constitution, that of free markets, but he did so with the full complicity of Congress this time. In 1965 Johnson successfully introduced Medicare as an addition to the Social Security program. Now, in addition to payroll withholdings for old-age retirement and unemployment insurance, employees and employers experienced payroll tax withholdings for old-age medical care. A year later, Johnson further intruded the federal government into health care, this time with Medicaid, a program designed to provide federal health-care subsidies to poor Americans.

Health-care expenditures as a percentage of GDP rose from 5 percent in 1960 to 9 percent in 1969. But the monster Johnson had created just kept on rolling. The trajectory was straight up. By 2005, health-care expenditures accounted for 16 percent of GDP.[13]

Some argue that government intervention in health-care markets has not been the causal factor. However, the undeniable fact is that federal spending for Medicare and Medicaid has grown at a dramatic rate since the government decided to make health services "more affordable."

The fundamental problem has been the interference of the federal government in private markets. Just as Herbert Hoover wanted to set the price of wheat and tomatoes in World War I, and the federal government two decades later told farmer Roscoe Filburn how much land he could use to grow his own wheat, now it told doctors and hospitals how much they would be reimbursed by the federal government's Medicare and Medicaid "clients" for specific medical procedures.

The subsequent nightmarish market inefficiencies helped drive up costs and fraud dramatically. More important, they set the stage for even further intrusions of the federal government into free markets, in health care and elsewhere.

Nixon continued Johnson's assault on the promise of free markets. In August 1971, he instituted an ill-advised program, the New Economic Policy, which temporarily froze wages and prices for ninety days, then extended those controls indefinitely.

In a statement evocative of George W. Bush's 2008 claim that he abandoned principles of the free market to save it, Nixon wrote of his wage and price control decision that "[h]aving talked until recently about the evils of wage and price controls . . . I knew I had opened myself to the charge that I had either betrayed my own principles or concealed my real intentions."[14]

The system of wage and price controls imposed by government bureaucrats failed badly. Ranchers and farmers refused to ship animals and produce to markets. Supermarket shelves went empty. By April 1974, the experiment had been abandoned.[15]

In the midst of all this expansionism in the executive branch, coconspirators in the judicial branch fueled the fires of federal interventionism. The judicial activism initiated with the *Wickard v. Filburn* decision in 1942 now blossomed at all levels of the federal judiciary.

The problem with the Republican Party during much of this time, according to Harvard scholar, Nixon staffer, and future New York senator Daniel Patrick Moynihan, was that it had no ideas:

> The Republicans cannot govern on any sustained basis in America. They simply do not have the intellectual or moral basis on which to build consensus. . . . They had no program, far less a mandate to put one in effect. They had almost no thinkers, almost no writers. . . . [Their] periods in office have been and are likely to continue to be little more than interludes brought on by Democratic internal dissidence.[16]

It was undoubtedly true that establishment Republican leaders, from Thomas Dewey in the 1940s to Dwight Eisenhower in the 1950s and Nelson Rockefeller in the 1960s, merely offered pale imitations of the New Deal. In the nineteenth century, the Democratic Party had offered a limited-government alternative to Hamiltonian centralization. In the first half of the twentieth century, no political group had one. Moreover, in the latter half of the twentieth century it would not be the Republican Party that offered such an alternative. Instead it came from an obscure band of Austrian economists and American writers and intellectuals who began to gain credence with a "fringe" group of conservative Republicans.

Journalist and author Henry Hazlitt popularized these ideas, beginning in 1938, when he reviewed Austrian economist Ludwig von Mises's classic work *Socialism* for the *New York Times*. Von Mises lived in Austria during the 1920s and '30s, and from there he witnessed firsthand the rise of national socialism in neighboring Germany and communism in the nearby Soviet Union.

Hazlitt's 1944 review of F. A. Hayek's *The Road to Serfdom* led to the popularization of that work. Soon economic arguments for an originalist construction of the Constitution and a restoration of the broken promise of free markets began to circulate among academics and intellectuals. Even Raymond Moley, a refugee from Roosevelt's "Brain Trust," came to agree with Hazlitt, von Mises, and Hayek.

In 1946, Hazlitt captured the essence of these ideas in the short classic *Economics in One Lesson*. Hazlitt succinctly demonstrated, with easily understood examples, the failure of government intervention in markets to account for the "second order" effects of those actions. Since people and markets behave rationally, he argued, any government policy designed by a simpleminded politician to have one outcome is certain to have unintended outcomes counter to the original intent.

Among the enthusiastic supporters of this philosophy was Lemuel Boulware, a public relations genius working for, of all companies, General Electric. Ronald Reagan, a movie actor on the downslope of his film career, who had been hired by GE to promote the company and "American ideals," was introduced to *Economics in One Lesson* by Boulware. Throughout the 1950s, Boulware tutored Reagan in these concepts, with an occasional assist from Hazlitt. Reagan in turn worked diligently to understand and communicate this new philosophy he was learning in simple television and radio broadcasts that could be understood by average Americans.

By 1964, the nascent conservative movement had found a Republican presidential candidate in the flawed Barry Goldwater, whose 1960 classic, *The Conscience of a Conservative*, drew heavily on the ideas of Hazlitt, Hayek, and their ideological ally William F. Buckley Jr., founder of the influential *National Review*.

Goldwater was right on most things, but wrong on civil rights, the one significant accomplishment for which Lyndon Johnson deserves great credit. It had been almost two centuries since the epochal statement had been made in the Declaration of Independence that "all men are created equal," but for the African-American population, that fundamental promise of equality had yet to be fulfilled. The Civil War had ended slavery, but the Jim Crow laws, entirely a product of the Democratic political establishment in the South, and the U.S. Supreme Court's "separate but equal" pronouncements in the 1890s had served to create a class of Americans who did not enjoy the full benefit of that promise.

It was Johnson, of course, son of the South and master of the Senate, who was uniquely positioned to pass the Civil Rights Act of 1964 and the related Voting Rights Act of the same year. Both pieces of legislation gave African-Americans the rights they had been deprived of by many states. There were nuances of argument made by opponents, especially from the Democratic South, that such policies violated the principles of federalism and states' rights. Most Americans, however, understood the fundamental principles of fairness and natural rights involved.

These principles had been voiced from the earliest stages of the republic—in 1765 by James Otis, who had specifically argued that rights of freedom applied to blacks and whites, and by Virginia's George Mason, whose original Virginia Declaration of Rights in 1774 had also applied to blacks and whites.

When the vote on the Civil Rights Act came to the Senate in June 1964, after lengthy filibusters from southern senators, it passed by a margin of 73–27. A higher percentage of the 33 Republican senators (27 senators, or 82 percent) voted in favor of the bill than of the 67 Democratic senators (46 of them, or 69 percent).[17]

But Goldwater suffered from the same problem of discernment that Republican presidential nominee Alf Landon had in 1936. Landon chose to focus on the supposed unconstitutionality of the very popular Social Security program and was wiped out by Roosevelt. Similarly, Goldwater, citing a very particular understanding of federalism, opposed the civil rights legislation. He was joined by five Republican senators from the South.

It was a mistake from which he could not recover.

Every fundamental principle of Americanism, as popularly understood, cried out in opposition. Among the African-American community, a perception about the differences between Democrats and Republicans solidified.

As recently as 1956, blacks had given 39 percent of their vote to the Republican, Eisenhower. In 1960, that number dropped to 31 percent. Many African-Americans were angered that Nixon had refused to take Coretta Scott King's phone call as her husband, Martin Luther King Jr., sat in a Reidsville Georgia State Prison cell where he had been imprisoned on trumped-up traffic charges; Kennedy had not only taken Mrs. King's call but had warmly encouraged her.

In his 1964 landslide victory over Goldwater, Johnson won 61 percent of the vote and took all but six states, and he took no less than 92 percent of the African-American vote. It's been virtually the same for the Democratic Party in every presidential election since then.

S ensing the impending disaster, the Republican Party turned to a great communicator in the last weeks before the vote to try to stop the landslide. In late October, Ronald Reagan delivered before a live national television audience what was subsequently simply called "the Speech." For the first time in almost a century, the nation heard a clear and articulate description of an alternative to the Hamiltonian centralized government that both major political parties had practiced for decades.

Most conservatives in the audience agreed on one thing: they had nominated the wrong man. Their champion, the man who could win, was Ronald Reagan.

W hen John F. Kennedy's young speechwriter Ted Sorensen made Winthrop's phrase "a city upon a hill" the cornerstone of Kennedy's 1961 speech to the Massachusetts General Court, it was just weeks before Kennedy's inauguration as president. Like Winthrop, Kennedy spoke of his desire that the type of governmental authority exercised in America be an example to the world. And, like Winthrop, Kennedy called each individual participant in that society to a higher duty—a personal responsibility to do his or her part to help create that example.* For Kennedy, this higher duty was framed as a call to patriotism—one that built upon Puritan concepts of state-enforced communitarianism. This historical precedent from his home state provided a convenient phrase upon which—when added to his Inaugural Address's famous "ask not" formulation—he could launch what could be considered a "statist" mutation of American exceptionalism. Kennedy's interpretation metastasized under Lyndon Johnson's leadership and Nixon's acceptance to create a massively intrusive federal government with an associated ruling political class.

It was an extraordinarily secular speech when contrasted with Winthrop's providential words from 1630:

> for we must consider that we shall be as a City upon a Hill, the eyes
> of all people are upon us; so that if we shall deal falsely with our
> God in this work we shall shame the faces of many of god's worthy
> servants, and cause their prayers to be turned into curses upon us
> till we be consumed out of the good land whither we are going.[18]

Kennedy and Sorensen's editing led to something more secular: "'We must always consider,' he said, 'that we shall be as a city upon a hill—the eyes of all people are upon us.'"[19]

The thirteen years between Kennedy's reintroduction of the phrase "city upon a hill" and Reagan's version of "a city upon a hill" in 1974 were some of the most tumultuous in American history. Kennedy's assassination in 1963 shocked, saddened, and forever changed the country. Johnson's subsequent Great Society dramatically increased the role

---

* Reagan would later add several elements to the meme that drew even more from Winthrop's vision. He kept Kennedy's concept that the United States was and should remain an example to the world, but added the providential and covenantal nature of our republic.

214 COVENANT OF LIBERTY

of government in domestic affairs, extending and adding to Kennedy's domestic plans, while race relations deteriorated and the Vietnam debacle unfolded.

During those years, the "city upon a hill" phrase that had been so breathtakingly inspiring when spoken by Kennedy deteriorated into the realm of the hackneyed. Lesser lights such as Johnson, Nixon, Hubert Humphrey, and a myriad of other politicos draped the phrase over speeches designed to sell increasingly uninspired policies. When delivered by such journeymen orators, Kennedy's soaring rhetoric descended into overused cliché, an ill-fitting overcoat draped upon the slumping shoulders of hollow men.

In the midst of the national self-doubt of the 1970s it was left to Reagan to reinvigorate the country by "rebranding" the phrase with new, deeper meaning. He publicly spoke of "a city upon a hill" as early as 1969,[20] but the phrase did not become associated with him at a national level until he spoke to the inaugural Conservative Political Action Committee (CPAC) convention in 1974. In that speech, he added back the providential connotations that Kennedy and Sorensen had removed in 1961:

> John Winthrop said, "We will be as a city upon a hill. The eyes of all people are upon us, so that if we deal falsely with our God in this work we have undertaken and so cause him to withdraw his present help from us, we shall be made a story and a byword throughout the world." Well, we have not dealt falsely with our God, even if He is temporarily suspended from the classroom.[21]

Perhaps more important, Reagan also added the notion of a constitutionally based covenant* as a key element of his "city upon a hill" in that 1974 speech:

---

* Kennedy, of course, honored the Constitution in his public statements and enforced it throughout his administration. He did not, however, as Reagan did, refer to it in his visionary description of "a city upon a hill."

The culmination of men's dreams for 6,000 years were formalized with the Constitution, probably the most unique document ever drawn in the long history of man's relation to man. I know there have been other constitutions . . . [that] say, "Government grants you these rights" and ours says, "You are born with these rights, they are yours by the grace of God, and no government on earth can take them from you."[22]

Though Reagan wouldn't add the word *shining* to the imagery until 1982, his first full year in the presidency, Americans understood what he meant.*[23]

He offered the rhetoric, at least, of a return to constitutional originalism. His "shining city upon a hill" was a vision of a strong and free America that upheld the constitutional covenant between God, the people, and their government. It was a different vision from the Kennedy/Johnson/Obama "city upon a hill," where the superior morality and intelligence of the political ruling class attempts to enforce its own idea of communitarian standards upon unwilling and uncooperative individuals. And though Reagan honored the higher intentions of Winthrop's "city upon a hill," he rejected that vision's biblical covenant for the more steadfast constitutional covenant.

By the time Reagan took office, federal spending under Jimmy Carter had increased to 22 percent of GDP. Despite his best efforts, Reagan was unable to cut that level over his eight years. This was due, in part, to strong resistance from a Democratic Congress, but it was also because many of his fellow Republicans didn't share his views. One of his first failures, for instance, came about because Tennessee Republican senator Howard Baker opposed his efforts to close the Department of Education, one of the best examples of federal government excess.

---

* Reagan probably heard the phrase "shining city upon a hill" on St. Patrick's Day, March 17, 1982, when Irish prime minister Charles J. Haughey spoke with the president at a luncheon held in Haughey's honor that day in the White House. "Irish people everywhere yearn for that day when their country will finally find peace and justice in unity, and they, in their turn, in their land, will create a 'shining city on a hill,'" Haughey reportedly told Reagan.

When Reagan was succeeded by George H. W. Bush, an establishment Republican who had once called Reagan's vaunted supply-side
philosophy "voodoo economics," the hopes for an alternative to the
Democratic leviathan faded. Bush only made it official when he went
back on his famous pledge to "read my lips, no new taxes."

It was in this setting that the eccentric Texas billionaire Ross Perot
entered the arena, offering himself up—twice—as an alternative to
Bush establishment Republicanism, essentially warmed-over, Clinton-
esque New Deal/Great Society Democratic dogma. But unlike Reagan,
Perot offered an unusual top-down form of populism that sought to cut
the massive public deficit with a laundry list of "efficiency cuts." More
significantly, Perot's overall program was based not on a devotion to
constitutional originalism, but instead on a kind of nationalistic protec-
tionism more characteristic of the Hoover Republican era. His famous
opposition to the North American Free Trade Agreement was master-
fully and improbably destroyed in a live "debate" on Larry King's CNN
show by none other than Al Gore.

In the 1992 presidential campaign, Perot gained 19 percent of the
popular vote, but he failed to win the electoral votes of a single state.
His legacy was to ensure the election of Bill Clinton and leave behind
the ruins of a chaotic and undisciplined third-party organization. His
Reform Party, which was dominated by personalities and dissatisfaction
with the current regime, offered no coherent, politically practical alternative to the dominant big-government philosophies of both parties.

Though this group could not be called a true ideological forerun-
ner of the Tea Party movement, it did foreshadow a kind of widespread
dissatisfaction with the existing political power structure, one that new
technologies and a new generation would exploit a decade and a half
later.

Chapter 10

THE BROKEN PROMISE OF DELIBERATIVE ACCOUNTABILITY AND THE RISE OF THE TEA PARTY MOVEMENT

As the twentieth century drew to a close, Americans of all stations in life realized that while we still believed our democratic republic was based on the concept of "the consent of the governed," those who did the governing thought no such consent was required. The deliberative accountability of the seventeenth-century New England town meeting was nowhere to be found in modern America. In its place stood a cynical system in which elected political officials spoke words they didn't believe to secure the votes of people they wouldn't listen to after the polls closed, in order to maintain the power that benefited themselves and the special interest groups that gave them the funds to maintain their power.

The average voter was repelled by this corruption but felt helpless, as one single citizen with limited financial resources and time, to correct the situation.

It was in Connecticut, proud home of the New England town meeting and the first state constitution, defender of the charter against the usurpations of the tyrant Edmund Andros, that the first counterattack was launched. In February 1991, newly elected governor Lowell Weicker, a self-proclaimed maverick and independent who had left the Republican Party and won election the previous fall, went back on the promise he had made that he would never introduce or support a state income tax. He was now convinced that Connecticut needed an across-the-board 6 percent state income tax, and he was committed to seeing it enacted.

On August 22, after six months of infighting and wrangling, the state senate, in whose chamber sits a chair made from the wood of the famous Charter Oak, passed by a margin of one vote Weicker's state income tax. Having passed the House already, the bill was whisked to the governor's office, where he signed it into law, sitting at the governor's desk also said to be made of wood from the Charter Oak.

That October, 40,000 citizens rallied at the state capitol in Hartford in opposition to the new income tax. But it was a case of too little, too late. The income tax has remained a fixture of Connecticut finances since, and the state's economic circumstances have not improved, nor has the state's budget, which continues to experience chronic deficits and overspending.

Eight years later, veterans of this failed grassroots protest arrived to provide moral support to a similar rebellion in Nashville, Tennessee. There local activists would wage a three-year campaign, known as the Tennessee Tax Revolt, that successfully beat back efforts by a turncoat Republican governor and greedy Democratic state legislators to introduce a state income tax.

The battle began in the fall of 1999 and ended with victory in the summer of 2002. The state constitution, ratified in 1870[1] as a condition of readmission to the Union after the Civil War, prohibited a state income tax on ordinary earned income.[2] This prohibition was confirmed by three unanimous decisions of the Tennessee Supreme Court.[3]

By the mid-1990s, Tennessee was one of only nine states with no state income tax. Democratic politicians and their public union allies—the Tennessee State Employees Union and the Tennessee Education Association—had long coveted the revenue from a state income tax. Now they were ready to go for it, confident that a more pliable state supreme court, amid a financial crisis caused by the introduction of TennCare, could be persuaded to find it constitutional this time around.

Most Tennesseans thought that Governor Don Sundquist stood in their way. First elected to Congress as a Republican in 1982, he served a gerrymandered district that stretched from Memphis to the suburbs of Nashville. During his six terms in Congress, he usually voted along conservative lines, receiving high ratings from the American Conservative Union and other similar groups. While campaigning for the 1994 and 1998 elections, he promised never to support the introduction of a state income tax.[4]

In a surprise address to both houses of the state legislature on March 29, 1999, Sundquist revealed his new tax plan. It was as close to an income tax as could be gotten without actually calling it an income tax. Corporations were to be charged a 6 percent excise tax on all employee compensation above $72,000. His plan landed with a thud. Talk radio hosts in Nashville skewered him for introducing what amounted to an income tax on the upper middle class. Soon legislators were flooded with angry e-mails and phone calls in opposition to the proposal.[5] The special session ended and the regular session resumed in April with no action taken by the General Assembly.

Every public poll at this time showed that 75 percent of the people of the state opposed a state income tax. But Sundquist was determined to have his way. In late October 1999, he secured a favorable opinion from the Democratic attorney general, Paul Summers, that an income tax would be constitutional.[6]

Local opposition, sparked by talk radio hosts Phil Valentine and Steve Gill, and aided by WWTN morning anchor Darrell Ankarlo and afternoon financial guru Dave Ramsey, began to coalesce. A group of grassroots activists was formed, called the Tennessee Tax Revolt. Ben Cunningham, a retired Internet entrepreneur, became a leader of and driving force behind the group. His technology skills would come in handy in his new vocation as a grassroots activist.

As the special session began, Cunningham and his group mounted an e-mail and phone call assault on legislators contemplating passage of a state income tax. Using the bullhorn of local talk radio hosts sympathetic to the antitax cause, the legislators received tens of thousands of e-mails and calls per hour. Next Cunningham and his allies introduced a new grassroots tactic—citizen activists began driving their vehicles around Legislative Plaza honking their horns. By the third week, as public opposition to the income tax mounted, it was clear that the proposal would not succeed.

Despite the grassroots victory in this battle, Governor Sundquist and his special interest allies continued the war for the balance of the term. They still had three more years, and were determined to use every minute of that time to concoct a plan that would thwart the will of the people.

The last gasp of the income tax effort came in the summer of 2002. Desperate to push a vote through on the last day of the legislative session, Speaker Jimmy Naifeh held the vote open for two hours. The car honking around Legislative Plaza was deafening. Naifeh's last-ditch effort failed. After three determined years, a focused, vocal, and energized group of conservative grassroots activists had finally defeated the state income tax.

S ix years later, on September 24, 2008, President George W. Bush addressed the nation about an urgent financial crisis. "Under our proposal," the president began as he pitched his financial industry bailout to the country in the nationally televised address, "the federal government would put up to 700 billion taxpayer dollars on the line to purchase troubled assets that are clogging the financial system."[7] Here came the Emergency Economic Stabilization Act of 2008. Bush would three months later candidly acknowledge that by supporting the Troubled Asset Relief Program (TARP), a bailout of huge banks mired in the subprime mortgage mess, he had "abandoned free market principles to save the free market."[8] Americans had the same reaction to his reversal as the citizens of Tennessee had to Don Sundquist's flip-flop on taxes.

In Weaverville, North Carolina, thirty-six-year-old Erika Franzi stared incredulously at her television, wondering if she had heard the president correctly.

> "Did you hear that?" I asked my husband. For a few minutes, I thought it was a joke. But the president said the same thing every time I replayed it on my TiVo. Soon it sunk in that the president I had supported and voted for had just made a statement in direct op-position to everything I believed in. He opened the door for Amer-ica to join the rest of the socialist nations on earth. And he did it without apology. The president of the United States had made a self-contradictory, nearly laughable statement. And it seemed to me what was left of our free market system would begin to crumble as a result.

Shaken, Erika pondered the implications of this announcement. She wondered about the details of how it would work. She understood that $700 billion would be given to entities that were "troubled." But who, she wondered, would determine which entities were "troubled"? Who would determine how much they got? Who would watch over how they spent the money? Who would watch over the watchers?

Republican presidential nominee John McCain had heard President Bush's speech that night as well. He reacted by famously suspending his campaign and flying to Washington to consider his vote. The suspen-sion amounted to nothing, and McCain joined the majority. He voted for the dreaded TARP legislation, which had gone through Congress at lightning speed, passing in the Senate by a 3-to-1 margin[9] and in the House by 263–171 votes.[10] On October 3, 2008, President Bush signed the bailout legislation into law within hours of its passage.

"Pretty quickly," Erika said, "I realized that the Treasury Depart-ment was now endowed with the arbitrary power to distribute an unprecedented amount of public funds. The people who were supposed to protect our interests, our representatives in Congress, had abdicated their responsibilities and duties. They had given away their rights to supervise the disbursement of the funds they had appropriated to some nameless, faceless bureaucrats who could do anything they pleased."

President Bush's signature on the TARP legislation brought to the surface deep doubts about the increasingly arbitrary nature of the exercise of federal power. To Erika and many others, the legislative branch no longer reflected the "sovereign majority"—the will of the majority of average Americans. True, the 110th Congress that passed the TARP legislation had been elected in accordance with the constitutional rules, election laws, and customs that had been in place for more than two centuries. But the great disconnect in America of 2008 was that this time-honored process had been corrupted almost beyond recognition.

As the Republican president continued to alienate the conservative base, the energetic, Internet-savvy, grassroots-driven Obama campaign ran organizational circles around him. McCain's resounding electoral defeat in November came as no surprise to anyone.

Barack Obama's 69 million votes were ten million more than John McCain's total. Obama's 53 percent to 46 percent advantage in the popular vote translated into an Electoral College wipeout, with his 365 electoral votes more than double McCain's 173.

The results were equally disappointing for Republicans in Congress. Democrats had a net gain of 24 seats in the House of Representatives, ending up with a 257–178 majority. Even worse, 53 percent of all congressional votes in the country were cast for Democrats, while only 42 percent were cast for Republicans. In the Senate, the Democrats gained eight seats, moving a 51–49 majority up to a more secure 59–41.[11]

Postmortem suggestions among disappointed conservatives were numerous. The most obvious idea was to nominate an actual conservative instead of a Republican in Name Only (RINO) for president next time around. Others pointed out the critical need to adopt and use new technologies effectively.

Liberals and Democrats dominated the Internet at the time, from the blogosphere to Facebook. The effective use of Facebook, combined with the liberal policies of Obama, had led to a 2–1 victory by Obama over McCain with voters under thirty.

The newest social media tool, however, Twitter, was one in which liberals had not yet cemented their dominance. Since it was relatively uncharted territory, this represented the most likely opportunity for conservatives to move ahead quickly. It was around this time that the Top Conservatives on Twitter list (TCOT) I created rapidly grew into an online community of more than a thousand activists. It was obvious to us that, despite the abysmal 2008 election results, conservatives could retake the House in 2010. All 435 seats would be up for grabs, giving us an opportunity to nationalize the election around conservative principles. If all Republican seats were held, a switch of 40 Democratic seats would put the Democrats in the minority.

But the establishment Republican voice was old, tired, and worn out. We were convinced—despite the cachet of cool attached to President Obama—that given a choice between his Big Government Liberal Voice and the True Conservative Voice, the country, since it still is "center-right," would have chosen the True Conservative Voice. Soon we launched a TCOT "Action Project"—Operation Conservative Majority in the House.

The Bush administration gave TCOT an opportunity to work together when it proposed to allocate some of the TARP money to General Motors and Chrysler. This was a stunning rejection of free market principles. George W. Bush's claims that "he had abandoned the free market to save the free market" seemed as ridiculous to us then as they do to the rest of the country today. We decided to combat this proposal, and once again, technology came to our aid as we took advantage of our ability to communicate rapidly with each other.

The past year had seen the arrival of free conference call services. All you had to do was dial the call-in number and you could participate. We arranged for James Gattuso, the Heritage Foundation's automobile industry bailout expert, to address a conference call of activists. Armed with his insight, we planned mass phone calls to members of Congress and a shipment of cartoon Piggies via Facebook social media. We sent a thundering herd of "Bailout RINO" Facebook gifts (graphic designers had created images of real rhinos with the four letters RINO on them) to the thirty-two House Republicans who had voted for the proposed auto bail-out when it passed the House by a significant margin the previous day.

The next day, the same bill failed to pass in the Senate.

With the number of TCOT members growing constantly—it was now over two thousand—the end of the efforts to stop the auto bailout marked the beginning of a larger effort to decide what this growing community of online conservative activists stood for. A Statement of Principles was needed.

On January 8, 2009, after consideration of various models, includ-ing those of the Heritage Foundation and the Cato Institute, and a con-ference call to confirm our consensus, we arrived at this:

> Here's what we mean by Conservatism—We believe in the re-turn to the concept of limited government in the United States. We support (1) limited government (2) free markets (3) individual liberty (4) a strong national defense. . . . Given the uncertainty sur-rounding the fifth pillar of the Heritage Foundation, "traditional values," [we] felt . . . it was best not to include this particular pillar [in our definition] of conservatism.[12]

Three weeks later, on January 28, 2009—eight days after Barack Obama had been inaugurated as the forty-fourth president—at 6:11 p.m. the House of Representatives passed the "Stimulus Bill" by a 244–188 margin.[*] The 800-page bill had first been made available to members of Congress less than forty-eight hours earlier. The speed of the process, with its self-evident disregard for more than two centuries of legislative deliberative tradition, was shocking. Congress spent virtually no time deliberating the bill—in

---

[*] All 177 Republicans voted against it, joined by only 11 Democrats.

fact, it's likely that the vast majority of members had not even read the bill before voting. Speaker Nancy Pelosi and her Democratic troops in the House, by their actions, had just signaled their rupture with the nation's customs and constitution, and their embrace of this new paradigm. They demonstrated the kind of absolute authority that James I would envy.

The Stimulus Bill passed the Senate by a 61–37 vote on February 10, 2009. The conference committee revisions were accepted by both houses on February 13, and on February 17, President Obama signed the bill into law.

Two days later, CNBC correspondent Rick Santelli launched the Tea Party movement with "the rant heard round the world." It lasted only about six minutes, during his regular reporting from the floor of the Chicago Mercantile Exchange. The Obama administration had just announced plans for a new bailout program—this time for mortgages— and Santelli took exception.

His six minutes were captured on video and went viral on YouTube. A dry reading of the transcript fails to capture the most compelling aspect of the rant—the tone of frustration and defiance.

> The government is promoting bad behavior. We certainly don't want to put stimulus forth, and give people a whopping $8 or $10 in their check and think that they ought to save it. . . . How about this, President and new administration: Why don't you put up a website to have people vote on the Internet as a referendum to see if we really want to subsidize the losers' mortgages or would we like to at least buy cars and buy houses in foreclosure and give them to people that might have a chance to actually prosper down the road and reward people that could carry the water instead of drink the water. . . . We're thinking of having a Chicago Tea Party in July. All you capitalists that want to show up to Lake Michigan, I'm going to start organizing. . . . If you read our Founding Fathers people like Benjamin Franklin and Jefferson, what we are doing in this country right now is making them roll over in their graves.[13]

Twenty-four hours later, Santelli's rant had been viewed 1.2 million times on CNBC.com—becoming the most viewed ever clip on the site. During that time, to accompany that clip, CNBC.com ran a poll that asked, "Would you want to join Rick Santelli's Chicago Tea Party?" Ninety-four percent of the 227,000 respondents said yes.[14]

The online conservative community we had developed at Top Conservatives on Twitter was poised to act. The idea Santelli suggested of holding a tea party in Chicago in July had spread through the Internet like wildfire. We knew that the world would never wait until July. The energy to undertake a proposed tea party protest existed now, and if that energy wasn't channeled properly, it would dissipate.

J. P. Freire, at the time the managing editor of *American Spectator* magazine, had started to organize a tea party in Washington, D.C.,* to take place a week from that day, at noon on Friday, February 27. In his Twitter message to me, he asked if we could help promote that event through the TCOT community. Using the Washington event as a base, we decided to organize a simultaneous national event, called the Nationwide Chicago Tea Party (the name was designed to communicate that we were following up on Rick Santelli's suggestion). Eric Odom, who had previously organized nearly twenty thousand online activists under the banner of the "Dontgo" movement the previous August in an effort to persuade Congress not to recess before they accomplished cost-cutting measures, agreed to organize a Chicago event. This would give conservatives around the country a rallying point and hopefully galvanize a growing conservative community of activists, both online and offline.

Eric, Stacy Mott (founder of the conservative women's network Smart Girl Politics), J. P., and I invited everyone on TCOT to join us in a call to launch this new project. On February 20, 2009, we were joined by about fifty activists, including several who would play im-

---

* The extent of the organizational activities at this time consisted of simply creating an event on Facebook for noon, Friday, February 27, at the Tidal Basin, near the Jefferson Memorial. The location of the event would later be switched to Lafayette Park, across from the White House.

portant roles in the future of the movement: Christina Botteri, who
would play a key role managing our social media communications;
Amy Kremer, who would later become chairman and spokesperson
for the Tea Party Express; Jenny Beth Martin, who would cofound
the Tea Party Patriots; Brooks Bayne, a social media wizard who organized the first Los Angeles Tea Party; Beulah Garrett, our favorite online conservative grandmother activist; and a graphic designer,
known as "illustr8r" on Twitter, from a blue state, who held conservative views but felt it was important to remain anonymous to avoid
losing clients. Illustr8r's artwork would become ubiquitous throughout
the Internet for both the February 27 Nationwide Chicago Tea Party
and the April 15 Tax Day Tea Party.* Local leaders who were on the
call included Tony Katz and Gary Aminoff in Los Angeles; Wendy
Herman in Corpus Christi, Texas; Stacie Burke in Franklin, Tennessee; Geoff Ludt in Portland, Oregon; Brad Marston in Boston, Massachusetts; Jason Hoyt in Orlando, Florida; Felicia Cravens in Houston,
Texas; James Dickey in Dallas, Texas; Brian T. Campbell and Jenny
Hatch in Denver, Colorado; Shelli Dawdy in Lincoln, Nebraska; and
Stephen Spinks in Florida.

Since TCOT, Dontgo, and Smart Girl Politics all had a growing
online footprint, we decided that these three online groups would form
the leadership team of a loosely knit group we now called the Nationwide Tea Party Coalition.

Every night for the next week, we held a two-hour conference call.
Participation increased dramatically each night. The calls were online
versions of a New England town meeting. I played the role of meeting moderator. Prior to each call, our leadership team focused on key
points we wanted to communicate to those who stepped up to organize
local events around the country. We offered very specific and focused
messaging—the theme was "Repeal the Pork or Retire." We suggested
specific signage, all revolving around the ethos of limited government—

* Her description on Twitter today reads "Digital illustrator for kids by day. Betsy Ross for Tea
Parties by night."

cut taxes, cut spending, limit the size of government, and respect the Constitution.

To help local activists, we set up a website where we provided specific, practical information on how to hold a rally (with suggestions on permitting and how to work properly with the local authorities, and, most important, instructions on the importance of cleaning up after the event) and how to communicate with local media—including a list of about forty ideas for signs, many of which would show up in later press coverage.

We also developed a strategy to capture the events of the day digitally—in either still images or video—and push them out quickly to friends in the conservative blogosphere and the mainstream media on the day of the event.

At this first tea party, on February 27, 2009, 30,000 people showed up in fifty cities around the country. Press coverage was mixed, but on balance we succeeded in communicating that there were plenty of Americans unhappy with the Stimulus Bill. Online conservative media gave it great coverage, thanks to the fact that we made images and crowd-count information available to them immediately. Local television, surprisingly, gave the fifty events decent coverage in almost every location. Network television paid no attention to us, and among the cable networks only MSNBC gave any live coverage at all. Fox News' Greta Van Susteren offered a few minutes in her program that evening, but otherwise, Fox News paid no attention to us.

We immediately decided to do it again on a much larger scale, with a Tax Day Tea Party on April 15, 2009. No one doubted that with six weeks' advance notice, that event would be bigger and better than the Nationwide Chicago Tea Party.

A week after the success of the Nationwide Chicago Tea Party on February 27, 2009, I received a private direct message on Twitter from Newt Gingrich. Would we, he asked, be interested in having his American Solutions group join the Nationwide Tea Party Coalition whose leadership team consisted of Eric Odom of Dontgo, Stacy

Mott of Smart Girl Politics, and me from TCOT as the fourth sponsor of the Tax Day Tea Party?

If Gingrich's group was added as a sponsor, it would add jet fuel to the movement. So far we were perceived as a group of activists on the margin, even though our message of the limited government ethos reflected the views of the majority of the American people. With the former Speaker of the House would come increased media visibility, and inevitably interest from Fox News, where he was a featured contributor. But Gingrich's record was viewed by many as questionable. He had been an able articulator of the limited-government ethos when he championed the Contract with America, which had propelled him to the speakership in 1994 during the Clinton administration. However, the perception was that during his four-year tenure, his accomplishments toward that goal had not matched his rhetoric. Worse yet, his successor, Dennis Hastert, had played a critical role in enacting the big-government Republican policies of the Bush administration.

It didn't take us long to do the calculus and conclude that the benefits of including Gingrich's group as a sponsor far outweighed the costs. (However, Eric was quick to point out that we were likely to lose a significant number of our libertarian supporters because of their dislike for Gingrich.) At the dawn of the modern conservative movement in the 1950s, *National Review* editor Frank Meyer argued that libertarians, "traditional" conservatives, and "social" conservatives should unite in their efforts to fight communism, government expansion, and the decline in civil society. Gingrich may have been wobbly and not as consistent a defender of the limited government ethos as some of our fellow activists might like, but he would certainly be a strong ally in our efforts to lend credibility to our nascent Tea Party movement.

We arranged a conference call between four members of our leadership team and Gingrich to extend an invitation for his group to join the Tax Day Tea Party. We thought Gingrich might be interested in learning something about what was really happening on the ground in America. We were quite surprised that, on this call at least, he wasn't.

Instead, Gingrich gave us a twenty-five-minute lecture on the importance of citizen activism in America.

The irony could not be ignored. We were the citizen activists who were on the cusp of launching one of the most significant movements in modern American history, and Professor Gingrich was instructing us on how to be activists. We, of course, listened politely, because we all recognized having him on board was a major coup that would significantly advance the impact of the Tax Day Tea Party the next month. I came away convinced that he intended to run for president in 2012, and that he saw the nascent Tea Party movement as a good vehicle to advance that cause. I didn't doubt his overall sincerity in supporting the limited-government ethos of the movement, but the lines between self-interest and altruistic love of country were so blurred as to be indistinguishable.

The official press release announcing "Newt Gingrich's American Solutions Comes to the Tea Party" was issued on Tuesday, March 17, 2009, less than four weeks before the Tax Day Tea Party event, and Gingrich's comments were on target. "The American people are fed up with Washington's irresponsible spending spree. . . . There are better solutions than big government and higher taxes to create jobs and get the economy moving again."[15]

Stacy Mott of Smart Girl Politics had perhaps the most interesting comments. "To me," she said, "one of the most remarkable things is that none of the three Coalition organizations existed a year ago. . . . All three of our groups focus on rapid-response citizen activism. We use the latest technology tools to coordinate the simultaneous activities of tens of thousands—and soon to be hundreds of thousands—of activists across the country."[16]

The digital ink wasn't dry on the press release when Gingrich caused a problem that irritated all of us so greatly that there were calls to kick him out of the Coalition. We had labored mightily since the inception of the Nationwide Tea Party Coalition to make sure that everyone in the movement understood that we united around the fiscal issues. We would leave the social issues off the table until the fiscal and constitutional issues had been solved. Our motto was "Save the Republic first, then let the traditionalist and non-traditionalists duke it out over social issues." But Gingrich endorsed the American Family Association's "Tea Party"—which placed an emphasis on social values—the next day. This group had no real supporters within the Tea Party movement, but had instead merely taken the list of local tea parties that we had posted at the Tax Day Tea Party website, claimed them as its own, and sent out press releases and e-mails to its e-mail list of conservative Christians touting the national tea party it was organizing.

We could not believe that Gingrich had allowed himself to get caught up with such a deceptive group. But there he was, in a YouTube video, endorsing this social-issues-driven phony co-opter* of the genuine Tea Party movement with the same degree of sincerity he had used to deliver ours. To make matters worse, there were rumors that a "religious" group that may have been associated with this "faux" tea party effort was sending out e-mail blasts in California that were blatantly antigay.

We were able to get the offending Gingrich YouTube video for the "faux" tea party event taken down and persuaded Gingrich's staff that he really needed to maintain a discipline on his public message that (1) our group's event was the only national Tea Party he had endorsed and (2) social issues were not in the mix. It all worked out within a week, but no one in local or national leadership really trusted Gingrich much after that.†

At seven o'clock on the morning of Wednesday, April 15, 2009, three dozen Tea Party activists, all carrying homemade signs, gathered in a Kroger grocery store parking lot in the small city of Richmond Hill, Georgia. It was the first tea party in the country that day, and it marked the beginning of the nationwide Tax Day Tea Party,

* The American Family Association is a legitimate group that promotes socially conservative values. Its claim that it represented the Tea Party movement was phony.

† Gingrich would further alienate the Tea Party when he endorsed the RINO Dede Scozzafava in the special election for New York State's 23rd Congressional District in October 2009.

an event that would bring one million Tea Party protesters together in nine hundred cities across all fifty states over the course of one day.[17]

Signs with words of fiscal responsibility and limited government reflecting the day's theme, "Repeal the Pork, Cut Taxes," were in good supply at Richmond Hill that morning, as were other signs that reflected "the limited government ethos,"[18] championing concepts such as fidelity to the Constitution, the sovereignty of the people, individual liberty, individual responsibility, and free markets. One energetic protester's sign read "Government of the Government By the Government For the Government."[19] Others read "Stop the Spending," "Fiscal Responsibility," and "Make Way for Liberty." Within half an hour, the early morning patriots were standing on all four sides of the main intersection in their small coastal town twenty miles southwest of Savannah, holding their signs up to the honking delight of most of the morning's commuters.

Seventeen hours later and six thousand miles to the west, one thousand Hawaiian Tea Party activists closed out their own tea party on the steps of the state capitol in Honolulu. The Hawaiian protesters matched the literary creativity of their Georgia counterparts with signs that read "Cut Taxes Not Freedoms,"[20] "Stop Stimulus Giveaways," and "Can the Pork."[21]

Fox News deployed three network stars and one well-known contributor to anchor live coverage of Tax Day Tea Party events from key cities around the country. During the afternoon, Glenn Beck stood on a stage outside the Alamo[22] in San Antonio, where rocker Ted Nugent warmed up the crowd of more than 15,000 with a boisterous solo guitar version of the national anthem.[23] In Sacramento, Neil Cavuto[24] stood on a stage with Lloyd Marcus, a black singer-songwriter whose original song, "The Tea Party Anthem," had turned him into "the Paul Revere of the Tea Party movement," in front of a crowd almost as large. That night former airline stewardess Amy Kremer joined Sean Hannity in Atlanta, where he broadcast his nightly program live from a stage in front of an estimated crowd of more than 20,000. In New York City that night, twenty-nine-year-old architect Kellen Giuda shared a stage with former Speaker of the House Gingrich, before a crowd of more than 5,000 in front of City Hall. Crowd sizes in the 10,000 range were reported in some surprising locales, including Madison, Wisconsin; Lansing, Michigan; Olympia, Washington; and St. Louis, Missouri.[25]

The day unfolded with very few difficulties, and no reports of violence. In Chicago, Eric Odom famously told Republican National Committee chair Michael Steele, "Thanks but no thanks," when Steele asked to speak at the event. "You're welcome to come and listen," Odom told Steele. "But we're not interested in hearing you speak. Frankly, you need to understand what we're telling you because so far, we don't think you do."

New media played a significant role in coverage of the event. From a studio in El Segundo, California, a team of two dozen media producers, talent, and support crew at Internet webcaster Pajamas TV broadcast the events live from around the country in a twelve-hour marathon.

The traditional national broadcast networks—CBS, ABC, NBC— paid little attention to the day's proceedings, though their local affiliates provided thorough coverage. Among the cable networks, Fox News covered it extensively,[26] while CNN and MSNBC covered it as if it were some kind of avoidable yet tragically awful national car wreck. CNN reporter Susan Roesgen conducted an argumentative and aggressive live interview with an activist whose views she obviously did not share. The five-minute video clip went viral, confirming the activists' impression that the mainstream media was irrevocably biased against them.[27]

Most mainstream media commentators seemed to not quite comprehend what motivated the activists of this nascent Tea Party movement. On CBS's *Face the Nation* that Sunday, Obama administration advisor David Axelrod, when asked about the tea parties, said, "I think any time you have severe economic conditions there is always an element of disaffection that can mutate into something that's unhealthy."[28] On CNN's *State of the Union* that same day, Democratic consultant and former White House advisor James Carville called the tea parties "harmless and damaging to Republicans." His broadcast counterpart, conservative William Bennett, lauded the activists but concluded, "I wish they had a little more focus to them."[29]

The activists, for their part, considered themselves neither unhealthy nor unfocused. They were, in fact, as ideologically motivated at the dawn of the Tea Party movement as the Founding Fathers were at the dawn of the American Revolution. Jefferson, Franklin, and Adams sought "to purify a corrupt constitution and fight off the apparent growth of prerogative power,"[30] as historian Bernard Bailyn argued. The homeschool moms, blue-collar dads, small business owners, and myriad other activists of the Tea Party movement sought to save the republic by forcing political leaders to honor the four covenantal promises that had been broken. They believed that if political leaders honored the fourth promise—to listen to, engage with, and honestly deliberate in full view of the sovereign people—the first three promises captured in the three core values of the Tea Party movement—constitutionally limited government, fiscal responsibility, and free markets—were likely to be honored as well.

It was precisely this unwillingness of elected officials of either party to listen that energized the Tea Party protesters to activism that day. The concept of the sovereignty of the people had, for so many years in American history, centered on the civic obligation to learn about the relative merits of candidates, vote in elections for the "best" candidates, and perhaps volunteer in or donate to the campaigns of particularly good candidates.

The Tax Day Tea Party protests suggested the beginning possibilities of an exciting new model for more engaged political activism by everyday conservatives. By dramatically increasing the amount of time in their lives they devoted to political activism, and using new technology tools of social media and communications, citizens could force elected officials to interact with them in ways that confirmed the idea that in a democratic republic, the people are sovereign.

I t's important to note here that the conservative nonprofit groups that many in the media and the left claim were responsible for launching the Tea Party movement had very little to do with the events up to April 15, 2009. FreedomWorks, which sponsored a large tea party event in Washington, D.C., on September 12, 2009, held a one-day training session that one organizer of a small February 27, 2009, Florida tea party rally attended prior to that event. In Arizona, an organizer affiliated with Americans for Prosperity helped organize an event in that state. On the April 15, 2009, Tax Day Tea Party event, both organizations had a hand in several other local events, but they were minor in comparison to the total of 900 events held across the country.

Indeed, the involvement of FreedomWorks and Americans for Prosperity during these first months was primarily because the movement could be a source of fund-raising. In that regard, it proved to be a very effective tool for them.

A fter the Tax Day Tea Party event, the Tea Party movement evolved in the kind of unpredictable chaos that has characterized many grassroots movements.

The most fascinating aspect of this evolution took place in thousands of local tea party groups organized around the country. The seeds of local groups in nine hundred cities around the country had been planted. In each of those locations, the single individual or half-dozen people who had put on their events began meeting to contemplate their next action.

By the end of July, the three core values of constitutionally limited government, fiscal responsibility, and free markets could be seen displayed on national and local websites around the country. There were variations on this theme (some groups added national defense, for instance, or secure borders, or individual liberty), but the clear focus on the limited-government ethos remained.

Collectively, individually, and collaboratively, the Tea Party movement had confirmed that our challenge was to save the republic first, and let the traditionalists and nontraditionalists duke it out later over the social issues.

With a clear long-term focus—returning conservatives to control of the House in November 2010—but lacking a short-term focus, the movement stalled for a bit. New tea parties were being formed all around the country, but the question of what to do next, especially after a series of anticlimactic Fourth of July events, remained unanswered. Nancy Pelosi and Harry Reid provided that answer.

The twisted legislative history of ObamaCare began in July 2009, when eighty-three-year-old Michigan congressman John Dingell introduced H.R. 3200, a two-thousand-page version of "health-care reform." Polls at the time indicated that a majority of Americans opposed such legislation, but Obama, Pelosi, Reid, and the Democratic majorities in both houses were determined.

When members of Congress met with their constituents in the August recess that followed, all hell broke loose. Local tea parties encouraged their members to attend the congressional town halls held during the recess and ask questions of their representatives about the legislation. The most common questions posed to the legislators by their constituents were all a variation upon this theme: since the majority of us oppose this legislation, and you yourself can't explain its merits to us, why do you intend to vote for it? Unused to responding to these sorts of challenges, the Democratic congressmen* stumbled badly as their constituents registered their disapproval.

When the shell-shocked Democratic congressmen and senators returned to Washington in September 2009, they realized that they wouldn't be able to push their health-care proposals through as quickly as they had imagined. Chastened by the town hall reactions, the Ways and Means and Education and Labor committees of the House slowed their review and legislative markup process to a crawl.

---

* As well as one well-known Republican senator, Arlen Specter of Pennsylvania, who would become first a former Republican (switching to the Democratic Party in late 2009) and then a former senator (after losing the Democratic primary).

The first sign that the Tea Party movement had electoral muscle came in the unlikeliest place of all—an obscure congressional district in upstate New York where a special election scheduled for November 2 now took on the form of a national referendum on ObamaCare. Democratic strategists were only too pleased to see that a serious tactical error by establishment Republicans in Washington and New York gave them the opportunity to add one more vote toward that needed 218 majority.

In May of that year, Barack Obama cleverly promoted John McHugh, the incumbent Republican congressman in New York's 23rd Congressional District (eleven counties that form an area stretching from north of Syracuse and Albany up to the Canadian border), to a position in his administration as secretary of the army. When McHugh accepted President Obama's nomination on June 2, 2009, the wheels were set in motion for a special election to replace him on November 2, the date selected by Governor David Paterson.

The district, and earlier versions of it, had been in Republican hands for more than one hundred consecutive years. In 2008, however, Obama had carried the district with 52 percent of the vote, and Democratic prospects in the special election were promising. The Democrats waited until after the Republicans had already picked theirs to name their candidate.

The eleven county Republican chairmen, who had the authority to pick the nominee, decided to hold four local meetings around the district, inviting all the candidates to speak. Afterward, all eleven chairmen would convene and, with each county chairman receiving a weighted vote depending on his or her county's Republican population, they would select the nominee based upon a majority vote.

The process was tainted by a few county chairmen who ignored the will of the rank and file expressed in these public forums. The candidate who received the nomination at a July meeting of the county chairmen, Dede Scozzafava, was an extraordinarily liberal Republican who voted more like a liberal Democrat. As she campaigned, she refused to state her position on ObamaCare. Based on her record, most conservatives in the district were quite certain she would vote in favor of it.

New York is one of the few states where minor parties can play a role in election outcomes. This is due to a peculiarity of its election law, which allows votes from two different party endorsements to be added cumulatively to a candidate's total. The Conservative Party is the most prominent minority party in the state, but other fringe parties, such as the Working Families Party, also have ballot slots in elections. An extra 5 percent from a Conservative line on the ballot for a Republican candidate can transform a 46 percent loser into a 51 percent winner.

Conservative Party State Chairman Mike Long had made it clear he would not support Scozzafava. When Doug Hoffman, an unpolished also-ran who was never a serious candidate for the Republican nomination, asked for the Conservative Party nomination, Long gave it to him.

Conservatives around the blogosphere took notice that the local Republican establishment had nominated a RINO. Democrats also recognized that Republican leaders had chosen poorly. With a three-way race now between Republican RINO Scozzafava, Conservative Doug Hoffman, and Democrat Bill Owens, the Democrats knew they had a chance. Democratic Party money began pouring in. All the usual liberal suspects, including the infamous SEIU, lined up to throw cash behind Owens.

Meanwhile, Scozzafava's fund-raising lagged, and Hoffman's climbed. Both the Club for Growth and former Tennessee Republican senator Fred Thompson endorsed him. Online donations from tea partiers across the country poured into the Hoffman campaign coffers. By the end of October, he had received more than $2 million.

A broad array of conservative new media leaders documented countless manifestations of Scozzafava's left-wing policies, ranging from support of the Obama stimulus package to support of "card-check" legislation to any number of social issues. In early October, Scozzafava once again equivocated on how she would vote on the proposed Obama-Care health-care takeover.

The Washington power brokers of the Republican establishment were strongly behind Scozzafava from the beginning, despite her liberal policies and the very high likelihood she would be a vote for ObamaCare. The National Republican Congressional Committee, for instance, spent close to $1 million supporting her candidacy. The Republican National Committee endorsed her, as did former Speaker Gingrich. Gingrich's endorsement drew a fierce backlash from the blogosphere. Red State's Erick Erickson pronounced him done as a legitimate candidate for the 2012 presidential nomination. The Tea Party movement, which had cautiously embraced Gingrich's early participation in the April 15 Tax Day Tea Party, now skewered him for his support of a candidate who embodied every aspect of a political ideology it despised.

Scozzafava was under the intense national pressure of the new conservative media, and outspent by both Owens and Hoffman; polls showed her support evaporating. By the end of October, she was barely registering double digits. On Friday, October 31, 2009, Scozzafava withdrew from the race. The next day she endorsed the Democrat, Bill Owens, knowing he would cast a vote in favor of the ObamaCare bill in the House. On the morning of November 3, Owens scored a surprising 50–45 percent victory over the Conservative candidate Hoffman. Scozzafava's endorsement of Owens was the decisive factor in his victory. Her public statements and the robocalls she recorded had moved undecideds into his camp.

Owens was flown down quickly to Washington from Plattsburgh. He was sworn in just in time to cast his vote on H.R. 3962, the latest version of ObamaCare. It passed by a vote of 220–215. The vote in the House that day would matter little in the end. Even with the victory in the 23rd District, the Democratic leadership would have to resort to outlandish legislative trickery to pass the baneful ObamaCare.

Senate Majority Leader Harry Reid took particular notice of the rising tide of public opposition and increasingly effective conservative grassroots activism. To Reid it was increasingly likely that government-mandated health care would be unable to pass if the rules were followed. Reid decided to resort to trickery, and House Ways and Means Committee chairman Charlie Rangel was just the man to help him with it. Eighty-one years old, Rangel had represented Adam Clayton Powell's former Harlem district in Congress since 1972. In 2010, he would be censured by the entire House for repeated violations of House rules, all related to his failure to disclose significant amounts of income in his federal tax returns. That scandal lay in the future. For now, however, Reid needed Rangel's help.

On September 17, 2009, Rangel had introduced a bill in the House, H.R. 3590, the "Service Members Home Ownership Tax Act of 2009," whose purpose was "to amend the Internal Revenue Code of 1986 to modify the first-time homebuyers credit in the case of members of the Armed Forces and certain other Federal employees." The bill passed the House on October 8 by a 416–0 vote.

On November 19, Harry Reid introduced his own version of H.R. 3590 in the Senate. He took the bill that had been unanimously passed by the House, renamed it the "Patient Protection and Affordable Care Act," deleted all its contents after the first sentence, and replaced it with totally different content.[31] What followed was the first pass of the Senate version of ObamaCare. This bill, H.R. 3590—which had originated for a totally different purpose—would be one of the two bills that the Congress would pass in March 2010 that would establish ObamaCare. By taking a bill that had already passed the House and replacing the content of the bill entirely with the ObamaCare provisions, Reid was likely to avoid a conference committee. The Senate could pass a bill with any content it wished. If the House accepted that bill without amendment, it could be sent directly to the president for his signature.

It was the type of legislative trickery usually reserved for minor bills. Reid's tactic was designed to subvert the constitutional legislative process on a bill that would affect 16 percent of the country's economy and that was clearly so unpopular with the public that it would not make it through the usual channels of a conference committee.

For centuries, the conference committee process had been sacrosanct in the legislative branch of the government. Any bill of any significance would go through this process. Only through this process of thoughtful deliberation did legislation carry the moral authority of popular consent.

Reid had to rely upon "legal bribery" to get the gutted and replaced H.R. 3590 passed in the Senate. With the "Cornhusker Kickback," a concession given to Democratic senator Ben Nelson of Nebraska, Reid secured the critical last vote in the 60–39 passage of H.R. 3590 in the Senate on Christmas Eve, 2009, which enabled Reid to beat a potential filibuster of the bill there.

Nelson forced Reid to include special protections in the bill for the state of Nebraska, protections no other state had. Included in the language of the law was a provision that the federal government would pay for Nebraska's expanded Medicare population forever. In forty-nine other states, from the fourth year on, each state had to pay for the expanded Medicare population. Only in Nebraska were these costs to be carried in the fourth year and beyond by the federal government. Estimates of the total windfall to the state of Nebraska resulting from this backroom deal topped $100 million.[32] Average citizens in the other forty-nine states were outraged, and most Nebraskans were embarrassed and humiliated by the shameful conduct of their own senator.[33]

The Senate bill also included an additional $300 million in Medicaid funds that would go only to the state of Louisiana. Pushed by Democratic holdout Senator Mary Landrieu, this "legal bribe" was dubbed by Republicans "the corrupt bargain" and "the Louisiana Purchase."[34]

The Tea Party had few resources with which to fight this, but we were determined, unlike the Republican leadership, to fight back against the Democrats. We decided to launch a project called "Take the Town Halls to Washington." The idea was to have large groups of constituents from around the country come to Washington and go directly to their members of Congress to explain why they should oppose ObamaCare. We focused on sixty-six members who were publicly undecided. We reminded them that if they failed to vote against ObamaCare, they would be voted out of office in November.[35]

Representative Michele Bachmann of Minnesota helped kick off the project at a press conference, telling Tea Party activists to "take the town halls to Washington, DC" to defeat the health-care bill.

Soon Tea Party activists began flooding into Washington on their own nickel, coming from faraway states, like Texas, Nebraska, and Tennessee. Patti Weaver, the leader of the Pittsburgh Tea Party, who had been with the movement from its inception, paid for two busloads to come down, and they packed a room with about sixty constituents of their congressman, Jason Altmire, who equivocated until the last minute. Ultimately he voted against ObamaCare and became one of the few Democrats in marginal districts who ended up being reelected in November 2010.

On March 17, 2010, Democratic congressman John Spratt* of South Carolina introduced H.R. 4872, the Health Care Education and Reconciliation Act of 2010. Less than a month earlier, Majority Leader Harry Reid had denied that the reconciliation process was on the table, yet here it was. And the ram-down came fast.

On Sunday, March 21, the House agreed to the Senate amendment to H.R. 3590—the bill that had originally been introduced for a completely different purpose by Charlie Rangel back in September and was now called the Patient Protection and Affordable Care Act—by a 219–212 vote. President Obama had promised to issue a meaningless executive order that claimed to limit the use of federal funds for abortions so that a dozen so-called pro-life Democrats led by Bart Stupak could publicly remove their opposition to ObamaCare.

The sleight of hand continued when later in that day, by a 220–211 vote, the House passed the Health Care Education and Reconciliation Act of 2010—the reconciliation end run that patched up the differences between the House and Senate plans. President Obama signed the first bill of the two-headed monster—the Patient Protection and Affordable Care Act—into law on Tuesday, March 23, 2010.

Two days later, the Senate passed the Health Care Education and

---

* Congressman Spratt was defeated for reelection in November 2010.

Reconciliation Act, with one amendment to the version passed Sunday by the House, by a 56–43 vote. This vote was quite noticeable, because it would not have been "filibuster proof" if the Senate had not broken its rules on reconciliation. The following week, President Obama signed the second bill into law.

Perhaps the most outrageous public statement by a contemporary political figure that reflects the arrogant, abusive, and deceptive exercise of legislative power required to pass ObamaCare was made at a town hall meeting in Hayward, California, on July 24, 2010.

Democratic congressman Pete Stark of California, an unpleasant and arrogant seventy-eight-year-old who had served in Congress for twenty consecutive terms without ever facing a serious challenger, responded emphatically when a constituent asked him, "How can legislation such as this [ObamaCare law] be constitutional when it seems to be in direct conflict with the Thirteenth Amendment? . . . If this legislation is constitutional, what limitations are there on the federal government's ability to tell us how to run our private lives?" Without blinking, Stark responded, "I think that there are very few constitutional limits that would prevent the federal government from rules that could affect your private life."

The constituent followed up: "My question is: How can this law be constitutional?—but more importantly than that—if they can do this, what can't they? Is your answer that they can do anything?"

Stark shot back authoritatively, "The federal government, yes, can do most anything in this country."[36]

By the fall of 2010, a string of stunning victories by Tea Party–backed Senate candidates in Republican primaries had establishment Republicans reeling. The Tea Party Express played a significant role in these victories, taking its bus tours, publicity machines, and advertising dollars to states in play. In Utah, upstart Mike Lee knocked off incumbent Bob Bennett, who ungraciously complained after his defeat about how little these tea party grassroots activists had appreciated all his years of hard work. In Nevada, Sharron Angle defeated Sue Lowden, the establishment-backed candidate, and in Alaska, Joe Miller upset Lisa Murkowski. In Kentucky, Rand Paul, Ron's son, defeated the Republican Party establishment favorite, Trey Grayson.

Even while establishment Republicans were wringing their hands that by nominating such untested Tea Party conservatives, Republican voters were dooming the possibility of general election victories in all of these states, the unintended consequence of these Senate primary battles was to give a sense of encouragement and hope to conservative Republican challengers in House of Representatives districts previously considered safely in Democratic hands.

Polling also indicated this trend. By the fall, the widely accepted mantra among pundits was that it was likely that the Republicans would take over the House. The unknown was now the margin of victory. Would it be merely a change in the majority, or would it be a historic mandate of the type Newt Gingrich secured when the Republicans took over the House in 1994 after being in the minority for fifty years?

Given the Democrats' record of constitutional destruction, and the high level of outrage, the Republican Party significantly underperformed in the November 2010 general elections. With a better coordination, the 63 net gain could and should have been over 100. And the Senate gain of 6 seats could and should have been 10 or 11.

Chapter 11

RESTORING THE SECULAR COVENANT: A TEA PARTY AMERICA BASED ON THE CONSTITUTION

P eople often ask me, What would America look like if it were run by the Tea Party? What they are really asking is, What activities of the federal government are properly constitutional and how much of our tax dollars should be spent on those activities?

Just as the Founding Fathers sought to restore the promise of the English Constitution in eighteenth-century America, the Tea Party movement seeks to restore the four broken promises of the American Constitution in twenty-first-century America. Even Alexander Hamilton and Thomas Jefferson, who disagreed on almost every other aspect of the Constitution, would be in agreement that restoring the broken promise of the fiscal constitution is central to the very survival of our country. In a spirit of national unity, then, we begin to paint our portrait of a constitutionally restored America by focusing on this point of agreement between the two legendary adversaries whose disagreements have defined the course of our nation's history. What would it take to restore that broken promise? Later on, we'll complete the canvas by describing the restoration of the other three promises—of plain meaning, free markets, and deliberative accountability.

THE 12 PERCENT SOLUTION RESTORES THE
PROMISE OF THE FISCAL CONSTITUTION

What percentage of the nation's economic output should be spent by the federal government? The Founding Fathers gave us their answer when they applied the simple principles of the family budget to the federal budget. No program during peacetime could be undertaken unless there was a corresponding tax that could pay for it. National debt was incurred only during times of war, when the survival of the republic was at stake. It was never to be used to finance current consumption.

When those principles were applied to the federal budget during the 142 years between 1789 and 1931, federal expenditures as a percentage of the nation's gross domestic product always stayed within the range of 2–4 percent.

In stark contrast to the Founding Fathers, today's Democrats think that federal expenditure as a percentage of GDP should be at least 24 percent. Most Republicans think it should be 20 percent. Some conservative Republicans have recently suggested that it should be as low as 18 percent.

Both the Democrats and the Republicans are wrong. Applying the tradition of the fiscal constitution to our contemporary circumstances, the maximum level that federal expenditures as a percentage of GDP should reach is not 25 percent, or 20 percent, or even the "wildly ambitious" 18 percent. Instead it should be 12 percent, half of what Democrat leaders believe it should be, and barely two-thirds of the level suggested by even the most conservative Republicans.*

Most Americans inherently agree with the idea that federal expen-

---

* In November 2011, the FreedomWorks-sponsored "Tea Party Debt Commission" released a detailed report that proposed a ten-year federal budget that would reduce federal expenditures to 16 percent of GDP by 2022. This report, I would argue, establishes an upper boundary of the level of federal expenditures that the Tea Party movement would support. Unlike the "12 percent" solution, however, which is a level based upon the historical traditions of "the fiscal constitution," the 16 percent standard is based on "post-war norms."

ditures are two times greater than what they should be. A recent poll, for instance, showed that voters believe that half of every federal dollar is wasted.[1] Anyone who has ever watched a federal program in action, or walked through a federal office building to see what the federal employees there are actually doing, would have a hard time disagreeing with this assessment.

In 2011, federal expenditures were 24 percent of GDP, a full 20 percent of our GDP more than during the peacetime years between 1789 and 1931. At a minimum, then, today we're devoting an additional one-fifth of our economic output to the activities of the federal government. Throw in the additional 15 percent that goes to state and local government, and you have 39 percent of our GDP being spent on public activities at the federal, state, and local level.

Today much of that money is being spent in different ways than in the past. Prior to 1931 most federal expenditures went to defense, with the balance split between interest on the national debt and "other"—the bare-bones executive offices at State, Justice, and Treasury. As late as 1962, 49 percent of federal expenditures went to defense, with only 3 percent devoted to antipoverty programs, 13 percent to Social Security, 6 percent to net interest, and 28 percent to "other." Today, however, the story is quite different. In 2010, 20 percent was spent on defense, 14 percent on antipoverty programs, 29 percent on Social Security, 11 percent on net interest, and 25 percent on "other."[2]

In an America governed by Tea Party principles—that is to say, governed by the original principles of the Constitution—federal government expenditures would be limited to those activities that are explicitly authorized in the enumerated powers of Article I, Section 8. There is no room for expenditures on "implied powers" in a Tea Party budget.

Unlike that earlier time in our history when there were clear distinctions between peacetime and wartime budgets, our contemporary world has constant defense needs. Given the threats of modern terrorism, it's almost a certainty that we will be "at war" for many years to come. From a budgeting perspective, the question is merely what level of expenditures will be sufficient to defend us during this ongoing war.

Since it's a bigger, more dangerous, and more highly interconnected world today than it was in 1931, and since maintaining the common defense is one of the enumerated powers in Article I, Section 8, we can look at the current level of defense spending—$687 billion in fiscal year 2011, which was 5 percent of the GDP and about 20 percent of all federal expenditures—as a necessary addition to the "baseline" provided by the peacetime budgets between 1789 and 1931. Similarly, net interest—over $200 billion in fiscal year 2011—was 1.6 percent of the GDP, and over the thirty-year period from 1970 to 2009 averaged 2.2 percent of GDP.[3]

Adding these numbers (5 percent for defense, 2.2 percent for net interest) to the 4 percent at the "top of the historical range from 1789 to 1931" gives us 11.2 percent or, rounded up, 12 percent of GDP as a contemporary budget consistent with the traditions of the fiscal constitution.

Cutting the budget in half, then, would restore the broken promise of the fiscal constitution.

That's a tall order, one that even the Founding Fathers would find daunting. If we were to wave a magic wand, and federal expenditures in fiscal year 2013 were cut in half from fiscal year 2011's level of $3.8 trillion, they would be reduced to $1.9 trillion. Since federal revenues were only $2.1 trillion and the difference, $1.7 trillion, was paid for by increasing the national debt, our magic wand cuts would allow us to cut federal tax revenues by 10 percent, from $2.1 trillion to $1.9 trillion. This relatively modest reduction in tax collection merely indicates how severely we've come to rely on debt to fund our current consumption.

The broken promises of free markets could be restored by two broad actions. First, by instituting a complete reform of the tax system that eliminates all deductions and credits. Second, by dramatically reducing the number and scope of federal regulations that constrain the economic activity of individuals, small businesses, and large corporations.

There is great evil in a 12 million-word tax code that authorizes the government to take money from certain groups of citizens and give it to other groups whose only difference is their ability to spend the money necessary to lobby for their own benefits from the U.S. Treasury.

The corrupt practice of providing federal subsidies and benefits to some economic enterprises, while withholding those same privileges from the economic enterprises of other individuals, represents an egregious violation of the individual rights of those denied the special privileges. This unconstitutional idea that the federal government has the right to pick winners and losers from among the citizenry not only infringes on the individual rights of the majority who do not receive the special treatment, but also has the deleterious effect of allocating scarce resources in ways that are not optimal for society as a whole.

More important, it undermines the moral authority of the entire federal government. From the entitlements granted to the children of uninjured Union Army veterans by the Republican "Billion Dollar Congress," to the special tax benefits to the sugar trust wrapped up in the 1894 Wilson-Gorman Tariff, to the bailouts of some Wall Street firms over others (Goldman Sachs was saved, Lehman Brothers was left to die), to the propping up of GM and Chrysler with massive loans, tax benefits, and the abrogation of property rights of the prior bondholders in those companies, to the subsidies for the production of ethanol by Iowa farmers, to the ill-advised "cash for clunkers" programs, subsidizing those who are failing in the market, penalizing those who are competing, is one of the greatest moral dysfunctions of our current society.

Removing any and all special tax breaks would create a tax code whose impact is neutral on economic activity. This would lead to the more efficient allocation of resources throughout the entire economy.

Eliminating subsidies for ethanol, for instance, would remove the negative second-order effects that they have created in the economy. Due to those subsidies, for instance, as much as a quarter of all American corn production is devoted to the production of fuel rather than food.

The unintended second-order effects of this policy? Food prices have increased, making it more difficult for the poor to feed themselves—not only here in the United States, but throughout the world.

Take this second-order effect, multiply it by tens of thousands of such subsidies, tax credits, and tax deductions, and you can see why our economy produces more of certain goods than an efficient market would create, and fewer of other goods.

The other action that would restore the broken promise of free markets would be to dramatically reduce the scope and size of federal regulation of business. When Thomas Jefferson wrote in 1774 that the tyranny of a single monarch had been replaced by the tyranny of 160,000 electors in England over 4 million colonial Americans, he could just as easily have been writing of today's tyranny, where several hundred thousand bureaucrats, overeager legislators, and activist judges hold sway over the 100 million Americans who either own their own businesses or work for businesses.

Nowhere is the burden of compliance with ever-growing regulatory requirements greater than with small businesses. Indeed, one of the greatest competitive advantages of business size in today's world is the superior ability large companies have to fund the onerous regulatory compliance requirements imposed by the federal government. And the bad news: under the Obama administration those requirements have continued to grow, rather than shrink.

While it's true that in some areas of business activity—such as the complex financial transactions of publicly traded companies—intelligent federal regulation is in the public interest, in contemporary America most regulations have the effect of thwarting the individual initiatives of small businesses. And most economic growth originates in those small businesses that carry the greatest regulatory burden—at least as measured as a percentage of their revenues.

Of all the four broken promises of the constitution, restoring the promise of plain meaning will require the most patience. It will be restored not in a matter of years, or even in a matter of successive presidential administrations, but instead over decades and generations.

The first challenge is to maintain within the populace the notion that the Constitution is the secular covenant by which we have all agreed to be governed. Then this fundamental belief must be passed on to subsequent generations. This will require a tremendous level of commitment toward civic education of our younger generation—adults under thirty, and children of all ages. How or whether such a commitment will be undertaken is beyond the scope of this book. However, given the natural organic development that has character-ized the Tea Party movement to date, it seems quite likely to be the case that such a commitment will emerge soon and in unexpected ways.

Today, at least, the supremacy of the Constitution is acknowledged by most, but not all, Americans. The idea is fought vigorously by the elites of the left. Indeed, the left has an entirely different set of guiding principles.

The core principles of the Tea Party movement are formed by devo-tion to the secular covenant of the American Constitution. The core prin-ciples of the left entail a complete rejection of the American Constitution and then its replacement under the "divine right of the state," a principle inimical to free markets but supportive of forced redistribution.

In such a world, the natural rights of the individual have been sup-planted by the collectivist wishes of the political elite. It's the natural evolution of William Jennings Bryan's collectivist majoritarian vision of forced Prohibition, Wilson's disdain for the Constitution and usurpa-tion of executive powers, the "fascist" sentiments of Hugh Johnson and FDR's National Industrial Recovery Act, and LBJ's paternalistic Great Society. The "Norman yoke" of English tyranny against which Jeffer-son and the other Founding Fathers had rebelled during the American Revolution has been replaced by the "Collectivist yoke" of elitist tyranny against which the Tea Party movement has revolted in the twenty-first century.

THERE ARE ONLY TWO CHOICES—THE TEA PARTY 12 PERCENT SOLUTION AND THE CONSTITUTION OR THE LEFT'S 36 PERCENT SOLUTION AND THE DIVINE RIGHT OF THE STATE

I can hear now the wailing and gnashing of teeth that the implementation of this 12 percent solution coupled with tax reform and regulatory reduction would arouse from critics on the left, the mainstream media, and the entire Democratic Party, as well as much of the Republican Party leadership.

"Draconian!" they would cry. "Heartless!" "What about the children?"

On this last point, there is some agreement. It is precisely for the children that we must make a choice between two starkly different visions of our future as a nation.

The Tea Party's vision cuts federal spending in half, limits the activities of the federal government to those specifically enumerated in Article I, Section 8 of the Constitution, and frees up 12 percent of our country's output for uses determined by private citizens and corporations acting independently.

The left's vision dramatically increases federal spending, increases the role of the federal government in all activities, and removes an additional 10–15 percent of our country's economic output from private citizens and corporations acting independently and places it in the hands of politicians and bureaucrats who will allocate those resources based on the political influence of eager and open-palmed interest groups.

Republicans who believe that their attempts to slightly reduce federal expenditures from current levels will stop the growth of the federal government are wrong. Government cannot be held static—or reduced in size and scope by a few percent. By their nature, statist governments can only grow. Their momentum and infrastructure require nothing less. Hoover's 6 percent of GDP in 1931 has grown to Obama's 24 percent in 2011. If government is not proactively cut, it will inevitably continue to grow. Within two decades, and left unconstrained, federal expenditures as a percent of GDP would quite likely grow by the same 12 percent by which they should be *cut* to approach pre-1931 norms.

Assuming that state and local government expenditures remain constant at the current levels of 15 percent of GDP, such an increase would raise federal expenditures to 36 percent of GDP and bring the allocation of economic output to public purposes in the United States to 51 percent—the same high level currently experienced in the debt-ridden, slumping economies of Europe. In France, which is at the higher end of the European spectrum, for instance, public expenditures as a percentage of GDP are at 52 percent. In Germany, at the lower end of the European spectrum, that number is 44 percent.[4]

Anyone who doubts that government's natural inclination to grow cannot be stopped by a Republican leadership committed to incrementally small "cuts" in federal expenditures need only look at the very recent track record. What happened to federal spending during the Congress that took office in 2011—a Congress where the House of Representatives was controlled by the Republican Party?

Amid much self-congratulation and ballyhoo, Republicans in the House and Democrats in the Senate passed a budget in April 2011 that the Republican leadership claimed would cut $38 billion from the federal government's 2011 budget.

But, as John Merline pointed out in *Investor's Business Daily*, "[In the first nine months of this year [fiscal year 2011], federal spending was $120 billion higher than in the same period in 2010, [recently released Treasury Department] data show. That's an increase of almost 5 percent. And deficits during this time were $23.5 billion higher."[5]

Budget cutting under Republican presidents Ronald Reagan, George H. W. Bush, and George W. Bush has fared no better. We have no reason to believe, therefore, that the current policies of "incrementally small" cuts of the Republican leadership will do anything to stop the growth of federal expenditures.

The simple truth of a federal government that has abandoned the fiscal constitution of our Founding Fathers is clear. Lacking external constraints, politicians will continue to transfer wealth from taxpaying Americans to politically connected interest groups of all sorts—corporate cronies, unions, or others. And these beneficiaries will aggressively resist any efforts by the rest of us to stop or limit these transfers.

W hat changes will our magic wand have produced? At the broadest level, here are eight:

First, everyone in America—private individuals and companies—will experience a 10 percent increase in discretionary income.

Second, financial markets will react favorably. Interest rates on our national debt will decline, and the country's recently downgraded credit rating will likely be upgraded instead.

Third, the number of civilian federal employees will be cut from 2 million to 1 million. These people will be in search of gainful employment.

Fourth, some recipients of federal "entitlement" payments will have their benefits reduced. Others—in particular current retirees receiving Social Security benefits—will continue to receive entitlement payments just as they were promised in the contract they agreed to when they contributed payroll taxes from their earnings to pay the retirement benefits of previous generations. Some "entitlement" recipients will stop receiving benefits entirely.

Fifth, some recipients of "antipoverty" program funding will have their benefits cut.

Sixth, federal departments and agencies whose functions are entirely without value, or are even of negative value, since they disrupt effective private markets, will be eliminated. In this category we would place the Department of Education, the Department of Energy, the Department of Housing and Urban Development, and numerous others.

Seventh, defense expenditures, while not necessarily cut, will be exposed to higher levels of scrutiny. But the standard ought not to be some artificial concept of "shared pain" across the various departments in the federal government, nor should it be an equally artificial comparison to other countries' levels of defense expenditures. The standard ought to be what amount of money is required to maintain a defense capability in troops, equipment, and systems sufficient to honor the constitutional requirement of Article I, Section 8 to "maintain the common defense."

Eighth, some private companies currently benefiting from crony capitalist loans and special income tax benefits—General Electric and Solyndra come to mind—will not receive federal funds.

I t is a well-known trick in Washington to justify expenditures on a worthless program threatened with cuts by placing into that program some line item that can arguably said to be important to some interest group. Old hands call this the "Washington Monument" trick. Years ago, a clever bureaucrat—faced with cuts to a particular pet project—ominously warned that if such cuts were made he would be forced to shut down the Washington Monument. It wasn't true, of course, but the threat carried the day.

Such threats have been made by bureaucrats and politicians since the beginnings of the republic. Politicians are no more or less venal and self-serving today than they were two centuries ago in the time of Hamilton and Jefferson, or a century ago in the time of Wilson, or decades ago in the time of Franklin Roosevelt.

What's different today is that the natural constraints on political pandering imposed by the fiscal constitution have been removed. Politicians are not required to choose between competing programs. Instead they have been enabled to pander in an institutional way.

The discipline of a budget has been replaced by the inexorable leviathan of the institution of the federal government, out to expand its scope and power at every instance. Because the nature of government is to expand, we face two very stark choices: Either we undertake the political actions necessary to cut federal expenditures to 12 percent of GDP, or we sit back and watch as the share of our economic output devoted to the federal government continues to grow from the current level of 24 percent, by half, probably to around 36 percent.

The beauty of the fiscal constitution of the Founding Fathers is that the discipline it imposed forced the establishment of priorities in the ordering of federal expenditures. The political wrangling among the competing forces may have caused the occasional ruffled feather among those interests who lost out in the expenditures battle, but it also freed up for private hands the resources not used by the federal government.

Those fights over scarce resources would be replayed with great intensity in a Congress and administration that chose to cut federal expenditures in half. Conservative and liberal analysts in the past have set forward competing views of how federal resources should be spent, but those conversations have almost always been about which programs should be added to the budget. Rarely in modern political history have any programs actually been cut.

Without delving too deeply into specific programmatic solutions—that, after all, would be the charge given to elected members of Congress and an elected president who would fashion a "Tea Party First Hundred Days" legislative plan—it's worth examining some of the arguments that might be advanced by those current recipients of federal largesse who would be hurt in a 12 percent solution.

The nondefense federal workforce would be cut in half, leaving one million federal employees searching for work—now the real wailing and whining begin. Let's first be very clear whose ox is being gored. Does anyone believe that eliminating one out of every two federal employees will have any impact on the ability of the federal government to perform the constitutional duties it's been assigned?

Certain areas—air traffic control, for instance, and the clerks who actually cut the Social Security checks—would not likely be cut. But other areas are filled with fluff.

There would be little loss to the nation with such cuts.

The AFSCME unions would be hurt, of course, as would the one million federal employees who lost their jobs.

But there are plenty of opportunities for gainful employment elsewhere in a Tea Party America, especially if spending cuts are accompanied by dramatic reduction in regulations. Wherever these million workers end up—in their own construction businesses, working as plumbers, teachers, or information technology specialists—won't their efforts in those arenas actually add to the country's overall economic growth?

I grant the critics that the transition would be uncomfortable. But most of the rest of the country has been forced to deal with such employment transitions. Federal workers ought not to be a privileged and protected class.

The need to reduce or eliminate entitlement payments for some, but not all, current recipients is a classic Washington Monument situation. Very few would argue that old-age retirement benefits to current Social Security recipients should be cut or eliminated. After all, those people have honored their part of the contract by paying Social Security taxes their entire working lives. It's really not their problem that the system is not actuarially sound, that it is truly a Ponzi scheme, in which current benefits can be paid only by increasing withholding taxes on the current workforce.

One long-term solution would be to remove all these programs from the category of federal government entitlement programs. Social Security could be replaced on a phased basis with any of a number of private savings plans. And the other entitlement programs could be replaced by a free market of philanthropic citizenship, whose financial resources would be provided voluntarily from citizens with significantly greater discretionary income, resulting from dramatic reduction of their own federal tax burden. That reduction would have come with a reduction of federal expenditures from 24 percent of the GDP to 12 percent or lower.

In contrast to Social Security, which, though a disaster in terms of long-term unfunded liabilities, at least in current income terms generates more tax revenues than expenditures, the programs of Medicare, Medicaid, unemployment and disability, and Temporary Assistance for Needy Families are all significantly cash-flow negative.

Social Security's positive current-year cash flow, however, is completely the result of a steady increase in payroll taxes. When the Social Security payroll tax was first introduced in 1936, for instance, payroll tax withholdings were 1 percent each from employers and employees, for a total of 2 percent of an employee's wages. Seven workers were supporting every one retiree. Those numbers have steadily worsened over the years. In 1960 total Social Security withholdings had jumped from 2 percent of an employee's wages to 6 percent. By 1970 it was 8.4 percent, and by 1990 it was 12.4 percent.[6] Meanwhile, the number of workers supporting one recipient receiving Social Security benefits declined from seven to three.

These payroll tax withholdings increased from 4.4 percent of GDP in 1971 to 6 percent of GDP in 2010.[7] Payment of Social Security benefits increased from 3.3 percent of GDP in 1971 to 4.8 percent of GDP in 2010.[8]

The fundamental economic flaw of this system is that it has always been one of transfer payments from the current generation of workers to the current generation of retirees. Benefit payments to retirees were based on political rather than economic calculations. Though the current generation of retirees paid into the system and has been promised benefits in the future based on those payments, those earlier payments were not invested in interest-bearing accounts with their names attached. And retirees will receive payments back over their lifetime that, after about seven years of benefit payments received, will exceed everything they put into the fund originally. It's simply unsustainable.

Most entitlement programs involve a transfer of income from tax

producers to citizens who have lower income for a series of reasons—
they don't have jobs, they're disabled, their jobs don't pay them enough
for them to purchase food, housing, or health care. Under our current
system (excluding Social Security for the moment), the 8 percent of
GDP devoted to these programs is far from efficient.

It's also true that in our 12 percent solution, some recipients of "antipoverty" program funding have their benefits cut, and we can be sure
that our Democratic consultants will cue up the "It's for the children"
commercials. But would children go hungry?

Americans are among the most generous people on earth when it
comes to charitable contributions. If, as part of the national discussion for removing the federal role in all these entitlement programs, the
public dialogue were to focus on the responsibilities of citizens to provide charitable, nonprofit, free market philanthropic solutions to their
local communities' problems, what would be the result?

In all likelihood you would see an amazing renaissance and dramatic growth of private, localized philanthropic solutions that would
fill in the gap left by the departure of the federal government from this
arena. Imagine how local communities would increasingly compete to
show the rest of the country that their brand of philanthropic citizenship was the best in the nation.

One need only look at the philanthropic history of the myriad private
charities—from public libraries to hospitals—started by Benjamin
Franklin to conclude that this "can-do" spirit of American philanthropy
would be far more successful than the tone-deaf, forced-taxation,
bureaucratic-imposition model under which we currently suffer.

The left believes that a more intrusive government is necessary to
prevent the proliferation of social injustice and poverty. Leftists say the
federal government can better deploy the extra 12 percent of the GDP
it now takes from corporations and private individuals than can those
private individuals.

But is this assumption true?

What would private citizens and corporations do with these extra
resources?

They would either save the money, spend it on something that was a priority and of importance to them, or invest it, possibly in their own business. Any three of these actions would boost economic activity throughout the country. Now imagine a nation of 100 million taxpayers all engaging in those productive activities simultaneously.

The removal of the federal government from many areas of entitlement expenditures, combined with increases in discretionary income among private citizens and corporations, would likely lead to increased civic engagement at the local level. Where the government once provided the so-called safety net, local churches and charities would step in even more than they have so far, and would probably deliver much more effective aid.

P olitically, how realistic is this 12 percent solution? That depends on the answer to this question:

> How much of their time and resources will those who believe
> in constitutional conservativism volunteer in the political arena and
> how effectively will they communicate and persuade a majority of
> Americans to agree with their views about the role of the federal
> government?

These first three broken promises will be restored only if the fourth promise—the deliberative accountability of the legislative and executive branches—is honored. This will require the active engagement of those of us who wish to restore the first three promises. Left to their own devices, politicians will gravitate naturally toward the acquisition and abuse of power, and the centralization of that power in their own hands.

The biggest message is that we—the average American citizens— weren't paying attention as the leadership of both political parties drifted steadily away from the principles of our secular covenant. Each successive year, the federal government added more powers, through congressional legislation, the assertion and exercise of administrative power, and a judiciary that increasingly failed to rein in governmental authority.

Consider the political and governmental impact of the Tea Party movement so far. When we held the first Tax Day Tea Party on April 15, 2009, the federal debt was $10 trillion. Democrats held the presidency, controlled the Senate by a 60–40 margin, and controlled the House by a 257–178 margin. If anyone other than those of us who attended the thousand Tea Party rallies that day had suggested the Republican Party would have a majority in the House come January 2011, the idea would have been considered crazy.

Two years later, on April 15, 2011, the federal debt was $14 trillion. Republicans now controlled the House by a 255–180 margin, thanks entirely to the Tea Party movement. Democrats still held the presidency, and they also maintained control of the Senate, by a 53–47 margin.

In the two years between those two events, the Tea Party movement scored an incredible political victory by removing the Democrats from control of the House. However, performance to date in reaching the most important measurement of success—limiting the size of government—has been dismal. In these two short years, the debt increased by 28 percent, from $10 trillion up to $14 trillion.

This significant political victory was the result of two years of tireless work from hundreds of thousands of volunteers, many of whom spent during that time anywhere from $1,000 to $20,000 of their own money on travel, organizational materials, press release fees, and the like. On average, these volunteers devoted between ten and fifty hours a week to the cause, and this includes those who had full-time or part-time jobs.

The Tea Party movement, among its supporters, has redefined the concept of citizenship, specifically by increasing the amount of time, money, and other resources citizens should consider it to be their duty to devote to political engagement. The change, quite simply, involves an order of magnitude.

Get-out-the vote efforts, of course, are not the only measures of political engagement. The most effective methods involve direct communication with legislators and other elected officials. There are two critical factors in having effective, meaningful dialogue with such officials. The first is to be knowledgeable and thoroughly familiar with the relevant issues. The second is to be a known political force who can have an impact on that political figure's reelection.

The near-term future of the Tea Party movement is clear. Two thousand twelve will be a year of focus on elections, at a level of even more intensity than 2010. The presidential election will see perhaps the highest level of engagement in modern American political history—the ground game will pit loosely organized and underfinanced local tea parties against highly financed union and left-wing nonprofit get-out-the-vote specialists. The troops on the ground will be there, though the unions will pull out all the stops. It will be the most spectacular battle in American political history, fought precinct by precinct. In a fair fight, we'll win, because our views represent the majority opinion of the American people.

Activists in the Tea Party movement can count on this, though. The special interests that support the policies of the divine right of the state—the Democratic Party, the unions, the corporations that thrive off cozy crony capitalist relationships with the federal government, the latest phony populist group—will devote every financial and human resource necessary to thwart our efforts to restore the four broken promises of the Constitution in the 2012 elections.

Is the 12 percent solution possible?

Certainly.

Will a magic wand make it happen?

Certainly not.

There are no magic wands in the American political system. Systemic problems as large as those we currently find ourselves in are not solved in a single election cycle.

But they begin with one election cycle, and they continue in each cycle thereafter. What was begun in 2010 will continue in 2012. We may not reach the 12 percent solution in this upcoming cycle, or in the cycle after that, or in 2016 or beyond.

Still, this much is true. We must press forward through political engagement to secure the 12 percent solution, or we will most certainly be subjected to the "Collectivist yoke" of the left's 36 percent solution.

But we have awakened from our long slumber, our purpose is noble, and our prospects are good.

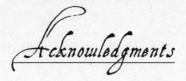

Acknowledgments

Two years ago Don Fehr of Trident Media read a column in the *New York Times* that mentioned my self-published book, *Rules for Conservative Radicals*. When Don contacted me and offered to represent me as a literary agent, I readily accepted. I am profoundly grateful for Don's friendship and outstanding representation.

It has been a great privilege to work with Adam Bellow, my editor at Broadside Books. I cannot speak of Broadside Books without also mentioning the excellence of associate editor Kate Whitenight.

My friends Jack Cashill, Ben Cunningham, and Mark Fitzgibbons, a clan of Celtic conservatives of whom Edmund Burke would be proud, provided invaluable insights and critiques of the work in process along the way.

I also want to acknowledge the contributions of numerous Tea Party allies with whom I've worked closely for the past three years. Most important, I want to thank Christina Botteri and Lorie Medina, whose own lives are models of selfless commitment to restoring the principles of American constitutionalism. Among the many others who have given generously of their time to the noble purpose of saving our republic, and have also been great friends to me, I want to thank Patti Weaver, Bill Hennessy, Amy Kremer, Judson Phillips, Teri and Don Adams,

Jamie Radtke, Mark Lloyd, Kellen Giuda, Rob Gaudet, David Webb, Milton Wolf, Robert Naegele, Stephen Kruiser, Glenn Reynolds, Michelle Malkin, Katrina Pierson, Tom Smith, Will McCullers, Dave Gardy, Dan Gainor, Tammy Bruce, Tony Katz, Zan Green, John and Gina Loudon, Jason Hoyt, Dan Riehl, Lloyd Marcus, Wendy Herman, Erika Franzi, JoAnn Abbott, and Brian T. Campbell.

I also want to acknowledge those who were significant intellectual influences on this book. I begin more than three decades ago with a group of scholars then at the Harvard Social Studies Department—Amy Gutmann, Todd Rakoff, and Don Gogel. Without the intellectual framework they provided, this book would not have been written. My most important recent influence is Georgetown Law School professor Randy Barnett, a brilliant scholar, champion of constitutional liberty, and friend to the Tea Party movement.

Finally, I want to thank my wife, Debye, and my daughters, Courtenay and Honor, who lived with *Covenant of Liberty* as much as I did.

Endnotes

CHAPTER 1: THE ENGLISH ROOTS OF AMERICAN LIBERTY

1. John Lilburne, *The Cause of Regal Tyranny Discovered*, quoted in Charles Harding Firth, *The House of Lords During the Civil War* (New York: Longmans, Green, 1910), p. 164.

2. Catherine Drinker Bowen, *The Lion and the Throne: The Life and Times of Sir Edward Coke: 1552–1634* (Boston: Little, Brown, 1956), p. 178.

3. David Howarth, *Images of Rule: Art and Politics in the English Renaissance, 1485–1649* (Berkeley: University of California Press, 1997), p. 53.

4. Alfred W. Pollard, ed., *Records of the English Bible* (London, 1911), p. 46, cited in *The Geneva Bible: A Facsimile of the 1560 Edition* (Peabody, MA: Hendrickson Bibles, 2007), p. 15.

5. Bowen, *The Lion and the Throne*, pp. 478–79.

6. J. G. A. Pocock, *The Ancient Constitution and the Feudal Law: A Study of English Historical Thought in the Seventeenth Century* (Cambridge: Cambridge University Press, 1987), pp. 5–15.

7. Bowen, *The Lion and the Throne*, pp. 482–502.

8. Edward G. Hudon, "John Lilburne, the Levellers, and Mr. Justice Black," *ABA Journal* 60 (June 1974), pp. 686–88.

9. Pauline Gregg, *Free-Born John: The Biography of John Lilburne* (London: Phoenix Press, 2000), pp. 193–95. There is no verbatim record of their conversation.

10. Ibid., p. 216.

11. Milton M. Carrow, "Administrative Justice Comes of Age," *ABA Journal* 60 (November 1974), pp. 1396–99. This article describes the significance of the 1970 Supreme Court decision *Goldberg v. Kelly*.

12. Gregg, *Free-Born John*, p. 267.

13. Ibid.

14. David Plant, "The Leveller Mutinies," British Civil Wars, Commonwealth and Protectorate, 2001–2011, http://www.british-civil-wars.co.uk/glossary/leveller-mutiny.htm.

15. Gregg, *Free-Born John*, p. 344.

16. Ibid., p. 357.

17. Jonathan Fitzgibbons, *Cromwell's Head* (Kew, UK: National Archives, 2008), p. 58.

18. Richard Ashcraft, *Revolutionary Politics and Locke's Two Treatises of Government* (Princeton, NJ: Princeton University Press, 1986), p. 190.

19. Ibid.

20. Gilbert Burnet, *History of My Own Time* (Oxford: Clarendon Press, 1897), p. 460. Burnet was no fan of James II, and was credited with completing the English translation of William of Orange's 1688 *Declaration of The Hague.*

21. George Henry Wakeling, *King and Parliament (A.D. 1603–1714)* (London: Blackie & Sons, 1897), p. 91.

22. E. Neville Williams, *The Eighteenth-Century Constitution, 1688–1815* (Cambridge: Cambridge University Press, 1960), pp. 10–16.

23. Ibid.

24. Michael Barone, *Our First Revolution: The Remarkable British Upheaval That Inspired America's Founding Fathers* (New York: Three Rivers Press, 2008), p. 181.

25. John Locke, *Two Treatises of Government*, edited by Peter Laslett, 3rd ed. (Cambridge: Cambridge University Press, 1988), p. 116.

26. Williams, *The Eighteenth-Century Constitution, 1688–1815*, p. 26.

27. Kate Davies, *Catharine Macaulay and Mercy Otis Warren: The Revolutionary Atlantic and the Politics of Gender* (Oxford: Oxford University Press, 2005), p. 45. Davies cites Macaulay's *Observations on Burke's Thoughts on the Present Discontents.*

28. Ibid.

29. Ashcraft, *Revolutionary Politics and Locke's Two Treatises of Government*, p. 590.

Chapter 2: American Constitutionalism and the Formation of the Secular Covenant

1. Vernon Louis Parrington, *Main Currents in American Thought: The Colonial Mind, 1620–1800* (Norman: University of Oklahoma Press, 1987), p. 118.

2. Ibid., p. 119.

3. Ibid.

4. Ibid., p. 120.

5. Ibid., p. 122.

6. Ibid., p. 123.

7. Nathaniel Bradstreet Shurtleff, *A Topographical and Historical Description of Boston* (Boston: Boston City Council, 1871), p. 478. The island in question is now known as Castle Island.

8. Kenneth Colegrove, "New England Town Mandates," *Publications of the Colonial Society of Massachusetts* 21 (1919), p. 412.

9. Ibid.

10. David Hackett Fischer, *Albion's Seed: Four British Folkways in America* (New York: Oxford University Press, 1989), p. 200.

11. Timothy Hall, *Separating Church and State: Roger Williams and Religious Liberty* (Urbana: University of Illinois Press, 1997), p. 87.

12. Perry Miller, *Errand into the Wilderness* (Cambridge, MA: Harvard University Press, 1984), pp. 35–36.

13. David S. Lovejoy, *The Glorious Revolution in America* (Middletown, CT: Wesleyan University Press, 1987), p. 155.

14. Michael Barone, *Our First Revolution: The Remarkable British Upheaval That Inspired America's Founding Fathers* (New York: Three Rivers Press, 2008), p. 231.

15. Parrington, *Main Currents in American Thought*, p. 124.

16. Ibid.

17. John Wise, *A Vindication of the Government of New England Churches* (Boston: Congregational Board of Publication, 1860), pp. 39–40, http://www.constitution.org/primarysources/primarysources.html.

18. Ibid.

19. Fischer, *Albion's Seed*, pp. 608–9.

20. Murray Rothbard, *Conceived in Liberty* (Auburn, AL: Ludwig von Mises Institute, 2011), p. 705.

21. Ibid.

22. James Otis, "Rights of the British Colonies Asserted and Proved," in Merrill Jensen, ed., *Tracts of the American Revolution, 1763–1776* (Indianapolis: Hackett, 2003), p. 21, http://teachingamericanhistory.org/library/index.asp?documentprint=267.

23. Walter Isaacson, *Benjamin Franklin: An American Life* (New York: Simon & Schuster, 2004), p. 243.

24. Ibid, p. 250.

25. Parrington, *Main Currents in American Thought*, p. 124.

26. Ira Stoll, *Samuel Adams: A Life* (New York: Free Press, 2008), p. 116.

27. Thomas Jefferson, *A Summary View of the Rights of British America*, 1774.

28. Demophilus, *The Genuine Principles of the Ancient Saxon, or English Constitution: Carefully Collected from the Best Authorities* (Philadelphia: Robert Bell, 1776).

CHAPTER 3: ALEXANDER HAMILTON AND THE BROKEN PROMISE OF PLAIN MEANING

1. Robert Yates, *Notes of the Secret Debates of the Federal Convention of 1787, Taken by the Late Hon Robert Yates, Chief Justice of the State of New York, and One of the Delegates from That State to the Said Convention* (Washington, DC: G. Templeman, 1886), http://avalon.law.yale.edu/18th_century/yates.asp.

2. Richard B. Morris, *Seven Who Shaped Our Destiny: The Founding Fathers as Revolutionaries* (New York: Harper & Row, 1973), p. 1. The phrase "founding fathers" was first used by then senator (later president) Warren Harding in 1916.

3. U.S. Constitution, http://www.usconstitution.net/const.txt.

4. Ibid.

5. Andrew Burstein and Nancy Isenberg, *Madison and Jefferson* (New York: Random House, 2010), p. 150.

6. Randy Barnett, *Restoring the Lost Constitution* (Princeton, NJ: Princeton University Press, 2004), p. 155.

7. Ibid.

8. Ibid.

9. Yates, *Notes of the Secret Debates of the Federal Convention of 1787*.

10. Burstein and Isenberg, *Madison and Jefferson*, p. 173.

11. U.S. Constitution.

12. Brian Lamb, *BookNotes: Stories from American History* (New York: PublicAffairs, 2001), p. 25.

13. Pauline Maier, *Ratification: The People Debate the Constitution, 1787–1788* (New York: Simon & Schuster, 2010), p. 69.

14. Harold Coffin Syrett, *The Papers of Alexander Hamilton*, vol. 9 (New York: Columbia University Press, 1962), p. 276.

15. U.S. Constitution.

16. "Ratification of the Constitution by the State of New York, July 26, 1788," from *Documentary History of the Constitution*, vol. 2 (1894), pp. 190–203.

17. Richard Brookhiser, *Alexander Hamilton, American* (New York: Free Press, 2000), p. 214.

18. Ron Chernow, *Alexander Hamilton* (New York: Penguin, 2005), p. 297.

19. Forrest McDonald, "The Founding Fathers and the Economic Order," Forum at the Online Library of Liberty, http://oll.libertyfund.org/index.php?Itemid=267&id=177&option=com_content&task=view.

20. "The First Bank of the United States," Office of the Clerk, House of Representatives, http://clerk.house.gov/art_history/highlights.html?action=view&intID=237. Some sources say the vote was 38–20.

21. Thornton Anderson, *Creating the Constitution: The Convention of 1787 and the First Congress* (University Park: Pennsylvania State University Press, 1994), p. 52, as he reconstructed them from the published notes from half a dozen of the delegates.

22. Ibid.

23. Walter Dellinger and H. Jefferson Powell, "The Constitutionality of the Bank Bill: The Attorney General's First Constitutional Law Opinions," *Duke Law Journal* 44:110 (1994), pp. 110–32, http://scholarship.law.duke.edu/cgi/viewcontent.cgi?article=1265&context=faculty_scholarship.

24. Harold C. Syrett, ed., *The Papers of Alexander Hamilton* (New York: Columbia University Press, 1961–87), p. 276, http://press-pubs.uchicago.edu/founders/documents/a1_8_18s11.html.

25. Ibid.

26. Larry E. Tise, *The American Counterrevolution: A Retreat from Liberty, 1783–1800* (Mechanicsburg, PA: Stackpole Books, 1998), p. 59.

27. *The Laws of the United States of America* (Philadelphia: Richard Folwell, 1796–1798), http://www.earlyamerica.com/earlyamerica/milestones/sedition/s-text.html.

28. Chernow, *Alexander Hamilton*, p. 558.

29. Richard N. Rosenfeld, *American Aurora: A Democratic-Republican Returns: The Suppressed History of Our Nation's Beginnings and the Heroic Newspaper That Tried to Report It* (New York: St. Martin's Griffin, 1998), p. 200.

30. Ibid., p. 533.

31. "US President—National Vote," Our Campaigns, http://www.ourcampaigns.com/RaceDetail.html?RaceID=59539n.

32. Andrew Jackson, "Why the United States Bank Was Closed," *America* 6 (1832), p. 111, http://www.lexrex.com/enlightened/writings/bank/jackson.htm.

Chapter 4: The Republican Party and the Broken Promise of Free Markets

1. "Founded by Hamilton: Paterson New Jersey Is One Hundred Years Old Today," *New York Times,* July 4, 1892.

2. "A Brief History of The Society For Establishing Useful Manufactures," Passaic County Historical Society Genealogy Club, 2000, http://www.rootsweb.ancestry.com/~njpchsgc/pce/sum.htm.

3. John Stancliffe Davis, *Essays in the Earlier History of American Corporations* (Cambridge, MA: Harvard University Press, 1917), p. 431.

4. "A Brief History of The Society for Establishing Useful Manufactures."

5. Ibid.

6. Douglas A. Irwin, "The Aftermath of Hamilton's Report on Manufactures," *Journal of Economic History* 64:3 (September 2004), p. 894. The SEUM prospectus explicitly stated its intent to manufacture two of these five proposed subsidized products—sailcloth and cotton manufactures.

7. Ibid.

8. Robert Francis Jones, *King of the Alley* (Philadelphia: American Philosophical Society, 1992), p. 173.

9. Davis, *Essays in the Earlier History of American Corporations*, p. 432.

10. Thomas Fleming, "Wall Street's First Collapse," *American Heritage,* Winter 2009.

11. Ibid.

12. Ibid.

13. "A Brief History of The Society for Establishing Useful Manufactures."

14. E. R. Wicker, "Railroad Investment Before the Civil War," a chapter in *Trends in the American Economy in the Nineteenth Century*, Conference on Research in Income and Wealth, National Bureau of Economic Research (Princeton, NJ: Princeton University Press, 1960), p. 506, http://www.nber.org/chapters/c2488.pdf. I use Shuman's estimates.

15. Ibid.

16. Calvin Colton, *A Lecture on the Railroad to the Pacific: Delivered August 12, 1850 at the Smithsonian Institute, Washington* (New York: A. S. Barnes, 1850), http://digitalcommons.unl.edu/etas/10/.

17. Ibid.

18. "Biographical Notes: Theodore Judah," http://www.inn-california.com/articles/biographic/tjudahbio.html.

19. Ibid.

20. J. David Rogers, "Theodore Judah and the Blazing of the First Transcontinental Railroad over the Sierra Nevada," unpublished paper, p. 9, http://web.mst.edu/~rogersda/american&military_history/THEODORE%20JUDAH%20AND%20THE%20BLAZING%20OF%20THE%20FIRST%20TRANSCONTINENTAL%20RAILROAd-Sierra%20Nevada-Rogers.pdf.

21. David Harward Bain, *Empire Express: Building the First Transcontinental Railroad* (New York: Penguin, 2000), p. 76.

22. Republican Party Platform (1860), *TeachingAmericanHistory.org*, http://teachingamericanhistory.org/library/index.asp?document=149.

23. Democratic Party Platform, June 18, 1860, Avalon Project at Yale Law School, http://avalon.law.yale.edu/19th_century/dem1860.asp.

24. 1860 (Southern) Democratic Party Platform, Blue and Gray Trail, http://blueandgraytrail.com/event/1860_(Southern)_Democratic_Party_Platform.

25. *Congressional Globe*, December 20, 1860, p. 169.

26. Bain, *Empire Express*, p. 106.

27. Ibid., p. 110.

28. Rogers, "Theodore Judah and the Blazing of the First Transcontinental Railroad Over the Sierra Nevada," p. 19.

29. Ibid., p. 20.

30. *Congressional Globe*, April 18, 1862.

31. *Congressional Globe*, April 10, 1862.

32. *Congressional Globe*, April 17, 1862.

33. Michael Tennant, "Dirty Deals on the 'Dark Continent' Perpetuate Pov-

erty," *New American*, December 23, 2010, http://www.thenewamerican
.com/index.php/world-mainmenu-26/africa-mainmenu-27/5622-dirty-
deals-on-the-dark-continent. Thomas DiLorenzo has also written extensively about the free market strategy successfully implemented by Hill
in the construction of the Great Northern Railroad. Ayn Rand is said
to have based the *Atlas Shrugged* character Asa Taggart loosely on Hill.

34. "Biographical Notes: Theodore Judah."

35. Ibid.

36. Bain, *Empire Express*, p. 161. Citing testimony of Secretary of the Interior
Usher years later before the United States Senate, Usher claimed Durant
told him that Lincoln selected Council Bluffs and that he held personal
title to seventeen lots of land there, held as collateral for a personal loan.
No other confirmation of this claim exists.

37. Ibid., p. 47.

38. Alexander Toponce, *Reminiscences of Alexander Toponce: Pioneer 1839–
1923* (Whitefish, MT: Kessinger, 2007), pp. 178–79.

39. James Surowiecki, "Durant's Big Scam," January 2003, http://www.pbs
.org/wgbh/amex/tcrr/sfeature/sf_scandals.html.

CHAPTER 5: WOODROW WILSON AND THE
DIVINE RIGHT OF THE STATE

1. Robert Higgs, "Why Grover Cleveland Vetoed the Texas Seed Bill," Independent Institute, July 1, 2003, http://www.independent.org/publica-
tions/article.asp?id=1329.

2. "American President: A Reference Resource: First Term Key Events in
the Presidency of Grover Cleveland," Miller Center at the University of
Virginia, http://millercenter.org/president/keyevents/cleveland.

3. Lawrence J. Korb et al., *Serving America's Veterans: A Reference Hand-
book* (Santa Barbara, CA: ABC-CLIO, 2009), p. 20.

4. Ronald J. Pestritto, *Woodrow Wilson and the Roots of Modern Liberalism*
(Lanham, MD: Rowman & Littlefield Publishers, 2005), p. 42.

5. John Milton Cooper, *Woodrow Wilson* (New York: Vintage Books, 2009),
p. 17.

6. James Henry Thornwell, "A Southern Christian View of Slavery," in *The
Annals of America: 1858–1865, The Crisis of the Union*, published by
Encyclopaedia Britannica, 1968, http://teachingamericanhistory.org
/library/index.asp?document=1124.

7. *Minutes of the General Assembly of the Presbyterian Church in the Confed-*

erate States of America, vol. 1 (Augusta, GA: PCCSA, 1861), pp. 55–59.

8. Ibid.

9. Woodrow Wilson, *Constitutional Government of the United States* (New Brunswick, NJ: Transaction, 2001).

10. Ibid.

11. Thomas E. Wood Jr., "The Limits of Presidential Power," *Daily Reckoning*, http://dailyreckoning.com/the-limits-of-presidential-power/#ixzz 1RL8MfMYQ.

12. John V. Denson, "American Mussolini," at www.lewrockwell.com.

13. Paul Johnson, *Modern Times: The World from the Twenties to the Nineties*, rev. ed. (New York: HarperPerennial Modern Classics, 2001), p. 16.

14. Cooper, *Woodrow Wilson*, p. 390.

15. Ibid. p. 405.

16. Witold Sworakowski, "Herbert Hoover, Launching the Food Administration," in *Herbert Hoover—the Great War and Its Aftermath, 1914–1923*, Lawrence E. Gelfand, ed. (Iowa City: University of Iowa Press, 1979), pp. 40–60.

17. Ibid.

18. Ibid.

19. Ibid.

20. Cooper, *Woodrow Wilson*, p. 406.

21. George H. Nash, *The Life of Herbert Hoover: Master of Emergencies 1917–1918* (New York: Norton, 1996), p. 84.

22. Earl S. Brown, "The Food Administration: A History of Switzerland County's Part in the World War," 1919, *MyIndianaHome.net*, http://my indianahome.net/gen/switz/records/military/WWI/food.html.

23. "Porter County Played Part in All of Nation's Wars," *Vidette-Messenger*, Valparaiso, IN, August 18, 1936, pp. 11–12, http://www.inportercounty .org/Data/PorterCountyCentennial/Sec4-11_WorldWar.html.

24. "On the Home Front Conservation Becomes Second Nature," Oregon State Defense Council Records, State Historian's Correspondence, Box 1, Folder 38, 52; Publications and Ephemera, Box 8, Folder 1,http://arc web.sos.state.or.us/exhibits/war/wwl/conserve.html.

25. "Madison County's Honor Roll—World War I," http://home.comcast .net/~ingallsam/WWI/food.htm.

26. J. R. Sutherland, *Burt County Nebraska in the World War* (Tekamah, NE: Burt County Herald, 1919), pp. 118–19, http://www.usgennet.org/usa/ ne/county/burt/bcww1/bcww1p29.html.

27. G. C. Fite and J. E. Reese, *An Economic History of the United States* (Boston: Houghton Mifflin, 1959), p. 515.

28. Nash, *The Life of Herbert Hoover*, p. 303.

29. Ibid., p. 289.

30. Fite and Reese, *An Economic History of the United States*, p. 515.

31. Mary Sennholz, *Leonard E. Read: Philosopher of Freedom* (Irvington, NY: Foundation for Economic Education, 1993), pp. 26–32.

32. Ibid.

33. Ibid.

CHAPTER 6: REPUBLICANS FAIL TO
OFFER AN ALTERNATIVE

1. Herbert Hoover, "The Challenge to Liberty," *Saturday Evening Post*, September 8, 1934.

2. Herbert Hoover, *American Individualism* (Garden City, NY: Doubleday Doran, 1929), p. 22.

3. David Hart, "Herbert Hoover's Last Laugh: The Enduring Significance of the 'Associative State' in the United States," *Journal of Policy History* 10 (1998), pp. 419–44.

4. Hoover, *American Individualism*, p. 22.

5. U.S. Bureau of the Census.

6. Hoover, *American Individualism*, p. 24.

7. Ibid.

8. Ibid.

9. Ibid., p. 22.

10. Carl Watner, "Chaos in the Air: Voluntaryism or Statism in the Early Radio Industry?" *voluntaryist.com*, no. 51 (August 1991), http://www.voluntaryist.com/articles/051b.html.

11. Ibid.

12. Ibid.

13. Ibid.

14. Ibid.

15. Ibid.

16. Richard Vedder and Lowell Gallaway, *Out of Work: Unemployment and Government in Twentieth-Century America* (New York: New York University Press, 1996), p. 77.

17. Ibid.

18. No. HS-47: Federal Government—Receipts and Outlays: 1900 to 2003, U.S. Census Bureau, *Statistical Abstract of the United States: 2003*, http://www.census.gov/statab/hist/HS-47.pdf.

19. Thomas Sowell, "The Myth of How the Great Depression Was Resolved," *Washington Examiner*, June 18, 2010, http://washingtonexaminer.com/node/75086.

20. Vedder and Gallaway, *Out of Work*, p. 77.

21. Murray Rothbard, *America's Great Depression* (Auburn, AL: Ludwig von Mises Institute, 2000), p. 265.

22. Christopher Cantrill, comp., "Recent and Budgeted US Federal Debt," *USGovernmentSpending.com*, http://www.usgovernmentspending.com/federal_debt_chart.html.

23. No. HS-47: Federal Government—Receipts and Outlays: 1900 to 2003.

24. Vedder and Gallaway, *Out of Work*, p. 77.

25. Rothbard, *America's Great Depression*, p. 265.

CHAPTER 7: HOOVER, FDR, AND THE BROKEN PROMISE OF THE FISCAL CONSTITUTION

1. James M. Buchanan and Richard E. Wagner, *Democracy in Deficit: The Political Legacy of Lord Keynes* (New York: Academic Press, 1977), p. 21.

2. Ibid.

3. Ibid.

4. Ibid., p. 1.

5. Brookhiser, *Alexander Hamilton, American*, p. 85.

6. Andrew White Young, *The American Statesman* (New York: J. C. Derby, 1855), p. 136.

7. Sarah Lacy, "Can America Function More Like a Fiscally Responsible Company?" *TechCrunch*, February 24, 2011, http://techcrunch.com/2011/02/24/can-america-function-more-like-a-fiscally-responsible-company-its-up-to-us-the-shareholders/.

8. Buchanan and Wagner, *Democracy in Deficit*, p. 1.

9. Lawrence W. Reed, *Great Myths of the Great Depression* (Midland, MI: Mackinac Center, 2011), p. 4.

10. Democratic Party Platform of 1932, American Presidency Project,

http://www.presidency.ucsb.edu/ws/index.php?pid=29595#axzz1b
RMa62Yw.

11. Reed, *Great Myths of the Great Depression*, p. 5.

12. Herbert Hoover, *Memoirs of Herbert Hoover*, vol. 3 (New York: Macmillan, 1951), p. 142.

13. Reed, *Great Myths of the Great Depression*, p. 5.

14. Adam Cohen, *Nothing to Fear: FDR's Inner Circle and the Hundred Days That Created Modern America* (New York: Penguin, 2008), p. 84.

15. Ibid., p. 104.

16. Ibid., p. 106.

17. Ibid.

18. Ibid.

19. Ibid., p. 217.

20. Ibid.

21. Ibid., p. 219.

22. Buchanan and Wagner, *Democracy in Deficit*, p. 22.

23. Ibid.

24. http://www.freeuniv.com/lect/rankin/Unit7B.htm.

25. Ibid.

26. Ibid.

27. Ibid.

28. Frank Freidel, *Franklin D. Roosevelt: A Rendezvous with Destiny* (Boston: Back Bay Books, 1991), p. 138.

29. Ibid.

30. "Heroes: Economy's End," *Time*, August 26, 1935, http://www.time.com/time/magazine/article/0,9171,748895-1,00.html.

31. Ibid.

32. Ibid.

33. Herbert Levy, *Henry Morgenthau, Jr.* (New York: Skyhorse, 2011), kindle location 1395.

34. Ibid.

35. Henry Morgenthau Diary, May 9, 1939, Franklin D. Roosevelt Library, Hyde Park, NY, Microfilm Roll #50.

36. Ibid.

37. Christopher Cantrill, comp., "Recent and Budgeted US Federal Debt," *USGovernmentSpending.com*, http://www.usgovernmentspending.com/federal_debt_chart.html.

38. "United States Unemployment Rate 1920–2008," *Infoplease.com*, http://www.infoplease.com/ipa/A0104719.html#ixzz1HBgvrVx5.

39. *No. HS-47: Federal Government—Receipts and Outlays: 1900 to 2003*, U.S. Census Bureau, *Statistical Abstract of the United States: 2003*, http://www.census.gov/statab/hist/HS-47.pdf. In reading these charts, keep in mind that until 1976 the federal fiscal year ended on June 30. Then a single transitional quarter was added and the fiscal year ended on September 30. In all these charts from 1928 to 1975, then, the period showing 1929, for instance, covers the twelve-month period beginning on July 1, 1928, and ending on June 30, 1929. Since Herbert Hoover was inaugurated in March 1929, his first full budget was 1930 (July 1, 1929–June 30, 1930). The Depression was said to have begun in a stock market crash in October 1929.

CHAPTER 8: FDR's ASSAULT ON FREE MARKETS
AND THE CONSTITUTION

1. George Bittlingmayer, "The 1920s Boom and the Great Crash," Center for the Study of the Economy and the State, University of Chicago, Working Paper No. 86, May 1993, p. 2.

2. *Wall Street Journal*, October 26, 1929.

3. Bittlingmayer, "The 1920s Boom and the Great Crash," pp. 2–3.

4. "Business: Big Pool Punned," *Time*, November 28, 1932, http://www.time.com/time/magazine/article/0,9171,744808,00.html#ixzz1SwbbjObD.

5. Hugh S. Johnson, *The Blue Eagle from Egg to Earth* (Garden City, NY: Doubleday, Doran, 1935), p. 91.

6. Gerard Swope, *Stabilization of Industry* (New York: National Electrical Manufacturers Association, 1931), pp. 1–16.

7. John T. Flynn, *Country Squire in the White House* (New York: Doubleday, 1940), p. 77.

8. Arthur Schlesinger, *The Crisis of the Old Order* (New York: Mariner Books, 2003), pp. 182–83.

9. David Hart, "Herbert Hoover's Last Laugh: The Enduring Significance of the 'Associative State' in the United States," *Journal of Policy History* 10 (1998), pp. 431–32.

10. Kathryn Jean Lopez, "Depressed by Government: Amity Shlaes's New History of the Great Depression," *National Review Online*, June 12, 2007, http://www.abebooks.com/docs/CompanyInformation/PressRoom/NationalReview-Amity_Shales-12June07.pdf.

11. Michael Hannon, "Clarence Darrow and the National Recovery Review Board," University of Minnesota Law School Library, p. 2, http://darrow.law.umn.edu/trialpdfs/National_Recovery_Review_Board.pdf.

12. James Q. Whitman, "Of Corporatism, Fascism and the First New Deal," Yale Law School Faculty Scholarship Series Paper 660, 1991, p. 772.

13. Johnson, *The Blue Eagle from Egg to Earth*, p. 172.

14. Ibid., p. 175.

15. Whitman, "Of Corporatism, Fascism and the First New Deal," p. 772.

16. Hannon, "Clarence Darrow and the National Recovery Review Board," p. 4.

17. Whitman, "Of Corporatism, Fascism and the First New Deal," p. 766.

18. "Recovery: Mixed Doubles," *Time*, September 10, 1934, http://www.time.com/time/magazine/article/0,9171,747887,00.html#ixzz1WMdLV8u2.

19. Ibid.

20. Jonah Goldberg, *Liberal Fascism: The Secret History of the American Left, from Mussolini to the Politics of Meaning*, Kindle edition (New York: Crown Forum, 2008), pp. 153–54.

21. Ibid.

22. Ibid.

23. Ibid.

24. Hannon, "Clarence Darrow and the National Recovery Review Board," p. 5.

25. Whitman, "Of Corporatism, Fascism and the First New Deal," p. 772.

26. Hannon, "Clarence Darrow and the National Recovery Review Board," p. 5.

27. Ibid., p. 6.

28. Ibid., p. 8.

29. Jonah Goldberg, "The Raw Deal: A Review of *The Forgotten Man: A New History of the Great Depression*, by Amity Shlaes," *Claremont Review of Books*, Winter 2007, http://www.claremont.org/publications/crb/id.1502/article_detail.asp.

30. Hannon, "Clarence Darrow and the National Recovery Review Board," p. 8.

31. Ibid., p. 10.

32. Ibid.

33. George F. Will, "Trifle with the Government? Just Ask Jacob Maged," *Washington Post*, September 16, 2010.

34. Burton W. Folsom Jr., "The NRA: How Price-Fixing Perpetuated the Great Depression," *Freeman* 59:3 (April 2009), http://www.thefree

manonline.org/columns/our-economic-past/the-nra-how-price-fixing-perpetuated-the-great-depression/.

35. "Recovery: Batteryman," *Time*, December 17, 1934.

36. Steve Horwitz, "Follow Up on the Schechters," http://hnn.us/blogs/entries/57686.html.

37. Hannon, "Clarence Darrow and the National Recovery Review Board," p. 11.

38. Leslie Shope, "Give a Man a Job!" *Brooklynology*, February 12, 2009, http://brooklynology.brooklynpubliclibrary.org/post/2009/02/12/Title.aspx.

39. Author's phone interview with Estelle Freilich, daughter of Joe and Lillian Schechter, August 29, 2011.

40. Hannon, "Clarence Darrow and the National Recovery Review Board," p. 11.

41. "Fireside Chat on Reorganization of the Judiciary, March 9, 1937," http://www.hpol.org/fdr/chat/.

CHAPTER 9: LBJ, RICHARD NIXON, AND THE
FINAL DESTRUCTION OF THE THREE PROMISES

1. Guian A. McKee, "*Lyndon B. Johnson and the War on Poverty*: Introduction to the Digital Edition," Miller Center of Public Affairs, Frank Batten School of Leadership and Public Policy, University of Virginia, p. 6, http://rotunda.upress.virginia.edu/pdf/american-cent/WarOnPoverty-introduction-USletter.pdf.

2. Randall Bennett Woods, *LBJ: Architect of American Ambition* (New York: Simon & Schuster, 2006), p. 17.

3. Ibid., p. 27.

4. Robert Higgs, "Why Grover Cleveland Vetoed the Texas Seed Bill," Independent Institute, July 1, 2003, http://www.independent.org/publications/article.asp?id=1329.

5. *Budget of the United States Government*, Office of Management and Budget Historical Tables, annual. See also http://w3.access.gpo.gov/usbudget/fy2004/pdf/hist.pdf and http://www.whitehouse.gov/omb/budget/fy2004/.

6. David Reynolds, *America, Empire of Liberty: A New History of the United States* (New York: Basic Books, 2009), p. 358.

7. *Budget of the United States Government*, Office of Management and Budget, Historical Tables, annual.

8. Adam Young, "A Retrospective on Johnson's Poverty War," *Mises Daily*, December 26, 2002, http://mises.org/daily/1126 .

9. Ibid.

10. "The Economy: We Are All Keynesians Now," *Time*, December 31, 1965, http://www.time.com/time/magazine/article/0,9171,842353,00.html.

11. "Letters to the Editor," *Time*, February 4, 1966.

12. Steven Hayward, "Nixon Reconsidered," Ashbrook Center at Ashland University, 1998, http://www.ashbrook.org/publicat/dialogue/hayward.html.

13. Ibid.

14. Daniel Yergin and Joseph Stanislaw, "Nixon Tries Price Controls," excerpt from their book, *The Commanding Heights* (New York: Simon & Schuster, 1997), pp. 60–64, http://www.pbs.org/wgbh/commandingheights/shared/minitextlo/ess_nixongold.html.

15. Ibid.

16. Hayward, "Nixon Reconsidered."

17. Jake Tapper, "Democratic Bigots," *Salon*, July 17, 2000, http://archive.salon.com/politics/feature/2000/07/17/rights/.

18. John Winthrop, *Model of Christian Charity*, 1630. Modern spelling provided by the author.

19. Theodore Sorensen, *Let the Word Go Forth: The Speeches, Statements, and Writings of John F. Kennedy 1947 to 1963* (New York: Dell Publishing, 1991), p. 57.

20. Phone interview by the author with Professor Richard Gamble, Hillsdale College, December 17, 2010.

21. Ronald Reagan, "City Upon a Hill," speech delivered at the first CPAC conference, January 25, 1974, http://www.presidentreagan.info/speeches/city_upon_a_hill.cfm.

22. Ibid.

23. Ronald Reagan, "Remarks of the President and Prime Minister Charles J. Haughey of Ireland at a Luncheon Honoring the Prime Minister, March 17, 1982," http://www.reagan.utexas.edu/archives/speeches/1982/31782c.htm.

CHAPTER 10: THE BROKEN PROMISE OF DELIBERATIVE
ACCOUNTABILITY AND THE RISE OF THE TEA PARTY MOVEMENT

1. *Journal of the Proceedings of the Convention of Delegates Elected by the People of Tennessee to Amend, Revise, or Form and Make a New Constitution for the State Assembled in the City of Nashville, January 10, 1870* (Nashville: Purvis Jones, 1870), p. 294.

2. Maclin Davis Jr., "The Constitutionality of the Proposed Tennessee Income Tax," Tennessee Tax Revolt, *Tntaxrevolt.org*.

3. Ibid.

4. Jeff Woods, "Read His Lips: Sundquist Ready to Crusade for Income Tax," *Nashville Scene*, October 7, 1999.

5. Ibid.

6. Davis, "The Constitutionality of the Proposed Tennessee Income Tax."

7. "President's Address to the Nation," September 24, 2008, http://georgewbush-whitehouse.archives.gov/news/releases/2008/09/print/20080924-10.html.

8. Jacob Weisberg, "The Complete Bushisms," *Slate*, March 20, 2009, http://www.slate.com/id/76886/.

9. U.S. Senate Roll Call Votes 110th Congress—2nd Session Question: On Passage of the Bill (H.R. 1424 As Amended), October 1, 2008, http://www.senate.gov/legislative/LIS/roll_call_lists/roll_call_vote_cfm.cfm?congress=110&session=2&vote=00213.

10. Final Vote Results for Roll Call 681, Clerk of the House of Representatives, October 3, 2008, http://clerk.house.gov/evs/2008/roll681.xml.

11. "House of Representatives: Big Board," *New York Times*, December 9, 2008, http://elections.nytimes.com/2008/results/house/votes.html.

12. "TCOT Statement of Principles," http://www.tcotreport.com.statement ofprinciples.html.

13. "Santelli's Tea Party," CNBC, February 19, 2009. You can see the original CNBC clip of the Rick Santelli rant at http://www.cnbc.com/id/15840232?video=1039849853.

14. "Santelli's Tea Party Outburst Sets CNBC.com Records," *Social Times*, February 20, 2009, http://www.mediabistro.com/webnewser/santellis-tea-party-outburst-sets-cnbc-com-records_b2797.

15. "Newt Gingrich's American Solutions Comes to the Tea Party," March 18, 2009, http://westernfrontamerica.com/2009/03/18/newt-gingrichs-american-solutions-tea-party/.

16. Ibid.

17. "Pajamas TV Final Estimate: April 15 Tea Party Attendance Exceeded One Million," April 30, 2009, http://www.reuters.com/article/press Release/idUS241221+30-Apr-2009+PRN20090430.

18. Amy Gardner, "Few Signs at Tea Party Rally Expressed Racially Charged Anti-Obama Themes," *Washington Post,* October 14, 2010, http://www.washingtonpost.com/wp-dyn/content/article/2010/10/13/ AR2010101303634.html. In October 2010, Emily Ekins, a doctoral student in political science at the University of California at Los Angeles, used the phrase "limited government ethos" as part of a study she had conducted of the content of 250 signs she personally photographed at a September 12, 2010, Tea Party rally held in Washington, D.C. She analyzed and categorized these signs, and concluded that the vast majority of them reflected the same "limited government" ethos displayed at the original 2009 Tax Day Tea Party event.

19. "Tax Day Tea Party in Richmond Hill GA—Updated," *Chickenhawk Express,* April 15, 2009, http://chickenhawkexpress.blogspot.com/2009/04/ tax-day-tea-party-in-richmond-hill-ga.html.

20. "Hawaii Tax Day Tea Party," April 15–19, 2009, http://www.flickr.com/ photos/macprohawaii/sets/72157616548101496/.

21. Tiffany Hill, "Web Exclusive: A Honolulu Tea Party," *Honolulu,* April 2009, http://www.honolulumagazine.com/Honolulu-Magazine/April-2009/Web-Exclusive-A-Honolulu-Tea-Party/.

22. "Glenn Beck 'On the Record' at the Alamo," *FoxNews.com,* April 16, 2009, http://www.foxnews.com/story/0,2933,516620,00.html.

23. "Ted Nugent at San Antonio Tax Day Tea Party," http://vimeo .com/4176791.

24. Liz Robbins, "Tax Day Is Met with Tea Parties," *New York Times,* April 15, 2009.

25. A list of the estimated crowd size in all nine hundred cities that held Tax Day Tea Party events on April 15, 2009, is available at http://www .surgeusa.org/actions/teapartycrowds.htm.

26. Alex Weprin, "Cable News Ratings: Fox News Stays on Top: CNN Falls to Third in Prime Demo, HLN Keeps It Close," *Broadcasting & Cable,* April 28, 2009, http://www.broadcastingcable.com/article/210239-Cable_News_Ratings_Fox_News_Stays_On_Top.php.

27. Chris Ariens, "Susan Roesgen Out at CNN," *TVNewser,* July 16, 2009, http://www.mediabistro.com/tvnewser/susan-roesgen-out-at-cnn_ b27854?c=rss. Ms. Roesgen now works for a local television station in New Orleans.

28. Peter Hamby, "Axelrod Suggests 'Tea Party' Movement Is 'Unhealthy,'" CNN Political Ticker blog, April 19, 2009, http://politicalticker

.blogs.cnn.com/2009/04/19/axelrod-suggests-tea-party-movement-is-unhealthy/.

29. Ibid.

30. Bernard Bailyn, *The Ideological Origins of the American Revolution* (Cambridge, MA: Belknap Press of Harvard University Press, 1992), p. 283. The adjective *prerogative* is used to describe powers that are granted exclusively to one person or group. In sixteenth- and seventeenth-century England, the term was most often used in association with the monarch. *Royal prerogative* referred to powers reserved to and exclusively exercised by the monarch. In the Bailyn quote, the word *prerogative* refers to powers reserved to and exclusively exercised by the English government—Parliament, prime minister, and king—acting in unison against the people of the American colonies.

31. Wesley J. Smith, "Obamacare: Senate Trick to Fast Track Passage," *Firstthings.com*, November 19, 2009, http://www.firstthings.com/blogs/secondhandsmoke/2009/11/19/obamacare-senate-trick-to-fast-track-passage/.

32. Jordan Fabian, "Obama Healthcare Plan Nixes Ben Nelson's 'Cornhusker Kickback' Deal," *The Hill*, February 22, 2010, http://thehill.com/blogs/blog-briefing-room/news/82621-obama-healthcare-plan-nixes-ben-nelsons-cornhusker-kickback-deal.

33. "Nelson Accused of Selling Vote on Health Bill for Nebraska Pay-Off," *FoxNews.com*, December 20, 2009, http://www.foxnews.com/politics/2009/12/20/nelson-accused-selling-vote-health-nebraska-pay/#.

34. Fabian, "Obama Healthcare Plan Nixes Ben Nelson's 'Cornhusker Kickback' Deal."

35. Alex Pappas, "Tea Party Coalition Plans to 'Take the Town Halls to Washington,'" *Daily Caller*, March 5, 2010.

36. "Congressman Pete Stark (D-CA)—Federal Government Can Enslave Citizens," *Virginia Right!* August 2, 2010, http://www.varight.com/news/congressman-pete-stark-d-ca-federal-government-can-enslave-citizens/.

CHAPTER 11: RESTORING THE SECULAR COVENANT:
A TEA PARTY AMERICA BASED ON THE CONSTITUTION

1. Jeffrey M. Jones, "Americans Say Federal Gov't Wastes Over Half of Every Dollar," September 19, 2011, http://www.gallup.com/poll/149543/americans-say-federal-gov-wastes-half-every-dollar.aspx.

2. *2011 Budget Chart Book*, Heritage Foundation, http://www.heritage.org/budgetchartbook/.

3. Congressional Budget Office, "Report on Federal Debt and Interest," December 2010, p. 25.

4. *2011 Index of Economic Freedom*, Heritage Foundation, http://www.heritage.org/index/ranking.

5. John Merline, "The Austerity Myth: Federal Spending Up 5% This Year," *Investor's Business Daily*, October 17, 2011.

6. Social Security Online, "Trust Fund Data," http://www.ssa.gov/OACT/ProgData/taxRates.html.

7. *The Budget and Economic Outlook: Fiscal Years 2011 to 2021*, Congressional Budget Office, January 2001, Table E-10, "Outlays for Mandatory Spending, 1971 to 2010, as a Percentage of Gross Domestic Product," http://www.cbo.gov/ftpdocs/120xx/doc12039/01-26_FY2011Outlook.pdf.

8. Ibid.

Index

About the Author

Michael Patrick Leahy is an innovative leader in both the tactics and strategy of grassroots conservative new-media activism. As cofounder of Top Conservatives on Twitter, Leahy helped to form the Nationwide Tea Party Coalition. With a BA degree from Harvard and an MBA from Stanford, he has more than two decades of private-sector experience in technology and communications. He is the author of several books, including *Rules for Conservative Radicals*. He lives in Tennessee.